THE LORD'S PRAYER

THE
LORD'S
PRAYER

Spiros Zodhiates

AMG
PUBLISHERS
Chattanooga, TN 37422

Second Revised Edition

ISBN 0–89957–049–6

Printed in the United States of America
03 02 01 00 99 98 –R– 6 5 4 3 2 1

To
WALDEMAR MURJAHN,

whose life and generosity
God uses as an answer
to many a prayer of God's
children everywhere.

Preface

Prayer is a mystery. We don't know how it works, but we know that it does. Conversation with our fellow human beings is one of the most precious endowments we possess. Would God leave us without the privilege of communication with Himself? A thousand times No!

But He is "up there" and we are "down here." He is pure Spirit, while we are both spirit and body. Our spirit communicates with fellow human beings through the tongue that is material, but in our prayers the material part of our makeup is bypassed and the spiritual within us communicates with God. That is why communication with other people is not as difficult as communication with God.

Nevertheless, as a demonstrable token of the reality and value of prayer, God often permits the results of prayer to be tangibly experienced in the material realm.

The Lord Jesus gave us a model prayer which has been repeated through the centuries of Church history, and its purpose was to teach us that the primary effectiveness of prayer is in the realm of the Spirit, rather than in the realm of matter.

To understand the Lord's Prayer is to attain some measure of comprehension of the mysteries that surround God, His attitude toward us and concern for us, and our behavior toward Him and our fellow men. In the Lord's Prayer you have a compendium of theology and anthropology. Jesus Christ came that God and man may meet, and no exercise of the soul makes that meeting more real than praying:

The Lord's Prayer

Our Father which art in heaven,
Hallowed be thy name.
Thy Kingdom come.
Thy will be done in earth,
as it is in heaven.
Give us this day our daily bread.
And forgive us our debts,
as we forgive our debtors.
And lead us not into temptation,
but deliver us from evil:
For thine is the kingdom,
and the power, and
the glory, forever. Amen.
                                    —Matthew 6:9–13.

As has been pointed out:

You cannot pray the Lord's Prayer
And even once say "I."
You cannot say the Lord's Prayer
And even once say "My."
Nor can you pray the Lord's Prayer
And not pray for another,
For when you ask for daily bread
You must include your brother.
For others are included
in each and every plea—
From the beginning to the end of it,
It never once says "Me!"

The study of the Lord's Prayer made a tremendous difference in my life as I wrote the thoughts that follow. It is my prayer for you that it will make a difference in your life also. My sincere thanks go to my Editorial Assistant, Mrs. Sybil Wilson, for her diligence in editing, enriching, and typing the manuscript.

Spiros Zodhiates

CONTENTS

Section I
Why, Where and How Should We Pray?

Section II
Our Father, Who Art in Heaven

Section III
Hallowed Be Thy Name

Section IV
Thy Kingdom Come

Section V
Thy Will Be Done

Contents

Section VI
Give Us This Day Our Daily Bread

Section VII
Forgive Us Our Sins as We Forgive
Them That Sin Against Us

Section VIII
Lead Us Not Into Temptation

Section IX
Deliver Us From Evil

Contents

Section X
The Doxology

SECTION I

Why, Where and How Should We Pray?

Why Do I Pray?

All Christians would do well to ask themselves, "Why do I pray? What is my motive in prayer? Is it to be seen or known as a man or woman of prayer? Is it so that I can impress others with my piety? Do I want a reputation as a wonderful Christian or a spiritual giant?"

In the Sermon on the Mount our Lord was teaching about almsgiving, prayer, and fasting—those public forms of worship so assiduously and zealously practiced by the Pharisees and the Scribes.

What concerned our Lord, and should also concern us, was not the practice of such pious acts, but the motive that lay behind them. In this sermon He was saying to the Jews in effect: "I am not so concerned with what you do in the way of religious observances as I am with *why* you do it. What is your motive? *Why* do you give alms, pray, and fast? What is the end you are seeking to attain?"

To our Lord, a desire for the notice and commendation of men for our acts of devotion and charity constituted one of the two basic elements of hypocrisy—the other being that of pretense and falseness which nullified all the public display. Someone has said that a hypocrite is a person who does not want to be holy before God, but only to *appear* holy before men. It was so with the Scribes and the

Pharisees. They didn't have the *reality* of righteousness, but they wanted the *reputation* for righteousness.

One thing our Lord wants us to understand is that *a good thing can become a cause for condemnation if it is wrongly motivated.* What clearer teaching of this truth could we have than that found in 1 Corinthians thirteen? Paul declares there that all eloquence (including eloquence in prayer), all faith, all knowledge, even self–sacrifice carried to the extreme of martyrdom, are useless and "profit nothing" apart from the motivation of love.

This indicates that it is possible for us to be engaged in all sorts of religious activities and observances that are simply so much "wood, hay, and stubble" (1 Cor. 3:12) because they are not done with a motive acceptable to God.

A person can belong to any religion, or to no religion, and still give alms, pray, and fast, but the teaching of Jesus is unique in its insistence upon purity of motive. Other religions than Christianity are mainly concerned with the zealous observance and practice of such acts of devotion and philanthropy. However, the fact that a person does these things does not thereby insure the approval of God. He is sure to ask that embarrassing question, "*Why* do you do them?"

In speaking of this hypocritical almsgiving, fasting, and prayer that was so distasteful to God because of its wrong motives, three times Jesus used the Greek word *apechō,* made up of the preposition *apo,* meaning "from" and the verb *echo,* meaning "have" translated in the Authorized Version as "reward."

When this term is used, it indicates "being paid in full with no balance due left over." If a person owed something and paid it in full, without anything more due, he would express this by the compound word, *apechō.* It is "to have one's reward or pay 'in full,' " and not just "to have."

The word *apechō* is used in Matthew 6:2 of those who were giving alms so that they could be commended by the onlookers. Jesus said in effect: "If you are giving alms in order to be commended by others, then you 'have your reward in full' [*apechō*]. God will give you nothing in the world to come. However, if you give alms in secret and receive no commendation for it down here, then you have a reward coming in the future."

The same word is used again in Matthew 6:5 in regard to those who pray publicly in order to be commended for their prayers. The verse says, "They have their reward in full [*apechousin*]."

Religious exercises, therefore, that are performed for the purpose of drawing the attention of our fellow men to ourselves are not acceptable to Christ. As one has put it, "Prayers which are meant for the ears of others will never reach the ear of God."

Never proclaim yourself to be a man or woman of prayer, nor allow others to call you that. Don't seek the reputation of a philanthropist, or of one who fasts. Be all of these, but let God alone know it. Don't give, fast, and pray so that others can say how wonderful you are. If you do, you "have your reward in full." As someone wrote, "Do good by stealth, and blush to find it fame."

The story is told of an artist who painted a picture of a friar in his canonical robes. When the painting was viewed from a distance, one would think the friar was in a praying attitude. His hands were clasped together and held horizontally to his breast; his eyes meekly lowered, like those of the publican in the Gospel; and the good man appeared to be quite absorbed in humble adoration and devout recollection. But upon closer scrutiny, the deception vanished. The book that seemed to be before him was discovered to be a punch bowl into which the wretch was all the while only squeezing a lemon!

That little story proves the point nicely: all that appears to be prayer is not true prayer in God's sight. Others may be deceived by it but not He. He looks into the heart to see what has inspired the words that have been uttered.

A little poem puts it succinctly:

> In all my prayers that I love to say,
> There is one moot question—
> Do I really *pray?*

Unless we have the right motives, we do not "really pray" at all.

Prayer Can Kill or Cure

In recent years the medical world has begun to experiment with a substance called curare. Used as a medication, especially as an antispasmodic, it has helped many people. Yet curare is a deadly poison used by the South American Indians to tip their lethal arrows. Strychnine is another poison that can be used as a medicine, serving as a tonic to the central nervous system. These substances can be helpful or harmful, depending upon the way they're used. They can literally kill or cure.

Prayer is like that, in a way. Based upon a proper understanding of the holiness and perfection of God, it's a wonderful "medicine" for our ills. Based upon a false concept of God, however, prayer can become destructive to our spiritual life rather than beneficial.

To borrow an illustration from nature, we know that a very slight shift in the position of the sun towards earth would change our earth from a habitable house to an inferno. What is now the source of life would become the source of death. Just so, a slight shift away from the truth in our concept of God can cause prayer to be changed from something that gives life to something that has a deadening effect upon our faith. Just as our natural life depends upon a proper relation of the sun to the earth, so our spiritual life depends upon a proper concept of God.

In themselves, our beliefs about prayer could actually cause our faith in God to deteriorate, instead of strengthening it. The reason this is possible is prayer can be a most frustrating thing if the person who is praying looks first at self and its needs, instead of looking first at God. This is why it's essential that our first realization in prayer be the holiness and perfection of God. We need to get a vision of His glory and adequacy before we begin to ask for the supply of our needs. Before we pray, we need an understanding of God and His character. In fact, if we don't have a true concept of Him we are apt to give up praying altogether, concluding that it's only a futile exercise of the imagination.

In at least one instance, wrong concepts of God and prayer were purposely *used* to kill faith. After the Russian revolution, one of the first goals of the Communists was to destroy all faith in God, especially among the children. In some schools, the children were instructed to go to the front of the room, kneel down, and pray to God for candy. When they opened their eyes, of course, no candy was there. The teachers taunted them with the fact that their "prayers" hadn't been answered. Therefore, it was obviously a waste of time to pray to God. The children were then told to pray to Lenin. As they were in prayer, the teacher quietly placed candy on each desk. The very act of prayer was used to convince the children of the futility of praying to God thus destroying their faith.

Even if our wrong concepts don't cause us to give up praying completely, they may at least cause us to draw the wrong conclusions. For example, as we observe the distribution of God's benefits and blessings, we may conclude that we are being denied what we need or ask because God doesn't consider us worthy or because we lack faith. Sometimes these are the reasons for our inadequate supply of resources, but not always. Remember the words of Christ as He discussed with His disciples the case of the man born blind, "Neither hath this man sinned, nor his parents: but that the works of God should be made manifest in him" (John 9:3).

If you pray, yet don't receive what you think God ought to give you, don't conclude that it's because of some injustice, mistake, or fault on God's part. Remember, He is perfect and holy. Also, don't conclude that it's necessarily because you lack faith or spiritual resolution or because you didn't spend a prescribed amount of time in prayer.

Are you experiencing frustration in your prayer-life? Maybe you need a new perspective. Instead of looking at yourself and trying to figure out what's wrong with your praying, go out and look at the stars. They bear mute but eloquent testimony to the perfection of God's natural creation and the precision of His natural laws. Remind yourself that the same God who rules over the natural creation also rules over the spiritual realm, including the realm of prayer. Doesn't it stand to reason that He maintains the same perfection and precision in the execution of His spiritual laws as He does in the execution of the natural?

How true it is: *to pray aright, we must know God aright.*

Prayer Begins With
a Sense of Need

When an architect designs a building, he doesn't begin with the roof but with the foundation. He begins his calculations on the ground rather than in the air. So it is with prayer—we build from the bottom up. And the foundation from which the edifice of prayer rises heavenward is our sense of need. Indeed, it's our sense of need that provides the stimulus to pray, for apart from it, it's doubtful we would ever pray at all.

Our sense of need always precedes our realization of the sufficiency of God to meet those needs. For instance, before a sinner seeks salvation, he must first realize his need for forgiveness. Then comes the recognition that salvation is found in sufficient abundance for all, in and through Christ.

A sense of personal inadequacy is an inherent part of man's makeup. On a horizontal level, this sense of inadequacy serves to create within us social instincts, for we are keenly aware that we cannot exist in isolation. God has made us social beings, and as such we instinctively grasp the truth of those lines in John Donne's poem, "For Whom The Bell Tolls," that state:

No man is an island, entire of itself;
every man is a piece of the continent,
a part of the main . . . .

Thus it is our sense of need that is at the base of all social interchange. This awareness that we are not sufficient unto ourselves makes society not only possible or desirable, but absolutely essential to our well–being. Imagine living all by yourself and never seeing, hearing, or speaking to another person. To live in such a state is to commit social and emotional suicide. We instantly recognize the severe personality disorder of the hermit or total recluse who shuns all contact with other human beings.

Just as our sense of need and dependence creates a social instinct and moves us toward our fellow man in the cooperative state known as society, it also creates a spiritual instinct that moves us toward God in prayer. Recognizing our need of others causes us to seek their company in social relationships; recognizing our need of God causes us to seek Him in the communion of prayer.

Our basic sense of aloneness and personal inadequacy and insufficiency can be only partially mitigated by our social contacts with other human beings. We can to some extent satisfy our need to communicate our feelings and to reveal our inner selves to persons of like mind. However, there is a point beyond which we cannot go in sharing our true selves with others. Our painful experiences of rejection and misunderstanding have caused us to be wary of revealing our most intimate feelings and yearnings to other humans, even those closest to us.

One person who had experienced many rebuffs and rejections in the process of seeking to share deeper thoughts and feelings wrote: "I have closed myself within myself, as the occupants of the medieval castle enclosed themselves for their protection not only within thick, impenetrable walls, but behind deep, impassable moats. And the drawbridge is up!"

It's our very need of expressing ourselves to someone who is totally understanding, sympathetic, and accepting, and our painful awareness that no human being can be all this to us, that drives us to God in prayer. Because we have learned to hide our deeper feelings from others, we are lonely. Surely God has implanted this sense of aloneness within us to cause us to seek communion with Him.

The drawn blinds in the house of bereavement suggest not so much a shutting out of the sunlight as a shutting in of the heart with its private sorrows that can't be shared with the world. Just so, when we shut the door of our prayer closet and seek to be alone in communion with our Heavenly Father, it's not so much a shutting out of others as the shutting in of ourselves with the One who knows us better than any other. We may desire the hushing of earthly voices, because we know that if they speak they will condemn, yet we long to hear the voice of the One who infinitely sympathizes with us and unerringly understands us. When the windows that look out upon the world are shuttered, we may look up through that window which is always open to heaven. When the strident voices of the world are hushed, we may hear more clearly that still, small voice that whispers within.

Who is there among our fellows that can understand our longings and yearnings? We can't even understand them ourselves! Nothing eludes our understanding like our deepest needs. Indeed, our greatest prayers are not those we utter but those whose very magnitude baffles expression. We may stifle these longings from others, simply because we can't articulate them. But the heart will speak to God when the tongue cannot. For such language of the heart, of what use is human fellowship? Our soul clamors for a sympathetic auditor, and apart from God there is no one who can meet the demand.

Like tides on a crescent sea–beach,
When the moon is new and thin,
Into our hearts high yearnings
Come welling and surging in,—
Come from the mystic ocean
Whose rim no foot has trod,—
Some of us call it Longing,
And others call it God.
                              —William H. Carruth

Astronomers, observing the movements of the planet
Saturn, came to the conclusion that these couldn't be
explained apart from the supposition that there was another planet, an unknown one, beyond it. They searched and
discovered Uranus and then Neptune. So is our human soul
attracted by the unseen. Invisible forces are exerting their
influence upon it. We have come out from God, and as
water seeks its level, surging ever onward toward its original source, the ocean, so the human spirit at every opportunity surges upward toward the level of its divine origin.
Thus St. Augustine wrote:

O Lord . . . Thou madest us for Thyself, and our
heart is restless until it
rests in Thee.

God Meets Our Needs
Through Prayer

Would it surprise you to learn that one of the basic laws of economics is also a basic law of prayer? It's the law of need (which creates what economists call "demand") and supply. This law is operative in all business transactions. When a person applies to the bank for a loan to buy a new car, he is putting this law into operation. The buyer has a need; the bank has the resources to meet that need. Such transactions require two parties.

Before a loan is contracted, there must be a borrower and a lender; before a gift is possible, there must be a receiver and a giver; before a legal will can exist, there must be an heir and a testator; before an organ is transplanted there must be a recipient and a donor.

Just as all these human transactions require a giver and a receiver, so does prayer. It's a sense of need that causes us to pray, but coupled with it must be a recognition of the abundant resources of God that are available to meet those needs.

God has all that we need, but though many of His common mercies are given freely to all, there are other gifts and graces that can only come to us through prayer. Thus James 4:2 says, "Ye have not, because ye ask not."

A benevolent father may desire that his son be equipped with a well–trained mind, but he can't present him with a disciplined and well–informed intellect as he would a camera or an automobile. Knowledge can't be imparted in such a way, though we sometimes wish it could! There must be personal involvement of work and study on the part of the one who is seeking knowledge. Therefore we see that desire for knowledge must precede its acquisition. We first have to want it.

Actually, nothing we enjoy as free human agents can be imposed upon us against our wills. Even love is impotent unless it is desired and sought—who hasn't heard songs and stories of unrequited love that was powerless to move the heart of the loved one to respond? If moral and spiritual gifts and qualities were forced upon us, they would be utterly worthless. God longs to endow us with all virtues, but if He imposed them upon us they would no longer be virtues, for the essential quality of virtue is that it be volitionally acquired. If God arbitrarily poured out His choicest gifts and graces upon us, we would become mere "dummy saints," much like a doll with a sweet expression painted on its face.

To force our will would be to annihilate it, for a will suppressed is a will destroyed. Therefore, however desirous God may be that we develop sublime moral qualities, He can't attain that end by forcing them upon us. It would not be the part of wisdom to destroy our capacity as free moral agents—the basis of our humanity—in the process of making us Godlike. Forcing His favors upon us would sink us to the level of beasts rather than elevate us to the height of divinity. Since righteousness can't be attained without personal volition, God withholds His great moral gifts until we seek them, thus rendering prayer an absolute necessity.

It is sometimes argued, "Why trouble God about our difficulties and needs? He knows all about them, so why not just leave everything entirely to Him and let Him see that all our needs are met?" We can't disturb God our Father more than by leaving Him alone, like a parent is disturbed when ignored by his child. Prayer isn't intended to intensify His love to us, but our love to Him.

Would the fact that you stand by the window watching and listening to your children's excitement over finding a bird's nest in a nearby tree mean that you don't want them to tell you about it when they come rushing in with the news? Would you, as a parent, say to them, "You don't have to tell me, I already know all about it"? Of course not! Love delights in being told what it already knows, for in the telling of the matter there is a new expression of the loved one's personality. What love revels in isn't the conversation but the communion, and God is love. Prayer is meant to be a love–tryst, and therefore the fact that God is willing and able abundantly to supply our needs doesn't preclude prayer.

Such abundance should rather serve as an incentive to pray. An indigent philosopher at the court of Alexander sought relief at the hand of that sovereign and received an order to his treasurer for any sum he should ask. He immediately demanded ten thousand pounds. The treasurer demurred at the extravagant amount; but Alexander replied, "Let the money be instantly paid. I am delighted with this philosopher's way of thinking: he has done me a singular honor. By the largeness of his request, he shows the high idea he has conceived of my wealth and munificence." God is honored in like manner.

A child who knows his father has nothing to give will be very reluctant to ask for anything at all, but one who knows his father is wealthy and generous will be emboldened to ask whatever he needs or desires. God is abundantly able to provide for all our needs. He has ordained that we come to Him with boldness in order to obtain what we need. Thus we are admonished in Hebrews 4:16, "Let us therefore come boldly unto the throne of grace, that we may obtain mercy, and find grace to help in time of need."

Sir Walter Raleigh one day asked a favor of Queen Elizabeth, who said to him, "Raleigh, when will you leave off begging?" To which he replied, "When your Majesty leaves off giving." Let us ask great things of God, expect great things, and let His past goodness make us instant in prayer.

Must I Go to Church to Pray?

The second occasion on which the Lord taught His model prayer to His disciples was not in Galilee, but in an unknown location. We read in Luke 11:1, "And it came to pass, that, as he was praying in a certain place, when he ceased, one of his disciples said unto him, Lord, teach us to pray, as John also taught his disciples."

The Greek text has it, *en topō tini*, "in an undetermined place." The Holy Spirit didn't want us to know the exact place, for I can well imagine that had it been revealed to us, we would have sanctified the ground on which our Lord prayed and where He sat to teach His prayer.

In spite of the fact that the exact place is unknown, apparently a group of Catholics have decided it was on the Mount of Olives. Today one can find on this mountain, across from the Temple area, the "Paternoster" Church, containing plaques engraved with the Lord's Prayer in a variety of languages.

Any place can be appropriate for prayer. Many people think that one has to be in a church in order to be able to pray, but our environment has nothing to do with prayer. It is significant that the Lord did not teach His disciples to pray while He Himself was in the Temple, which was the center of Jewish worship. Prayer is first mentioned in Genesis 4:26, "Then began men to call upon the name of the Lord." Where? We are not told. But prayer was established before particular places of worship were even designated.

In Luke's Gospel we have several references to the places where Jesus prayed. One such place was at the River Jordan, in Perea, where He was baptized. In Luke 3:21 we read, "Now when all the people were baptized, it came to pass, that Jesus also being baptized, and praying, the heaven was opened." The Greek word for "being baptized" is in the aorist tense, which implies "after He was baptized," or "when His baptism was completed." This participle "praying" is *proseuchomenou*, "while He was praying." He was possibly still in the water, or He may have just walked out of the water and while standing on Jordan's bank was praying. We are not told what He said. Perhaps He was not praying audibly at all.

The Lord Jesus often chose isolated desert places in which to pray, thus indicating that He considered these places equivalent to the closet to which He advised us to retire in order that we might speak to our God in private. He advises privacy in prayer, but this can be in any place, whether it is a desert area or a private room.

The Lord Jesus is never recorded as having closeted Himself in any synagogue for the purpose of prayer, possibly in order not to suggest that we need a place of public worship before we can engage in private prayers.

In Luke 6:12, we read "And it came to pass in those days, that he went out into a mountain to pray, and continued all night in prayer to God." Why did He go to a mountain? Just so He could enjoy privacy. This is made clear in Matthew 14:23, "And when he had sent the multitudes away, he went up into a mountain apart [privately, by Himself] to pray; and when the evening was come, he was there alone" (See also Mark 1:35 and 6:46, 47).

19

In Luke 5:16, we read, "And he withdrew himself into the wilderness, and prayed." In Luke 9:18 it says, "And it came to pass, as he was alone praying, his disciples were with him . . ." Apparently His disciples were nearby, but the Lord was praying by Himself. This was also the case in Luke 11:1—"And it came to pass, that, as he was praying in a certain place, when he ceased, one of his disciples said unto him, Lord, teach us to pray . . ."

He must have been praying alone. During the last week of His life, the week of His passion, the Lord wanted to pray in the Garden of Gethsemane on the Mount of Olives. Luke 22:41, 42 says, "And he was withdrawn from them about a stone's cast, and kneeled down, and prayed, saying, Father, if Thou be willing, remove this cup from me: nevertheless not my will, but thine, be done."

Thus we see that, as far as the Lord Jesus was concerned, He prayed anywhere He could be alone with God. That is the highest kind of prayer, when we can commune with God from the deepest recesses of our hearts without the distractions caused by the presence of others. Prayer is basically a private matter of communication between the individual and God.

However, although our Lord did most of His praying in private places, whenever He wanted to reveal deep truths, especially truths regarding His relationship with the Father, He made His prayers public, thus using them as a vehicle for His teachings.

Such a prayer is found in Matthew 11:25, 26: "At that time Jesus answered and said, I thank thee, O Father, Lord of heaven and earth, because thou hast hid these things from the wise and prudent, and hast revealed them unto babes. Even so, Father: for so it seemed good in thy sight." (See also Luke 10:21, 22.)

Another instance of Jesus' public prayer is in John 11:41, 42: "Then they took away the stone from the place where the dead [i.e., Lazarus] was laid. And Jesus lifted up his eyes and said, Father, I thank thee that thou hast heard me. And I knew that thou hearest me always: but because of the people which stand by I said it, that they may believe that thou has sent me."

And finally, the longest public prayer of Jesus is recorded in John chapter seventeen. In this prayer, as in the others mentioned, our Lord spoke of His special and unique relationship with the Father.

Where did the Lord Jesus pray these public prayers? The first, in Matthew 11:25, 26 and Luke 10:21, 22, was in Galilee—probably out in the fields—as the seventy disciples were ready to go south to Judea by way of Perea, which lies to the east of the Jordan. The second public prayer was over Lazarus' entombed body in Bethany, hardly two miles from Jerusalem. The third was in a garden on the Mount of Olives.

In no instance did the Lord pray publicly in a public place of worship, either the Temple or a synagogue. How different from those who consider the church as just about the only place fit for public prayer. Would we not do well to follow the example of Jesus and to consider the hills, cemeteries, and gardens as appropriate places for such prayer?

Of course, this is not to suggest that public places of worship should not also be places of public prayer. When our Lord drove the merchants and the money changers from the Temple, He said, "My house is the house of prayer; but ye have made it a den of thieves" (Luke 19:46).

The point is that Jesus did not teach, either by precept or example, that it was necessary to "go to church" in order to address His Father publicly. He had a spontaneity and naturalness in prayer that is the mark of all who live in close and constant communion with God. How impoverished we shall be if we insist on restricting our public prayers to the church. How much better if we learn to pray as He did, in all places and at all times, "making of the wide world a temple."

What Posture in Prayer?

Thomas Adams, one of the Puritan preachers, wrote: "If He be 'our Lord,' let us do Him reverence. It hath ever been the manner and posture of God's servants, when either they offer anything to Him (Matt. 2:11) or pray to receive anything from Him (Ps. 95:6), to do it on their knees. When he bestows favor or honor be it but a knighthood, men kneel for it. In that holy place, where men receive the forgiveness of sins, the honor of saints, so gracious a pardon, so glorious a blessing, there be some that refuse so humble a gesture to the Lord Himself. Never tell me of a humble heart, where I see a stubborn knee."

Prayer involves spiritual respect. This is demonstrated externally by our physical posture. But it doesn't necessarily follow that the person who prostrates his body thereby humbles his soul before God and engages in spiritual communication with the Lord.

Let us look now at some of the postures of prayer recorded in the Scriptures:

In the Bible, *bowing the head or the body* often symbolized the bowing of the spirit of man before God:

Genesis 24:26: "And the man *bowed down his head*, and worshiped the Lord" (this refers to Isaac).

When deliverance was announced to Israel, "they *bowed their heads* and worshiped" (Ex. 4:31).

After the Israelites' firstborn children were spared at the time of the Passover, we are told that "the people *bowed the head* and worshiped" (Ex. 12:27).

After Moses received the second tables of the law, he "bowed his head toward the earth, and worshiped" (Ex. 34:8).

Another physical posture assumed in prayer was that of kneeling. In 1 Kings 8:54 we read, "When Solomon had made an end of praying all this prayer and supplication unto the Lord, he arose from before the altar of the Lord, from *kneeling on his knees* with his hands spread up to heaven." (See also 2 Chr. 6:13.)

Ezra prayed in a similar manner as we read in Ezra 9:5: "And at the evening sacrifice I arose up from my heaviness; and having rent my garment and my mantle, *I fell upon my knees,* and spread out my hands unto the Lord my God."

Psalm 95:6 advises us, "O come, let us worship and bow down: Let us kneel before the Lord our maker."

It is written of Daniel while he was in exile in Babylon that he "went into his house; and his windows being open in his chamber toward Jerusalem, he *kneeled upon his knees* three times a day, and prayed, and gave thanks before his God, as he did aforetime" (Dan. 6:10).

Still another posture in prayer is *falling on one's face before God* In Numbers 20:6 we read, "And Moses and Aaron went from the presence of the assembly unto the door of the tabernacle of the congregation, and they *fell upon their faces:* and the glory of the Lord appeared unto them."

Joshua 5:14 says, "And Joshua *fell on his face to the earth,* and did worship, and said unto him, What saith my lord unto his servant?"

Of Elijah it is said, "And Elijah went up to the top of Carmel, and he cast himself down upon the earth, and put *his face between his knees*" (1 Kings 18:42).

2 Chronicles 20:18 says, "And Jehoshaphat *bowed his head with his face to the ground*: and all Judah and the inhabitants of Jerusalem fell before the Lord, worshipping the Lord."

Of the Lord in the Garden of Gethsemane it is written, "And he went a little further, and *fell on his face*, and prayed, saying, O my Father, if it be possible, let this cup pass from me: nevertheless not as I will, but as thou wilt" (Matt. 26:39).

Another posture is that of *standing*. Of Solomon it is written in 1 Kings 8:22, "And Solomon stood before the altar of the Lord in the presence of all the congregation of Israel, and spread forth his hands toward heaven."

Our Lord said in Mark 11:25, "*And when ye stand praying*, forgive, if ye have ought against any: that your Father also who is in heaven may forgive you your trespasses."

Never do we find any of God's saints praying with their knees crossed. Should we? I was deeply shocked when I saw that posture in prayer by some American missionaries in Cairo, Egypt, when I first came to know the Lord Jesus Christ. Crossed knees indicate a position of familiarity. A person granted an audience with the sovereign of Great Britain is instructed not to cross his legs while in the presence of royalty. In the East, it is considered a sign of disrespect to cross one's knees when in the presence of a venerable person. It is safest to avoid over–familiar postures when praying, lest the heart be made irreverent toward God.

Another of the Puritans wrote: "God is Lord of my body [as well as of my spirit]: and therefore challengeth as well reverent gesture as inward devotion. I will ever, in my prayers, either stand, as a servant, before my Master, or kneel, as a subject, to my Prince."

The Model Prayer and Why It Was Given

"**M**ore things are wrought by prayer than this world dreams of," wrote Alfred Lord Tennyson, "wherefore let thy voice rise like a fountain . . . night and day." But if prayer is the most powerful force in the world, it is also no doubt the most neglected and the least understood. And perhaps no prayer is so universally known and repeated, yet so little understood, as the one commonly known as "The Lord's Prayer."

Actually, in the light of the intended purpose of this prayer, this lack of understanding seems highly ironic. Woodworth observes "Clearly the object of the Lord's Prayer was not to teach prayer in the abstract, but rather *to correct false notions regarding communion with God,* and to advance the disciples in a knowledge of *the Father* as revealed by *the Son.*"

As we begin our analysis of the prayer, let us look first at the circumstances under which it was given. As our Lord emerged from a night of prayer, His waiting disciples saw how changed His countenance was. It radiated a glory that was not of this earth. What an effect prayer had on Him! One of them, perhaps yearning for a touch of this radiant glory upon his own life, and feeling keenly his lack of it, said to Him, "Lord, teach us to pray."

This is the heart–cry of millions today, for the desire to pray is instinctive in man. Yet so often even the true believer feels his inadequacy in this area. And of those who do pray, many have such a false view of prayer that it has become for them only "vain repetitions." Some almost seem to regard prayer as a form of "magic" incantations which, if repeated often enough and fervently enough, will produce (hopefully) the effects they desire.

In answer to the request of His disciples, the Lord gave them a model prayer. It's a very simple prayer, and it wasn't meant to be used exclusively. We are to pray *after this manner,* not *always with these words,* but always in this method, always in this spirit, and always for some or all of the things summed up in these brief sentences.

The prayer is indicative of what we ought to pray about and also of how we ought to pray. Hugh Latimer, reformer and martyr, said: "As the law of love is the sum and abridgement of all other laws, so is this prayer the sum and abridgment of all other prayers. All other prayers are contained in this prayer; yea, whatsoever mankind hath need of as to soul and body, that same is contained in this prayer."

As brief as it is, when we explore its true meanings we can begin to realize that it is the perfect response to that heart–cry of the race, "Teach us to pray."

The late Dr. Adolph Saphir wrote: "It is a model prayer, and as such commends itself to the most superficial glance—approves itself at once to the conscience of man. It is beautiful and symmetrical, like the most finished work of art. The words are plain and unadorned, yet majestic; and so transparent and appropriate that, once fixed in the memory, no other expressions ever mix themselves up with them; the thought of substituting other words never enters the mind. Grave and solemn are the petitions, yet the serenity and tranquil confidence, the peace and joy which they breathe, prove attractive to every heart.

"The Prayer is short, that it may be quickly learned, easily remembered, and frequently used; but it contains all things pertaining to life and godliness. In its simplicity it seems adapted purposely for the weakness of the inexperienced and ignorant, and yet none can say that he is familiar with the heights and depths which it reveals, and with the treasures of wisdom it contains. It is calm, and suited to the even tenor of our daily life, and yet in times of trouble and conflict the Church has felt its value and power more especially, has discovered anew that it anticipates every difficulty and danger, that it solves every problem, and comforts the disciples of Christ in every tribulation of the world.

"It is the beloved and revered friend of our childhood, and it grows with our growth, a never–failing counselor and companion amid all the changing scenes of life. And as in our lifetime we must confess ourselves, with Luther, to be only learning the high and deep lessons of those petitions, so it will take eternity to give them their answer."

In What Sense is This "The Lord's Prayer"?

I t is interesting to note that the prayer commonly known as "the Lord's Prayer" was actually given on two different occasions. The first time was in Matthew 6:9–13, as part of the Sermon on the Mount of the Beatitudes in Galilee. In this instance, it is given as part of a more general teaching of Jesus on almsgiving (Matt. 6:16–18). The second time the prayer was given is recorded in Luke 11:1–4.

Is it not possible that when the disciples heard the prayer first given on the Mount, they did not fully comprehend that Jesus was, in effect, "teaching them to pray"? It seems as though the Lord were saying to His disciples: "I have already given you what I consider the 'model prayer,' although you may not have fully grasped the significance of it at that time. Now you have asked me, once again, to teach you to pray. I cannot improve upon the prayer I have already given. I have nothing to add or to detract, for this model is all–inclusive and complete. Therefore, I can do nothing better than to repeat that which I have already given you once before." Thus the prayer as recorded in Luke chapter four is given in essentially the same form as the one recorded in Matthew 6:9–13.

Whatever the reason for the repetition of the prayer, about which we can only speculate, the very fact that our Lord did give it in practically the same form on two different occasions should indicate to us that He felt it could not be improved upon and that it contained all the elements of true prayer.

The prayer is called "The Lord's Prayer," not because it was expressive of Christ's relationship with His Father, or of His own needs, but simply because it was taught by Him. The possessive form is used in the same sense as when we speak of "Lincoln's Gettysburg Address," thereby indicating that the address was authored and given by Lincoln. Just so, "The Lord's Prayer" means that the prayer was formulated and given by the Lord.

It was not "His" prayer in the sense of being the prayer that He, Himself, prayed. "His" prayer in that literal sense is found in John chapter seventeen, where He pours out His heart to His Father just prior to His death on the cross.

However, when the term, "the Lord's Prayer" is used in regard to the prayer recorded in John chapter seventeen, the possessive is employed in the sense of personal use and expression of personal concerns. This prayer was actually prayed by Jesus, and represented His personal relationship with His Father.

In titling "The Lord's Prayer," we use the possessive in the same sense as when we refer to "God's grace," We do not mean that grace which is needed by God personally, but the grace which originates and has its source in Him, and which is granted to us humans by Him.

The conclusion at which we have arrived, then, is that the prayer was composed by Him and taught by Him, and in that sense is the Lord's prayer, but it was not His personal prayer. He never used this prayer Himself.

Theocentric Prayer

Edward Pell said: "To Jesus a man does not really approach God in prayer so long as his mind is centered in himself; he approaches Him only when he is more concerned about God's interests and will than his own, or when he is struggling to put God's interest ahead of his own."

When we come to speak to God, we shouldn't think first of ourselves, but of His honor and glory. When we kneel to pray, our first thought shouldn't be of all that God has done for us, nor all we've done for Him. Nor should we think of all we need or want God to do for us in the future. We should think of God Himself: His holiness, His absolute rule, and the necessity of His will being done on earth.

This agrees basically with the other teachings of the Lord Jesus Christ, such teaching, for instance, as we find in the Sermon on the Mount: "Seek ye first the kingdom of God, and his righteousness; and all these things shall be added unto you" (Matt. 6:33).

Unfortunately, our prayers are for the most part anthropocentric. *Anthrōpos* means "man" (human being), and *centric* means "having to do with the center." By nature the center of all our thoughts, concerns, and prayers is not God, but man. We're too concerned about ourselves when we pray, instead of being concerned with God—His holiness,

His rule, His will. Isn't it true that when we pray we sub-consciously feel that God's chief business is to concentrate on us? We almost seem to conclude that He isn't a good God if we're not the center of His concern!

Have you ever realized that there's a parallel between the Lord's Prayer and the Ten Commandments? In Matthew 22:34, 35 we find the Pharisees coming to Jesus in order to tempt Him. They asked Him if one who failed to keep one of the commandments would be guilty of breaking all of them. In verse thirty-six they asked Him, "Master, which is the great commandment in the law?" Similarly, we ask, "What is the greatest thing we ought to pray about?"

We need to remember that in the Christian life there is unity and balance. We are actually facing a dual relation-ship. There is a vertical relationship and a horizontal one. The one affects the other. On the one hand we have man's relationship with God; on the other, man's relationship with man.

Because this is true, the Lord's Prayer is divided into two sections. The first three petitions—"Hallowed be thy name," "Thy kingdom come," and "Thy will be done in earth, as it is in heaven" concern the person of God Himself. The other three or four petitions (it all depends on how you look at them as to whether you consider them three or four) deal with us human beings, and particularly with the person who is praying. "Give us this day our daily bread": this concerns our daily sustenance. "Forgive us our debts (or our trespasses) as we forgive our debtors (or those who trespass against us)": this deals with our own sin. "Lead us not into temptation": this deals with our encounters with temptation. "Deliver us from evil": this deals with the evil that is in us and around us.

We see that there are three petitions concerning God and three or four concerning man. The fact that the first

33

three deal with the Person of God indicates that this should be our first concern when we pray. We should center our prayers upon God Himself, for He's the center of the universe and of all things, not we. This is the basic lesson we learn from the Lord's Prayer.

Prayer Is an Expression of Relationships

"Our questions about prayer are not basically questions about prayer. They are questions about God," said one author. If we study closely the answer Jesus gave to the query of the Pharisees concerning the greatest commandment, we find that it answers some of our questions about prayer also.

How did He answer them? "Jesus said unto him, Thou shalt love the Lord thy God with all thy heart, and with all thy soul, and with all thy mind. This is the first and great commandment" (Matt. 22:37, 38). As we examine the Ten Commandments, we find that the first four deal with man's relationship to God. That's the vertical relationship I mentioned earlier. We can't treat our fellow humans right unless we are right with God. Then, in verse thirty-nine, the Lord went on and summarized the last six commandments in this way: "Thou shalt love thy neighbour as thyself."

We see this same pattern repeated in the Lord's Prayer. And the simplicity and beauty of this prayer are seen in the fact that it recognizes this dual relationship of God to man and of man to his fellow men, to which I have previously referred. Prayer ought to lead to the examination of our relationships with God and with our fellow men, because none of us lives unto himself or dies unto himself.

Thus, the first thing that our Lord is teaching us here is to say, "Our Father." He is bringing to light a new relationship with God. It is no longer that of a subject to a powerful king who stands far away observing our actions, waiting to punish us or impose certain duties upon us. It is rather the affectionate relationship of a child to a father.

In the Scriptures only the New Testament presents God as a Father of individuals, and He is introduced that way by the Lord Jesus Christ. He gives God a new name, that of "Father." In the Old Testament we do not find this. There the only references to God as "Father" are in connection with His relationship to Israel as a nation (Is. 63:16, Jer. 31:9). But the concept of the eternally and infinitely omnipotent God who comes down and establishes a Father–child relationship with individuals is not shown in the Old Testa-ment.

James Thirtle says in his *Interpretations of The Lord's Prayer*: "Israel had no such conception of God: in her forms of worship she still deals with One who is distant and unreconciled. The 'Our Father' symbolizes 'Liberty, Equality, and Fraternity.' as these are found in the standing and fellowship of believers: the liberty of the sons of God, the equality of such as are partakers of a heavenly calling, and the fraternity of those who have been made joint–heirs with Christ of the everlasting kingdom."

We find that such a revelation of God as Father is given in John 1:18: "God, no one has seen at any time" is what the Greek text says. But the English translation goes on to say, "the only begotten Son." The term "only begotten" immediately gives the impression that the Son was born of the Father. I don't know why this word, *monogenēs*, was translated as "the only begotten." It actually should be "the only one of the same family, the unique one." Observe that the Lord Jesus Christ is here called "the Son." He is the Son who has always been in the bosom of the Father. The Greek text says, "The One being in the bosom of the Father" (author's literal translation). The Son brought the Father out of His hiding place. The Greek word is *exegesato*. He "exegeted" Him.

Dr. G. H. Gilbert wrote: "The first recorded sentence of Jesus (Luke 2:49), and that which was probably His last (Luke 23:46), both contain the name 'Father.'"

How You Ask Makes a Difference

"Johnny," said the teacher, "if someone on the playground said to you, 'Get out of my way!' what person and mood would that sentence express? Johnny thought for a moment, then said brightly, "Mean person, bad mood!" He may have been a little mixed up about his English, but Johnny was smart enough to know that it's not always *what* you say that counts, it's *how* you say it!

That's true even in the Lord's Prayer, for it contains petitions expressed in two distinct ways. The first three petitions are in the third person singular of the imperative mood.

The first is, "Hallowed be thy name." It's not, "*Hallow* thy name," as though we were commanding God to hallow it. "Let it be hallowed," we say, as if there were a certainty about its being accomplished, although mixed with the certainty is the expression of personal participation in making it possible.

God's name is holy. The universe can never rob God of one iota of His intrinsic holiness. The fall of man, even into the very depths of sin, did nothing to make God any less holy. His character is immutable. The whole universe testifies to God's moral perfection, to His holiness, and to the fact that He has a definite plan that nothing and no one can annul.

The second petition, like the first, is in the third person singular imperative "Let thy kingdom come." In the Greek it's *hagiastheto*— "Let it be holy, thy name"; *eltheto*—"Let it come, thy kingdom." The third petition is similarly structured: *genetheto*—"Let it be done, thy will." Three things are mentioned: the holiness of God's name or God Himself, the kingdom of God, and God's will. These involve God's character, creation, and purpose. What part does man really play in all these, as far as God is concerned?

God's character is His own; we can't affect that, although we can affect His actions. Nothing we can do can make God more or less mighty, more or less just, more or less merciful. Nothing we can do can affect His creative power.

As far as His kingdom is concerned, we aren't the creators of it, it exists apart from us and is handed down to us. We can only accept or reject, choose or refuse, the kingdom. Our response to it determines our destiny, but we don't create it.

His will and His purpose are sovereign. We seek to find them, not for the purpose of changing them, but for the purpose of conforming to them.

How ridiculous it would have been if Christ had taught us to pray, "Father, *make* Thy name holy, *bring* Thy kingdom, *do* Thy will." Such a direct imperative would have given us the idea we could command God to perform what might not be possible apart from our involvement. Prayer is not meant to give such a concept of God!

God is sovereign in His character, His creation, and His purpose, whether we cooperate with Him or oppose Him. None of these three elements can be changed, for they are spiritual elements, eternally and infinitely interwoven into the very fiber of God's being. If they could change, then we would have a God who is not steady and dependable. True, these elements are the concern of the first three petitions of the Lord's Prayer, but the fact that they are in the third person imperative clearly indicates that their meaning is, "Let Thy name *be* holy," "*Let* thy kingdom come," "Let thy will *be* done," and not "Let us assist you, God." He permits and expects us to assist Him, but He doesn't want us to think we can help to *make* God what He already is.

When it comes, however, to the next four petitions, dealing with us and our physical and spiritual needs, there is a definite shift in the kind of imperative used. It's no longer, "Let it be," but is a direct petition in the second person singular. It is:

> You (Thou) give us (second person singular)
>   our daily bread.
> You (Thou) forgive us (second person singular)
>   our sins.
> You (Thou) deliver us (second person singular)
>   from the evil one.

There is more audacity manifested when it comes to our own needs of bread, forgiveness, protection from temptation, and freedom from the presence and influence of the devil.

We have a sense of responsibility for what happens to us, but we also realize that God's direct involvement is necessary. That which pertains to God's character, work, and purpose, He can manage on His own. When it comes to our own physical and spiritual well–being, we can't make it on our own, and therefore we have the petition for God's immediate involvement.

The Lord wanted us to realize this fundamental fact as we pray: there is nothing we can do to change God. He is immutable. However, there is always something God can do to change us. Without Him, none of our needs can be met. When He meets those needs, however, it's not according to our understanding of them, but according to His. For we see only darkly and know only partially, being limited by time and space, while He sees and knows us in the context of His eternal and infinite plan, in relation to all else He has made.

SECTION II

Our Father, Who Art in Heaven

The Brotherhood of Prayer

The Lord's Prayer was taught primarily to the disciples, who were Jews. That's one of the reasons Jesus taught them to say "Our Father" when they prayed (actually, in the Greek it is "Father ours"). The Jew was always conscious of being one of God's chosen people. In his prayers the Jew was the epitome of exclusiveness. He, out of all nations, was "the selected man." He was hedged round about with varied ceremonies from his cradle to his grave that served to impress upon him with the most grave significance that he was a peculiar man, not reckoned among the nations, but standing alone as God's particular, favored creature.

Jesus came in order to put an end to the concept of God having favorites. No longer do we stand to pray as Jew or Gentile, Barbarian or Scythian, bond or free. The lines of demarcation are now abolished and we stand to pray as one family, though we may have many differences in some aspects. We stand as one family to say "Our Father." He who stands by himself, not entering into the communion of the saints, not realizing that he is a member of the "body of Christ," is not standing in the position the Master would have him occupy.

We realize, however, that there are times when prayer must begin with the individual and his own need. He must cry aloud for pardon, for the removal of some great, separating cloud of sin, or for the gift of some necessary grace. The publican wasn't wrong to pray, "God be merciful to me a sinner" (Luke 18:13).

But, in reality, after one has become a child of God, prayer is no longer an individual matter but a collective one. Enter into your chamber if you will, and shut your door and pray in secret to the Father—alone with God, alone with your own sins and cares and desires—that you may pour them all out before the throne. But even as you open your lips in what you call "The Lord's Prayer," its first word (in Greek it's the second word) gives the lie to the theory that prayer is an individual matter: "Our Father."

It makes me realize that in prayer *I am not alone.* I am one with the members of God's family, which is also my family. My weak prayer is caught up into the great stream of prayer that goes up forever from God's family. The strength of my prayer is that it is not simply mine; that the moment I fall upon my knees I am no longer an individual man or woman talking to God, but a member of the family of God, a sharer in that human nature which Christ has carried to the right hand of God.

The communion of saints is what gives life and force to prayer, comfort and confidence to those who pray. *On my knees I cannot be alone.* My prayer, as weak, as feeble, as helpless as it is, is organically united with the prayers of the whole Church. We are all members of one body. We belong to an association for intercessory prayer. No part of this great organism can be touched with disease without the mischief vibrating through the whole, and no new strength can be gained that does not spread to each part, filling the whole with new energy.

We must avoid two things in prayer: selfishness and vagueness. We correct the one when we understand that all real prayer has an element of intercession in it; we correct the other when we fix our thoughts on the special needs of others. The more we pray for them that they may be better, may be more fit for the work of God, the more we shall have succeeded by God's grace to make our own selves better.

The Lord's Prayer makes us realize that we have duties and obligations to that family which is God's and ours. How can we look up to God and say "Our Father" when we are excluding any from their full share of that love? How can we say "Our Father" and then virtually add, "As I am Thine in a sense that my brother is not—give *me* something, forgive *me* something, save *me* from something"? What would you think of a child who rushed to his father when the house was on fire and cried, "Oh, save *me*! I'm your firstborn!" You couldn't help seeing the meanness and the selfishness of such a cry. What you would expect him to say, and what you, yourself, would surely say, is this: "Oh, Father, how can I help you save my mother and brothers and sisters!"

It is this selfish "I" and "me" that has been the greatest curse, not only of the world system, but even of the Church. While common prayer to the Father suggests a common interest, and helps to keep the common bond alive and vital, sin separates. The sinner is an egotist. The motto of the world is "Every man for himself." An isolating principle is at work in everyone who has turned his back on the Father, the result of which is seen when, in the language of the world's own shrewd vernacular, his one thought is for "number one."

This isn't to suggest that the individuality of the child is lost in the family, for it is always maintained, and God never loses sight of us as separate personal entities. He continues to deal with each of us on an individual basis.

Though it's necessary that each one of us pray for himself and say, "Father, give me my daily bread, forgive me, lead me," at the same time, everyone whose heart beats with the new life not only sings a new song but breathes a new prayer—the prayer that rises in concert with all the family and that opens with the cry, "Our Father."

How many are you going to include in that little possessive pronoun "our"—only the members of your church and denomination, or all those who have the same right as you to call God "Father"? Actually we are debarred from properly using the Lord's Prayer until we learn to exercise a large, boundless charity. Only let us feel how many there are to be included in that word "our," and we shall reverently pause before we venture to use it, lest our lips should be saying what our heart or our actions deny.

Dr. Charles Stanford, in his book on *The Lord's Prayer,* said: "The waves are many, the sea is one; the boughs are many, the vine is one; the stones are many, the temple is one; the children are many, the family is one; and as one family we say, 'Our Father.' "

God Is Not the Exclusive Father of Anybody

We might have no right to pray to God as our Father in heaven if we fail to realize the presence and the importance of those who live around us. The Lord didn't teach us to address God as only an individual Father. We're not to think of Him simply as "My Father," but as "Our Father," whether we pray privately or publicly.

Let us not misconstrue the fact that our Lord taught us to say "Our Father" as meaning that He intended this prayer for public use, therefore using the plural form "our" instead of the singular "my," The context in which this prayer is given and the teaching just preceding it (Matt. 6:6) clearly indicate that it was intended to be an individual, private prayer, offered in one's closet, a private place. True, we must each come to God as our own individual Father, but without thinking for one moment that we are His only child.

Woodworth says in his *Sermons on the Lord's Prayer*: "When thou prayest alone, shut thy door—shut out as much as thou canst the sight and notice of others, but shut not out the interest and the good of others; say, 'Our Father.' "

We must always remember when we approach God in prayer that He is the Father of others besides being our own personal Father. Bishop Christopher Wordsworth wrote concerning this: *"Pater hēmōn*—'Father of us.' Not *emou,* nor *hēmetere*—'my Father.' He lays the foundation of prayer in love. If God is our Father, we should honor Him as His children; and if He is the Father of us (*hēmōn*), it follows that we should love one another as brethren."

Someone asked a certain man what his creed was. He replied, "The first two words of the Lord's Prayer. 'Our Father.' " These words speak of our relationship to the One above us and to the ones around us. To have God as my Father is a privilege. But the realization that I am not His only child is filled with meaning and responsibility. I cannot ask God to bless me while at the same time neglect to bless those around me.

He who believes that he is the *only* object of God's care becomes demanding. Few parents are satisfied with only one child in the family. To share parental love and care is very healthy in the development of character and the proper attitude toward parents. When there is more than one child in the family the child ceases to consider the father's provision as being all for himself. There is a realization that it must be shared with brothers and sisters. Thus when we come to God we must recognize that His other children have equal rights with us.

When we realize we are only part of God's family this causes us to be more considerate of others. We learn to look at our seemingly unanswered prayers as perhaps the answered prayers of others. For instance, a farmer was praying for rain that his crops needed at a critical time. The rain didn't come, and as a result he lost his crop for that season. Later that year he was sharing this puzzling experience of unanswered prayer with a relative who lived several miles downstream on the river that flowed near his farm. The man said, "How glad I am that God didn't answer your prayers for rain at that time! We had found that there was a serious fault in the dam just above our community, and we were all earnestly praying that the spring rains wouldn't come until it could be repaired. God answered our prayers, but denied yours. But it was better for you and those in your area to lose one crop than for those of us here to lose all, and maybe even our lives!"

Only as we realize the full implication of the "our" in the Lord's Prayer shall we rejoice in our brother's prosperity and feel concern for the welfare of others. After all, even when God gives us what we ask of Him, He doesn't give it just so that we may enjoy it by ourselves, but rather that we may share it with others. Therefore we are not to pray except as members of a great family. We are not even to pray for general and common blessings for ourselves without asking God to grant the same blessings to our neighbor also.

If you feel that God doesn't answer your prayers, examine your relationship with others in His family. The Father in heaven won't listen to any child who doesn't wish his brothers and sisters well, much less to one who wishes any of them ill. If His gift to you will cause harm to others, it is wisdom on the part of the Father to deprive you of what you request. In reality He is doing you no harm but good. God is duty–bound to withhold from us that which we intend to use selfishly. Why should He give us something that by its very nature will harm others or our relationship with them?

This attitude is not to be a mere pretense. We are to be sincere in this, as in all aspects of our praying. We must interrupt the "Our Father" if we know that we have no respect for the rest of His family or are out of fellowship with a member of His family. Until that condition is corrected, we can't properly proceed with the prayer. If we call God our Father in common with others, we must be willing to call the rest of His family brothers and sisters with the same cordiality with which we call Him "Father."

The Lord's Prayer ought to knock out of us all social, economic, and denominational distinctions. You can't pray the Lord's Prayer sincerely if you consider those who don't belong to your particular denomination strangers to God, in spite of the fact that they, also, have trusted in the finished work of Christ on Calvary's Cross. The Lord's Prayer constantly breaks down the differences that separate us and magnifies our common faith. No two children of the same family think or act exactly alike, and yet in their differences they can have the same parents.

The rich must not despise the poor and the poor must not envy the rich. We must always be affectionately concerned about others in our Father's family. We must never feel so separated by something from someone that we cannot truly pray with and for him, and that we cannot carry his sins to God's throne with the earnest wish that they be forgiven as well as our own, or cannot desire that he receive everything that is truly for his good.

Nothing dishonors a father more than the squabblings among his children. How God as a Father must weep every time we call Him "Father" and yet don't truly act as brothers.

The Lord here teaches that the only true brotherhood is that which rests on God's Fatherhood. It is all because of Christ, through whom we realize God's Fatherhood by our adoption into His family. Because Christ is mine, all who are in Him are in my family. Because Christ has come we are "no more strangers and foreigners" (Eph. 2:19).

The Lord's Prayer exactly reverses the natural order which man adopts in drawing near to God. It teaches us to think not only of ourselves, but also of all the other members of the family of God. Most importantly, it teaches us to think first of God, placing Him before all others and above all else.

Jesus Christ Introduces God to Man as Father

Martin Luther once said: "The little word 'Father' spoken forth in prayer by a child of God exceeds the eloquence of Demosthenes, Cicero, and all the most famous orators the world has ever known." But what man would ever have dared approach God in prayer as "Father" if it had not been for the revelation of Him in that relationship to us by the Lord Jesus Christ? It is He who introduced this concept of God to us.

Whatever else this means, it must first of all mean that He is a personality. He is not to be identified simply as a power, or as "nature." Nor is He an "idea." You give the title of "Father" only to a person. Unfortunately, there are many people who believe in God without considering Him a person. They conceive of Him as something abstract. They say that He is an "intelligence," a "power," behind all that has come to exist.

To define adequately the word "personality" as it applies to God would be an impossibility, because man's concept of personality is but a projection of himself and therefore extremely limited.

Philosophers tell us that our idea of God can only be anthropomorphic. This means that we imagine God to be similar to ourselves. We conceive of Him as having the same shape as we, making Him only a projection of ourselves. We can only think of others in terms of ourselves, having the same appetites, desires, and philosophy of life. But if others differ radically from us in these areas, we cannot possibly comprehend their culture or their philosophy of life unless we are able to become acquainted with their way of life and to observe it objectively. Otherwise, there is no true basis of comparison. So it is with our idea of God.

It is true that He is a person. The problem is that God, though a person, is not like us. Because of this, we can have no accurate concept of His personality apart from divine revelation. Without it our ideas of God will continue to be anthropomorphic, and we will conceive of him as having the shape and the basic characteristics of man.

We can only imagine Him as an extension of what we are. Therefore, we mistakenly attribute human limitations to an infinite and eternal God. When we do this we bring him down to our level and make Him equal to us. This equality, if it be true, makes Him a God incapable of helping us. Consequently, the concept of an anthropomorphic God leads to a humanistic religion.

In the Old Testament, God is presented as infinite, eternal, and all–powerful. When He speaks, the earth trembles, and the people take off their shoes and stand in awe and adoration before Him. Then along comes Jesus Christ and tells us that when we pray we can say, "Our Father who art in heaven." It is not so much a matter of contrast as it is a matter of a fuller revelation of the true nature of God being given to us through our Lord. We see Him revealed through Jesus Christ in a way that the people of the Old Testament did not fully see Him, though they may have caught glimpses of His revelation at times.

A man who was leading in prayer at a large meeting called upon "the great and holy God" and addressed Him at length in many majestic terms of the Old Testament—as being infinitely removed from sinful humans and also utterly remote and unapproachable. Never once did he call Him "Father" or speak to Him as His child. One dear old saint, having endured all he could of this, murmured aloud, "Why doesn't someone give the poor man a New Testament?"

What Jesus was trying to tell us is that this God of whom we read in John 1:18, whom no one has seen at any time because He is infinite, eternal, and invisible, is present everywhere. Yet at the same time He cannot be limited to any one place.

A little girl saw a sign written by an unbeliever that read, "God is nowhere." Someone asked her what it said, and she, slowly spelling out the letters, replied, "Oh, it says, 'God is now here.' " This is the mystery of Christ. He brings God, who is everywhere, to the individual. God, who is considered by some to be "nowhere" is "now here", among us and in us. He is out in the universe encompassing space, and yet I can come and speak to Him just as I would speak to my earthly father.

Once again, look at that wonderful verse:, John 1:18: "God no one hath seen at any time." The only One of the same substance and nature, who belongs to the same family, is the unique Son. He is called the "Son" because His purpose in coming to the world was to reveal the Father and to teach us that God could become our Father. He is the only One who, by virtue of being of the same essence as Deity, has this unique relationship of Son to the Father. He has always been in the bosom of the Father. There is an intimate relationship and familiarity that exists between these two Personalities of the Triune God. To be "in the Father's bosom" is to be in an affectionate position.

So it was the Son who brought the Father to us. He who was thought to be at a great distance is brought close to us. Jesus Christ has made Him more understandable to man.

This is the revelation of God that we find in the Person of Jesus Christ.

God is Father to all human beings in Himself. But this relationship is appropriated only by those who believe in Jesus Christ. The Fatherhood of God is realizable only in and through the Person of Jesus. But the fact remains that God considers Himself as a tender and affectionate Father of all human beings. The story of the Prodigal Son that we find in Luke chapter fifteen very wonderfully demonstrates to us the relationship of God with humanity and the relationship of humanity with God.

God Was Not a Father to Jesus in the Same Way He Is to Us

Bishop Westcott wrote: "The oldest Greek poets spoke of Zeus as 'the father of gods and men' under the imagery of patriarchal life, and they made him like to themselves. Philosophers spoke of the Father of the universe, recognizing something more than an arbitrary connection between the Creator and the creation, but they added that 'it is hard to gain a knowledge of Him, and impossible to communicate it to the world.' The Hebrew prophets spoke of the Lord as the Father of Israel, forming and disciplining the chosen people with a wise and tender love. But Christ first added the title 'My Father' to that of 'Our Father.' It is through the revelation of the Son that we can each find our personal fellowship with a Father in heaven."

Truly Jesus Christ is the only One who could and did reveal God as Father to the human race. But when it comes to the relationship between Jesus and the Father, we note a difference. In John 10:15, the Lord Jesus Christ refers to God, not as "Jehovah," but as "Father." He says, "As the Father knoweth me, even so know I the Father." He is declaring that His knowledge of God as Father is equal to God's knowledge of Him as Son. Being a father, I know my child, but this doesn't necessarily mean that my child knows me equally well. In 1 Corinthians 13:12 we read that we "know in part," but He knows fully.

There is a difference in the mutual relationship that exists between God the Father and God the Son, and the mutual relationship that exists between God the Father and human children. Whereas the Son knows His Father equally as the Father knows Him, we as children of God do not and cannot know Him equally as well as He knows us. There is a unique relationship between Jesus Christ, the Son, and God, the Father.

As the late James Thirtle said: "In revealing the Father, Christ made known One whom He knew. His speech was of 'the Father,' 'My Father,' 'My Father and your Father.' We do not find, however, that the Master Himself used the prayer which He gave to His disciples: He said 'Father' without the 'Our,' and herein, as in other respects, showed Himself to be 'separate from sinners.' " (*The Lord's Prayer, An Interpretation Critical and Expository,* London: Morgan & Scott, 1915:65.)

When the Lord Jesus Christ was touched by Mary Magdalene at His post–resurrection appearance at the sepulcher, He referred to His Father in a distinctive manner. He said, "Touch me not [or, 'Do not continue touching me' as the Greek text has it]." What reason did He give for this? "Because I go to *my Father* and to *your Father.*"

Don't conclude that because Jesus Christ is called "Son," He must necessarily be a creature. We are creatures, but He is equal with the Father, He is co–eternal and infinite. He has always been in the bosom of the Father.

The only way for my son to come to know me fully is for him to acquire the same degree of maturity, growth, and understanding that I have. But the Lord Jesus has always been with the Father—there has never been a time that He didn't know the Father as the Father knew Him.

Is the Son of God Himself God?

Tertullian said, "Only God could teach us how He wished to be addressed in prayer." In view of this statement, it is highly significant that the Lord Jesus in His prayers always addressed God as Father, except in one instance when He employed the prophetic language of Psalm 22:1 in reference to His cross and its consequent shame. In this instance He said, "My God, my God." It's the only time in the New Testament in which our Lord prayed and didn't call God His Father.

As I have previously pointed out to you, the Greek text of John 1:18 says, "God [without the definite article which means, 'God in His infinity, eternity, and essential being as Spirit'] no one has ever seen" (author's literal translation). John isn't referring here to God's voluntary appearance in a partial or localized form, but to God in His totality. No one has seen Him in that way at any time. Both believers and unbelievers agree on this first declaration concerning the invisibility of God. In His totality, where is He? Can you touch Him? Can you see Him? No one can.

It's somewhat like standing on the shore and saying, "I see the ocean." Do you? You actually only see a part of it, because of your limitations. Nor can you have any true conception of its immensity.

God in the Old Testament revealed Himself in various theophanies, or voluntary appearances. But He never appeared in His totality and His infinity. It is impossible for a finite being to see an infinite being, if we can call Him a "being." Therefore the first part of John 1:18 declares that no created being can comprehend or see God in His infinity and in His eternity.

We know that the sun is the source of all light. Yet only a child in his ignorance dares to try to look into the face of the sun itself. We who are older know that to do so can result in blindness, because our eyes are unable to bear its brightness. We can only know the sun through what is revealed of it in the light and heat it sheds and in the colors by which it is reflected from the earth. The light of the sun reveals all else, and we use it to see by and to search out all other things, but the sun itself is beyond our ability to penetrate with our sight. How much less, then, can we expect to look directly at the sun's Creator, and to search out the brilliance of His glory, before whom all other suns are but darkness?

That Russian astronaut who went up in space and said, "I couldn't see God up there," unwittingly spoke biblical truth. God can never be seen by man unless He reveals Himself in a definitive form that is within the range of human visibility and comprehension.

The second part of verse eighteen tells us how Jesus Christ came to reveal God. He is referred to as "the only begotten Son," but as we have already learned, the word in Greek is *monogenēs,* which actually means, "the only one of the same family, the unique Son." It contains the same word from which our English word "genealogy" is derived. *Genos* is "kind" or "race," and *logos* is "study." "Genealogy," therefore, is "the study of the human race or family." The Lord Jesus was not declared to be "the only one who was born," but "the only one of the same race, the only one of the same substance," as the Father.

In order for Jesus Christ to be able to reveal God in His entirety, He had to be the One in whom the Godhead bodily and physically dwelt, and Paul declares this to be true of Him in Colossians 2:9. For Christ to be able to reveal the Father, He had to be of the same character, substance, eternity, and infinity as His Father. "The only one of the same family, the unique Son," who has always been with the Father, revealed Him to us.

The reason the Lord Jesus is called "the Son," is not only because He was born of the Father, but also because He has the same characteristics of deity as the Father. This relationship between God the Father and God the Son was indicative of the relationship that was going to be made possible as a result of mankind receiving the work of Christ. We, too, can become the sons of God. We can consciously know God as our Father.

Many people are confused about this. If you were to ask a Jehovah's Witness if he believes Jesus Christ to be God, he would say "No, He is only the Son of God." But there is no difference in essence between the Father and the Son, for the Son was "the only One who has always been in the bosom of the Father," and He brought Him out for us to see.

God Never Relinquishes His Claim of Fatherhood

A sign in front of a church said, "If God doesn't seem as close to you as He once did, who do you think has moved?" Since it is obvious that not all men today are living in a filial relationship to God, who has moved? Was it God, or was it man?

Is God the Father of everybody? In recent years any reference to the universal Fatherhood of God has come to be regarded as a tenet of liberal theology. Because of this, we sometimes flippantly reject the term, "the Fatherhood of God," thinking it implies that everybody is a child of God. But this does not logically follow. I believe that God is the Father of everyone in Himself, and that He created man so that He could be a Father to everyone in and through Jesus Christ. What we must realize is that, although He is the Father of all potentially, He is not the Father of all in actuality.

Remember that in John 8:44 our Lord, speaking to unbelievers, and knowing the lives that they led, said, "Ye are of your father the devil and the lusts of your father ye will do." Does this mean that God has relinquished His right to be a Father to all His creatures? No, He is still the Father of the unbeliever as well as of the believer.

A mother was sitting on the floor beside the bed of her sleeping son, loving and kissing him. When her husband came in, he asked her why she was doing this. She replied, "Because he won't let me love him like this when he is awake." That is just a dim illustration of the affectionate love of a parent for His human creatures that is always in the heart of God.

Do you recall what James says about the character of God? He declares, "With [God there] is no variableness, neither shadow of turning" (James 1:17). God is not changeable. He doesn't vary His attitude or His character. He is always the same—a God of love. We have proof of that in 1 John 4:8, which says, "God is love."

As Beecher once said: "The sun does not shine for a few trees and flowers, but for the wide world's joy. The lonely pine on the mountaintop waves its somber boughs and cries, 'Thou art my sun!' And the little meadow violet lifts its cup of blue and whispers with its perfumed breath, 'Thou art my sun!' And the grain in a thousand fields rustles in the wind, and makes answer, 'Thou art my sun!' So God sits, effulgent, in heaven, not for a favored few, but for the universe of life: and there is no creature so poor or low that he may not look up with childlike confidence and say, 'My Father, Thou art mine!' "

The trouble, however, is that through Adam's disobedience man estranged himself from God as a Father. He has lost the intimate relationship of sonship, which Jesus Christ came to restore for those who receive Him as Savior. But God has not abdicated His relationship as Father to all humanity.

Do you think that the father in the story of the prodigal son, when his son chose to run away from home and indulge in riotous living, ever ceased for one moment to consider himself the father of that child? Of course not! Someone said to a father whose son was living in utter sin, "Why don't you turn him out? Why do you tolerate him?"

He replied, "I can't turn him out, I'm his father."

The most amazing thing about the character of God is that no matter what you do to Him, He still loves you as a Father.

Jesus called those who would not follow Him "sons of the devil" because they were doing Satan's will. But He had never wanted them to do so. It was their own choice. It was just like the choice of a child who leaves his home and attaches himself to someone who has influenced him in the ways of sin. He may say to this person, "I am going to adopt you as my father." But does that real father who has been forsaken by his son ever relinquish the rights and claims of fatherhood toward that child, and does he change his feelings toward him? If you're a father, ask yourself if you would do so. Would I? Impossible!

Truly there is no changeableness in the nature of God. Man, woman, you can put a dart in His heart and what you will hear from Him is, "I still love you like a Father." That's the nature of God.

Therefore we must be careful to make the distinction between what God considers Himself to be and what we have chosen to become in our relationship to Him. He considers Himself a Father to us all, but most people have made themselves the children of Satan by running away from God. They are wayward children, but that is not His will for them. He still has the attitude of a Father toward everyone.

It Is We Who Change toward God, Not He toward Us

We have seen that the Lord Jesus Christ is the only One who could have revealed the Fatherhood of God to us. In fact, that is the very thing He came to do. Truly God is a Father, as far as He is concerned. His whole attitude toward all men is that of a Father, but the trouble is that our attitude is not that of sons. When we are saved through Jesus Christ it is not God who becomes our Father, but we who become His children. It's not He who changes His identity, attitude, and relationship toward us, but we who change ours toward Him. We become His sons and daughters.

This is what is called in the New Testament the doctrine of adoption. When we come to Him through Christ, He accepts us as returning, wayward children. From the far country of sin we enter the fellowship of His family.

A biblical illustration that will help to make clear this love of God for His rebellious and wayward human creatures is that of Absalom. He was so disobedient and rebellious that he broke his father's heart and finally lost his own life. Absalom's wickedness and rebellion could not destroy David's love for him. After Absalom was dead, David mourned for him in 2 Samuel 19:4, "O my son Absalom, O Absalom, my son, my son!"

David never stopped considering Absalom his son, but Absalom considered himself a stranger to his father. I believe that this is the way God feels toward men. In the story of the Prodigal Son, it was not the father who turned away from the son, but the son who went away from the father.

Let us consider this beautiful doctrine of adoption. Romans 8:15 says, "For ye have not received the spirit of bondage [of slavery] again to fear . . . ." Those who do not consider God as their Father are certainly slaves to fear. Observe, however, that through salvation we ". . . have received the Spirit of sonship [or adoption], whereby we cry, Abba, Father."

The change is not in the attitude of the Father, God, but in the attitude of the son, man. It is he who realizes that now, through Jesus Christ, God is his Father, and that he has been adopted into the family of God.

Romans 8:23 also speaks of adoption when it says, "And not only they, but ourselves also, which have the firstfruits of the Spirit, even we ourselves groan within ourselves, waiting for the adoption, to wit, the redemption of our body." Observe that there is an adoption that is spiritual and one that is physical. We are still expecting the redemption of our bodies to take place at some time in the future. The moment that a person comes to know Jesus Christ, he or she receives the One through whom this future adoption will be realized.

The Lord Jesus Christ is the "adoption agent." He takes a child who is completely estranged and brings him to the One who is potentially his Father. That One has always had the attitude of a Father, and has always had the desire to be a Father to that child. All the adoption agent does is to take the child and bring him into relationship with God, the waiting Father.

However, this adoption that we experience when we receive the Lord Jesus Christ and come into the fellowship of God's family is a spiritual one. Because we have not yet received the adoption of our bodies, they are still subject to all kinds of disease and infirmities. My head is still subject to the headaches, and so is yours. But the day is coming when this body of ours is going to be redeemed, is going to be adopted, and will become similar to the resurrection body of the Lord Jesus Christ. The doctrine of adoption is a wonderful truth, isn't it? God is our Father, but we can only become His children through the Lord Jesus Christ.

I once was an outcast stranger on earth,
A sinner by choice, and an alien by birth;
But I've been adopted, my name's written down,
An heir to a mansion, a harp, and a crown.
I'm a child of the King, a child of the King:
With Jesus my Savior, I'm a child of the King.
—Harriet E. Buell

Is Jesus the Savior of All Men?

We have seen that God, in Himself, is indeed the Father of all people. But we have also seen that whether that relationship is taken advantage of or not depends upon the acceptance or the rejection of the finished work of Jesus Christ. It is through Christ that we appropriate Him as our Father. We have not all become children of God. Or, to put it another way, we may be His children by creation, but some of us are in the Father's house and some of us are not. Some of us are obedient children and some are strangers to the Father while living in the Father's world.

Some would tell you that this teaching is not scriptural, and that it is not true that God is the Father of all people. But there is a verse I want to point out to you that would shock many people, concerning His being the Savior of all people. It is 1 Timothy 4:10: "For therefore we both labor and suffer reproach, because we trust in the living God, who is the Savior of all men." Have you ever noticed that? "Who is the Savior of *all men*." Is He, or is He not? He is. Christ died for all men: "For God so loved the world, that he gave his only begotten Son . . . ." (John 3:16). He loved the world and gave His Son for the whole world.

Is He the Savior of all people then? Yes, He is. But observe the words that are added at the end of 1 Timothy

4:10: "specially of those that believe." Actually, in Greek, the word for "those that believe" is *pistōn*. It means, "of the believing ones," or "of the believers." Now do you begin to see? He is the Savior. Christ is God the Son, and His blood has been shed once and for all. It is not going to be shed again for anyone. His sacrifice is finished. On the cross He cried out and said, "It is finished!" It is as though He were saying, "I have done my part of redemption."

> Free from the law, Oh happy condition,
> Jesus hath bled, and there is remission;
> Cursed by the law, and bruised by the fall,
> Grace hath redeemed us, once for all.
> Once for all, O Sinner, receive it;
> Once for all, O Brother, believe it.
> Cling to the cross, the burden will fall,
> Christ hath redeemed us, once for all.
> —P.P. Bliss

Whether you reject it or not is your business. It is your responsibility, and you will bear the results of your choice. God always gives man the privilege of choice, but He predetermines the consequences of that choice. In other words, you can't choose both the way that you shall go and the results of that way. God is the Creator, the Maker, of the laws that govern life. True, you have the privilege (if one could call it a privilege) of disobeying a law, but you do not have the privilege of avoiding the consequences.

Now, it is not always true that you are caught immediately when you transgress God's laws. You may suffer the consequences of your bad choice soon, or they may be delayed for a time. What often causes people to misunderstand the laws of God is that the consequences of disobedience sometimes seem long delayed. For instance, "The wages of sin is death" (Rom. 6:23), both physical and spiritual. The skeptic sins and says, "Death, where are you?" It isn't always immediate, whereas the consequences of disobeying certain physical laws are very immediate indeed. Consider the consequences of breaking the natural "law" of gravity. The moment you jump off a building, down you go, because gravity is pulling you toward the center of the earth.

But because God in His mercy often delays the application of the spiritual consequences of sin, we have presumed upon this and taken advantage of it. Be very careful of this. I believe that one of the greatest tragedies of the human soul is that the Father has His arms open to receive His prodigal child, and all the while that child may be saying, "Well, I can take my time and He'll still be there when I get ready to turn to Him."

Let me once again bring this wonderful verse, 1 Timothy 4:10, to your attention: "We trust in the living God, who is the Savior of all men, especially of those that believe." It really corroborates all that I have said so far as to the Fatherhood of God potentially existing for all men but not necessarily being experienced by all men. Not all have become His children, not all have become believers, but the only way to become one is through the acceptance of Christ's death as having taken place once and for all for you and for the whole of humanity.

Adoption and Predestination

What a privilege it is to have God as our Father! How important it is to make sure we are adopted into the family of God! We have seen that, as far as God is concerned, He considers Himself a Father to all, yet not all people are the children of God. You will recollect that when our Lord was speaking to those who were estranged from Him He said, "Ye are of your father, the devil." Did this mean that God had abandoned His position as a Father to all men? No.

There is one thing we must understand. Whatever happens in the world, whether in the lives of unbelievers or believers, happens as the result of either the direct or the permissive will of God. Read the book of Job and you will find that every time Satan tempted, tried, or tested Job, it was only after he had received permission from the Lord to do so. So, although God has not abandoned His position as Father to the unbelievers, He has in His permissive will allowed them to be estranged from Him. And He has allowed Satan to control their lives, up to a point, so long as this estrangement continues.

We have thus far looked at two verses that speak of the adoption of men into the family of God: Romans 8:15 and Romans 8:23. But there is another verse in Romans that we should consider. Remember that Romans 9—11 deal with the relationship of Israel to God. Romans 9:4 says, "Who are Israelites; to whom pertaineth the adoption, and the glory, and the covenants, and the giving of the law, and the service of God, and the promises." We see here that the Israelites were adopted into the family of God.

Another verse that speaks of adoption is Galatians 4:5: "So that he may redeem [or, buy over] those under the law, that we may receive the adoption of sons" (author's literal translation). The possibility of adoption is there, but it only belongs to those who receive it.

All of these verses speak of the adoption of mankind. We never see in them the concept of God becoming the Father of the individual. It is, rather, God being the Father of all and man becoming the child of God at the time that he enters into a saving knowledge of the Lord Jesus Christ.

And of course there is that key verse in John 1:12: "For as many as received him, to them gave He authority to become the children of God . . ."—not for Him to become their Father, for He has always been that, but for the one who believes to become the child of God. When you are saved it is not God who changes in His nature, but you who become a new creature and a child of God.

Ephesians 1:5 contains a word that has become a bone of contention for theologians. The verse reads, "Having predestinated us unto the adoption of children by Jesus Christ to himself, according to the good pleasure of his will." What does that mean? In order to understand this verse there is another passage that we must look at first, and that is Romans 8:28, 29, "For we know that to them who keep loving God, all things work together for the good to them who are the called according to his purpose" (author's literal translation). Observe verse twenty-nine especially: "For whom He did foreknow, them, he did also *predestinate*" (the same word that we find in Ephesians 1:5).

73

So His predestination is not arbitrary, but is according to His foreknowledge. In other words, He knows how you are going to respond. He allows the Gospel to be preached to you, but He knows beforehand whether you are one of those who are going to be His children. And it is sure and certain that He is going to attract each of these to Himself.

The Advantages of Having
God as Father

The director at a camp for delinquent girls instructed the counselors not to refer initially to God as "Father," since most of the children had experienced extreme rejection and abuse in their relationships with their own fathers. Instead, the director suggested the counselors refer to God as "Lord," "Savior," or "Friend," until the children could be led to a clearer knowledge of God's true character of love. To hear God referred to as "Father" would have created a mental block for these girls, for they would have thought of Him as remote, rejecting, harsh, or even cruel. This was what the word "father" meant to them.

Child abuse is at an all–time high in the world, and one is sickened by the daily accounts in the news of fathers who beat, starve, torture, molest, and even murder their own children. How sad that children should so often be disappointed or even emotionally shattered and spiritually shipwrecked because of the character and actions of their earthly fathers. To make your child wish he or she were someone else's child instead of yours is to have failed as a father.

Not all earthly fathers are the same. Some greatly endear themselves to their children, while others repel them. The attachment of a child to a father isn't automatic. It greatly depends upon the father's character and resultant behavior toward the child. If you're one of those who is disappointed with your earthly father, try God, for there are many advantages to having Him as your Father.

One of the advantages is that He always meets His responsibilities toward His children. He never acts from selfish motives. Earthly fathers are often selfish. Their treatment of their children doesn't always have the ultimate good of the child as its goal. For instance, a father may disregard the innate abilities of his child and try to force him into a profession that will meet his own proud expectations. He wants his son to maintain the same social and economic position he has attained. A father who is a physician may try to force his son to take up the study of medicine so that his practice can be continued and family tradition upheld. Who hasn't seen the sports–loving father who tries to force his frail, book–loving son into a sports career simply to satisfy his own ego?

A father who acts in this manner is making a great mistake, for his will should never be forced upon his child. God as a Father never forces us to comply with His will. He recognizes our individuality and allows us to find ourselves. He gives us our basic abilities, and He provides the essential environment in which we can develop them. God provides the blueprints for our lives, so to speak, but the building of them is left to us.

Another of the advantages of having God as Father is that He never discriminates in His dealings with His children, although we may sometimes think He does. However, this isn't to say that He treats them all equally. Does any earthly father treat his children with complete equality? If he does, he may lead them into rebellion against him. In fact, it's impossible to treat them equally, because of the capacity of their constitutional abilities. Not all our children are equal in intelligence or aptitude. A wise parent first finds out the capacity of each of his children, and then tries to fill that capacity with contiguous and congruent opportunities for appropriate development.

For instance, a child who is able to articulate well should be led to a profession that requires such ability: teaching, preaching, law, politics, and so forth. However, to try to influence a child who isn't fully committed to the Lord to become a preacher would be an injustice to both the cause of Christ and to himself. Fatherly guidance depends not only upon unselfish motivation but also upon wisdom and discernment. Here is the basic difference between God and human fathers: our wisdom and discernment are often deficient, but His are always perfect. He is the personification of wisdom.

He knows us best because He created us. There is a great difference between God's creating of His children and the begetting of children on the part of an earthly father. No earthly father ever has an inherent, full and unerring knowledge of his children. "We know in part" is a maxim that also applies to the knowledge a father has of his children. God, however, knows us fully, and therefore whatever He allows or directs in our lives is always for our ultimate good and growth as He sees it.

God's motivation toward His children is always holy and unselfish, and His arrangement of the circumstances of our lives is based on His unerring wisdom. As a Father, He will never take advantage of us. Nor will He ever act in our lives, either in guidance and provision, from a partial or faulty knowledge of us.

The Name "Father" Implies Relationship and Trust

Why did the Lord Jesus introduce God primarily to us by the name of "Father"? Because above all else, God's Fatherhood implies family relationship. The basic reason Christ came to earth was to make us God's children by providing Himself as the ransom for the satisfaction of God's justice. As we note in Exodus 34:7, God does not let man's sin go unpunished. But instead of punishing the sinner He punished His Son. This was not an injustice on His part toward the Son, for the Father and the Son are one and God was in Christ reconciling the world unto Himself (2 Cor. 5:19). Through faith in what His Son did for us, we become God's children. When we are born again, through becoming members of God's family, the name of Father and what it implies of our relationship to Him takes precedence over every other revealed name and relationship of God. Our first concern, then, is that He truly be our Father.

Christ not only presents God as Father because of the sense of filial relationship that this title invokes, but also because the use of this endearing name arouses within us a response of love toward Him. Strength and power may serve within themselves to produce a response of fear, but love toward the strong one will produce instead a response of security.

Who hasn't seen a strong, muscular giant of a man, whose strength and size would tend to arouse fear in other men, being pummeled and pulled about by his little child? Would a stranger have dared walk up to such a man as Abraham Lincoln, for instance, and begin to act with such presumptuous familiarity that his strength would be used against him? Hardly! And yet, Abraham Lincoln was one of the fondest and most gentle of fathers. As one reads his biographies, he is impressed with the gentleness with which this giant of a man treated his boys.

Others may well fear the strength of such a man, but to the child who knows him as "Father" there is only trust and security and a sense of complete freedom. There is no fear in the child's response to his father's strength, though of course there is always a healthy respect for it. Instead, there is great security and complacency in the knowledge that this strong one is his ally and protector from all who might seek to harm him.

Before we proceed to the point of seeking to have our needs met through prayer, it is imperative that we have a proper recognition of the qualities of God's character and of His intents toward us. God's name as "Father" shows the filial relationship that we are to have toward God and He to us. We must learn to love God for Himself alone, without any consideration of His gifts to us. It depends upon our concept of God whether our religion uplifts our life, or our life degrades our religion and smites with the leprosy of selfishness and superstition even our most holy things.

What good would it do us if we were able to obtain all the comforts and luxuries of earth, yet were not properly related to the Giver of them and had not a proper appreciation of His character? How would we like it if we were surrounded by comfort and luxuries, and yet everyone around us held a low opinion of us and shunned contact with us?

We would rather have less and be appreciated by others. The relationship is the important thing, not the material benefits derived from it. Does any father want his children to regard him as merely a source of material comforts, or does he not first of all want the love and respect and esteem of their hearts?

Just so, God, our Heavenly Father, is far more concerned that our attitude toward Him be right than that our needs be met. The relationship is fundamental, while the supplying of the needs is incidental. He wants us to have the proper attitude of love and respect and reverence toward Him as our Father, and He wants to be able to regard us and treat us as His loving, obedient, and reverent children.

Does a Child of God Have Legitimate Right to All That Is God's Simply Because It Is Available?

Queen Elizabeth and Prince Philip of Great Britain brought up their children in a simple—and in some ways even austere—manner. Though possessing great wealth, they didn't want their children to be spoiled by it, but rather to develop high moral character and a disciplined way of life. Other sovereigns of England and of Europe, among them Queen Victoria, were brought up with this same simplicity and even severity, as far as their way of living was concerned. They were thus trained for the awesome position of authority and responsibility they would one day occupy.

How wise these parents were! They didn't yield to the expediency of making their affluence available freely to their children and thereby spoiling them. Wise parents don't automatically put at the disposal of their children all that they possess in the way of material riches. They provide for their children's needs out of their abundance, but they guard against giving them too much.

They do this because they know that wealth that isn't wisely managed can become a curse instead of a blessing. Rich people who haven't learned to handle their wealth wisely can become a problem to themselves, to society, and to God. But the rich who are wise and prudent can be a means of great blessing to the world and can bring great glory to God by the benevolent use of their riches.

Our Heavenly Father owns everything, and we're His legal heirs, but His wealth is only apportioned to us according to His wisdom and will. When an earthly father prepares a will, he may designate his children as his sole heirs, but the will limits the inherent rights of the legal heirs by its stipulations. The existence of a will necessitates a division and apportionment of wealth among the heirs. Each person will receive the portion the father has willed him to have, and some may receive more than others. Thus we can say that a father's abundance can become his child's only if the father wills it and in the measure he wills it Likewise, the apportionment of our Heavenly Father's abundance to us is always according to His will.

The truth is, however, that God's love sometimes causes Him to act like a father who gives his children more than they need or deserve, simply because He loves them so much. Why doesn't God exercise His omniscience and give each of us what we deserve, instead of giving so abundantly to all, whether or not they ask for it? Why does it seem that His love overpowers His justice?

In Romans 2:4, Paul tries to explain why God shares an undue measure of His riches with us: "Or despisest thou the riches of his goodness and forbearance and longsuffering; not knowing that the goodness of God leadeth thee to repentance?"

The word translated "goodness" in the Greek text is *chrēstotēs* and *chrēston*. It's a fascinating word that must be distinguished from another Greek word, *agathōsunē,* also translated "goodness," which occurs in Romans 15:14; Galatians 5:22; Ephesians 5:9; 2 Thessalonians 1:11.

In Galatians 5:22, both words occur. *Chrēstotēs* is translated "gentleness" and *agathōsunē* is translated "goodness." Since both words are used to indicate two different characteristics of the fruit of the Spirit, there must be a difference between them.

To understand the meaning of *chrēstotēs,* we must view what Christ meant when He stated that the old wine is *chrēstoteros* (better) than the new wine (Luke 5:39). It refers to the mellowing of the new wine with age. Also, in Matthew 11:30, Christ's yoke is called *chrēstos.* That means it has nothing harsh or galling about it. When Christ asks us to take up His yoke to discipline ourselves in order to follow Him He infers that this disciplining or restraining isn't bad in itself. It has potential future goodness in its purpose, even though it may not appear good during the time it's being exercised.

Agathōsunē, on the other hand, is actual, apparent, and instant goodness. You can't mistake something that is good in this sense from its face value, as you can some things that appear evil and yet have potential good results. For instance, a sickness can be mistaken as evil, but it has potential good as its ultimate result. God is *chrēstos,* and *Christos* (Christ) spelled with an iota (i) becomes *Chrēstos* with an ēta (h), to show us that God sometimes goes out of His way to give us more than we deserve so that He may win us more fully to Himself. It's God's abundance shared in disproportion to our deserts, so that we may never excuse our attitude of unbelief toward God on the ground of His insufficient or miserly supply. Therefore, Romans 2:4 would read, "Or do you contemptuously consider the riches of his *chrēstotēs* [His goodness, His over-abundant supply], ignoring the fact that God's *chrēstotēs* [goodness, abundant supply] means to bring thee to repentance?" God's *chrēstotēs* is potential *agathōsunē.* God's abundant provision when we don't deserve it is not for the purpose of spoiling us, but for the purpose of showing us that He doesn't treat us as we deserve, thereby leading us to repent of our sin.

R.C. Trench in his *Synonyms of The New Testament,* states that God's *chrēstotēs* has the harmlessness of the dove with nothing of the wisdom of the serpent. God never means His abundance to harm us, but to help us. The fact that we sometimes allow it to harm us is our own fault. The same can be said of why God permits privation and suffering. His *chrēstotēs* may be expressed through abundance or privation, but in both instances He is seeking our ultimate good.

God's ultimate aim isn't expressed in material gifts and temporal benefits, but in the formation of moral excellence in human character. Therefore God doesn't intend us to regard our physical surroundings and circumstances as the ultimate expression of His perfect will for us, but rather as an arena that gives us the opportunity to realize His moral aim. "God . . . worketh in you to will," as Paul says in Philippians 2:13. As He works in us to will, He also works in us to pray.

Prayer is never to be regarded as an ingenious, labor–saving expedient that obligingly secures for us life's material resources and thus saves us the inconvenience of having to work for them. God doesn't do for us what we can do for ourselves. Prayer isn't a substitute for work.

Prayer is an appropriation of what is already ours as children of God, rather than a securing of what was never intended. Let us not be discouraged if we don't always receive what we ask.

Don't Ask God to Give You What You Think You Deserve

"Let me help, Mommy!" says little Susie to her busy mother. She then proceeds to make the bed with crooked covers and strange looking humps in the middle. Having finished, she stands back with a satisfied sigh and says, "Didn't I do good, Mommy?" Her mother, casting a dubious eye at the normally well–made bed, replies, "Yes, dear, you certainly did a good job!"

Now, does that mother need Susie's help to do the work of her household? Not really. In fact, some of Susie's initial efforts at "helping" will probably seem to make more work for her mother, instead of less. But she knows that Susie needs to learn how to make a bed. She also knows that Susie needs to feel that her contribution to the work of the household is important, for this is essential to her concept of herself as a vital part of the family.

In like manner, we might ask "Does our Heavenly Father really need our help with the work of running His household?" Not really, for He is self–sufficient and sovereign, and as such He isn't dependent on man for fulfillment of any of His needs or the attainment of any of His purposes.

Why, then, does He demand that we love Him, that we adore Him, that we worship Him, and that we preach the Gospel and help the poor? Because in being His co–workers we reap a blessing for ourselves. God's love is utterly pure and unselfish in this respect: He never asks anything of us for His benefit, but only for ours. This is in contrast to the love of earthly fathers, which is rarely utterly selfless and pure in its motives.

The eternal and infinite God condescends to the intimate relationship of a Father to you and me, and He allows us the high honor of working as members of His household. Actually, there is a far greater difference between God and His children as co–workers than between the mother and little Susie. His condescension is such that He allows us to help Him. His power is such that He could force us to do so if He chose. He doesn't force us, but if we choose, we can become His children and as such can help God to accomplish His work as Father of His vast family.

We must understand, however, that in doing so we contribute nothing essential to Him. By helping our earthly fathers, we may add something, because they're limited and need our help. But not so with God. He's limitless, and He could easily bring all His purposes to fruition without our aid or cooperation. He condescends to accept our service because He knows it will result in our growth and conformity to His likeness.

Since God doesn't really need our help, we shouldn't do what we do for Him as though He could be brought under obligation because of our contribution. Our work for Him should be purely a response to His love. If we expect God to treat us as paid employees, we're going to be extremely disappointed in the end.

Our Lord gave us a most revealing lesson in Matthew 20:1–16, the parable of the laborers. In this story, the owner of the vineyard went out and enlisted laborers to work in his vineyard. He agreed to pay the first ones hired a salary of one dinar (a day's wages) for a 12–hour workday. They wanted a work contract and they got it. But all the others, who worked for nine, six, and three hours, as well as the one who only worked for one, agreed to work for him on the basis of the mere promise that he was going to reward them justly. He wouldn't reveal how much that was going to be.

The time for payment came. The paymaster started with the last recruit, who had worked for only one hour. He was paid one dinar, the same as the employer had agreed to pay for a 12–hour workday. When it came, however, to payment for the man who had worked 12 hours, it was as agreed, one dinar. This man became angry with the employer and complained that it was unjust to pay as much for one hour's work as for a 12–hour day. The employer replied that the man had received the amount he contracted for. But the employer was pleased to give more to the one who had gone to work without any contractual agreement.

The lesson the Lord wanted to teach through this parable was that it's better to depend on God's mercifulness than to treat Him as a strict employer who is obligated to us because of the work we've done for Him.

So it is in prayer. Don't treat the high privilege of communion with God as though it were a mere business transaction with an employer. Don't try to strike bargains or enter into contracts with God. Treat Him as your loving Heavenly Father. Enter into the labor of His vineyard in dependence upon His gracious provision rather than according to your expectation of what He should give you. Instead of demanding justice according to your concept of what you deserve, rely upon His mercy and generosity.

After all, God's will toward us isn't static, but dynamic. It may be altered by our attitude toward Him. If the laborer who worked for one hour had demanded 1/12 of a dinar, he would have been given that and no more. It's very unwise to tell God in prayer what you believe you deserve and should have. How much better to leave it to Him to give what He thinks you should have. Which would you rather have God do—give according to your measure, or according to His? Once again, we're reminded to what great extent our prayers depend upon a correct view and appreciation of God.

The worker in the parable who complained against his employer for being unjust should have found fault with himself instead. Prayer truly has a boomerang effect, for God's actions toward us are the bouncing back of our attitudes toward Him. If we treat Him as an employer, and prayer as a mere business transaction, He'll have no other choice than to treat us as employees. If, however, we treat Him as our Father, He'll reciprocate by treating us as His beloved children. This is what He wants.

For after all, prayer isn't the establishment of a claim but the appropriation of it. It's the badge of partnership, the insignia of sonship. When we pray, we are exercising the sublime prerogatives we have inherited as the sons of God, and are entering into the active cooperation of our wills with His.

Praying to God Who Is Spirit

We are used to beginning the Lord's Prayer, "Our Father, who art in heaven," but did you know that the verb "art" is not in the original Greek text? A literal translation of the Greek is: "Father of ours, the One in the heavens." Why is there no verb in the Greek text? Because there has never been any particular time when God was not "in the heavens." In the Greek, whenever a verb is missing, it indicates limitless time. If this prayer said, "Our Father, who art in heaven," it would mean that the Father was in heaven at the particular time the prayer was made. The Lord Jesus Christ, however, wants us to know that our Heavenly Father has always dwelt in the heavens. He was, is, and ever will be in heaven. It is the permanent dwelling place of God.

In reality, it is not only God the Father who has always been in heaven, but also God the Son in His Deity, and God the Eternal Holy Spirit. As far as the Holy Spirit's deity and coequality with the Father and the Son are concerned, we know that in Hebrews 9:14 He is called "the eternal Spirit." One author wrote: "Among the names and titles by which the Holy Spirit is known in Scripture, that of 'the eternal Spirit' is His peculiar appellation—a name, which in the very first face of things, accurately defines His nature, and carries with it the most convincing proof of Godhead."

He said this because he knew that none but God is eternal. If the Holy Spirit is eternal, then He is God. If He is God, then His dwelling place is "in the heavens." 1 John 5:7 says, "For there are three that bear record *in heaven,* the Father, the Word [the Son], and the Holy Ghost: and these *three are one.*" 1 Peter 1:12 tells us that He is the "Holy Ghost sent down from *heaven.*"

Referring to the Son's coequality with the Father and with the Holy Spirit, Colossians 2:9 tells us very plainly that "In him [referring to Jesus Christ] dwelleth all the fullness of the Godhead bodily." This verse declares that while Jesus Christ was on earth He was all of the Godhead in bodily form. At the same time however, as a totally spiritual being He was "in heaven."

In speaking to the Samaritan woman at Jacob's well, the Lord Jesus revealed the nature of God. In John 4:24, He said, "God is a Spirit." The Samaritan woman had pointed to Mount Gerizim, where the Samaritans worshiped, indicating that this was God's dwelling place. She was disturbed because she thought that Jesus (who had just come from Jerusalem) believed that since Mount Moriah was the site of the Jewish Temple, it was where God dwelt. She had a concept of a limited and a localized God. If God is on Mount Gerizim, He cannot be on Mount Moriah. If He is here, He cannot be there.

The answer the Lord Jesus Christ gave her purposed to eliminate this concept of a God who was limited through localization. Jesus, by His answer, showed her plainly that God is not present in any one particular place to the exclusion of being fully and equally present in every other place. So He indicated to her and to us that the essence of the Deity is spiritual, and that God is fully a spiritual entity. God was on earth in the person of Jesus Christ but at the same time He was in heaven.

The Psalmist said: "Whither shall I go from thy spirit? or whither shall I flee from thy presence? If I ascend up into heaven, thou art there: If I make my bed in hell, behold, thou art there. If I take the wings of the morning and dwell in the uttermost parts of the sea; even there shall thy hand lead me, and thy right hand shall hold me" (Ps. 139:7–10).

This is why the Lord Jesus instructed His disciples that when they prayed they should say, "Our Father, the One in the heavens." It is as if He were saying to them, "Don't think, because I am among you just now, that God your Father is not still in heaven. I am the embodiment of Deity. At the same time, you have God also in heaven. I am God among you, whom you can see with your own eyes. He is God in heaven, whom you can't see with your physical eyes. And He, being Spirit, can be in more than one person, and can be everywhere present at the same time."

Sales said, "As the birds, wheresoever they fly, always meet with the air; so we, wheresoever we go and wherever we are, always find God present." And Augustine wrote, "God is a circle whose center is everywhere and whose circumference is nowhere." Whoever we are, wherever we may be within His vast creation, we are all, so to speak, "in the middle of the circle." No point in space is nearer God than any other point. This is what we mean when we say that God is omnipresent. The word literally means "all or everywhere present."

But how did Jesus Christ know that God was in heaven? Because He was God Himself, on earth. It is as if He were saying, "I know that He is God in heaven, because I am God on earth. The only difference is that I have a bodily form, and He doesn't." This doctrine is most important for us to understand. If God is in heaven, can He also be on earth simultaneously? Yes, indeed! He is a spiritual entity, but at the same time He is a personality. This is what the

Lord Jesus Christ wanted to indicate to his disciples: "God is your Father in heaven, and I am God, His Son, here and now among you. You are not praying to a God whom you can touch with your hands, although you can touch me. Now, being God-Man, I am temporarily on earth, but the God to whom you are praying is the same One to whom those before you have prayed. He is the same One to whom future generations will pray. He is the God who fills the heavens."

The Invisibility of God

The Lord Jesus Christ told us that we should address God as "Our Father, the One in the heavens." He was the same Father–God whom Abraham, Isaac, and Jacob knew. He is the same Father that our posterity will have. As we have already noted in John 1:18, the nonexistence of a verb in the Greek text indicates the timelessness of the dwelling of God in the heavens. There is no time that the heavens are not full of His presence. A literal translation of the verse is, "God [eternal, infinite], no one [no human being] has ever seen; the only begotten [*monogenēs*, the only one of the same family, or the only unique] Son, who has always been in the bosom of the Father, he himself has revealed him" (author's translation).

The first part of the verse is a statement concerning the invisibility of God. God, who is eternal, infinite, and in His essence Spirit, no one has been able to see at any time. No creature with its inherent limitations could or can at any time see God in His totality, eternity, and infinity.

The second part of John 1:18 speaks of Jesus Christ as co–equal and co–eternal with God. Since this is true, He is the only One who is capable of revealing the Father to us. This part of the verse has a verb in the participial form, *ho ōn,* "the One being in the bosom of the Father." It is not, "the One who now is or was" but, "the One who has always been." This verse declares that there has never been a time when the Lord Jesus Christ, in His eternal state, has not been in the bosom of the Father. When He came down here to earth, He took upon Himself flesh and appeared before us as the God-Man. At the same time, however, He was in the bosom of the Father in His essence as Spirit.

There is an essential difference between God and us. Whenever we speak of the eternal and infinite Creator, we must conceive of Him as being timeless and spaceless. That is, as Spirit. However, we as creatures are totally limited by time and space, and we are only able to think in those terms. This is why we cannot possibly conceive of the Deity in His totality, eternity, and infinity. The only One who could eternally and infinitely dwell with God was Jesus Christ, because He was equal and coeternal with God.

No creature could possibly see God in His eternity and infinity. Jesus Christ, however, could reveal to us where and who God is, and tell us that His attitude toward us is that of a father. No one but Jesus Christ could tell us this because no one else is able and qualified to know the essence and disposition of God. Remember that, when Jesus Christ as the God-Man was speaking to the woman at Jacob's well, He was at the same time in heaven as Spirit. This is what John 1:18b means when it says, in the Greek, "Who being at all times in the bosom of the Father." As God, as a spiritual, self–existent Being, Jesus was never separated from God the Father.

God Is a Person

O ne of the greatest revelations that the Lord Jesus Christ wanted to make as He taught us this prayer was when we pray, we are addressing not a power but a personality. We must not attribute wrong meanings to the word "person" or "personality." When we speak of a person, we usually think of a human face. And it is also true that when we think of others we usually conceive of them as the extension of our own personality. So, when we speak of God as a person, we tend to think of Him as an extension of ourselves.

He is not that, however. This is why God is a mystery to us. The concept involved in comprehending His personality is entirely different from the concept involved in comprehending human personality. He is a purely spiritual being, while we are made up of spirit, soul, and body. At the present time we cannot possibly know God fully, but the time will come when our natures will be changed and we shall become spiritual beings. Only then shall we know Him as He knows us. There is no limitation to His knowledge of us, but there is a limitation to our knowledge of Him. However, it is plainly evident that "Our Father, the One being in heaven," refers to a personality who can love and exercise His will.

The Lord Jesus Christ describes God as dwelling in the heavens. Heaven is a place, but again when we speak of a place we must not think of God as dwelling in a limited space. A place, for us, involves a limited space. But this is not true of God, who is limitless in His own essence. There is no address of heaven as there is an address of a person's home. We are dealing with an entirely different concept when we speak of God being in heaven than when we speak of ourselves being at such an address. We must not think of heaven as a limited, literal place, having the limitations of places as we know them on earth.

When God speaks to us, He accommodates Himself to our understanding and comprehension. He uses terminology that is understandable to us, in order to convey concepts that are beyond us. Have you ever had a mathematician try to explain abstract mathematics to you? Unless you are an equally capable mathematician, you will find it difficult to understand him. But you don't reject him just because you can't understand him. If you can hardly understand another human being who is beyond you in certain fields of knowledge, just imagine, then, our difficulty in understanding God, who is the infinite, the eternal One. And we have the same difficulty in comprehending His dwelling place.

Therefore, when we think of God or of His dwelling place, we must recognize the limitations of our ability to understand both. The dwelling place of God cannot be any smaller than He is. His dwelling place must be a spiritual location, since He, Himself, is Spirit. God is a living person to whom we can speak. He is conscious of all that exists within Him and around Him and therefore He is conscious of our coming to Him. But we must not make the mistake of conceiving of His personality as having two eyes, two ears, a nose, and a face like ours. He is a spiritual person, who can love, feel, and hear. He can recognize and is recognizable. A personality has distinctive features, although the features of God's personality are not similar to ours.

The first thing that the Lord Jesus Christ wants us to realize is that when we speak to God we are speaking to the Father. The Father can have a stick in His hand, or He can have open, loving arms. But picturing the Father in such ways is simply an accommodation to our limited comprehension and imagination. God is a Father who is pure Spirit, yet He dwells in heaven. He is a person who loves you and cares for you. However, He does not necessarily have human features. We must never think of God in an anthropomorphic manner. He is not in the form of man, but is Spirit. We, being men, can hardly understand pure Spirit. Nor can we understand the makeup of His personality. Nevertheless, He can have fellowship with us, and we with Him. As William Temple once said, "Christ does not reveal all that is meant by the word 'God.' There ever remains the unsearchable abyss of Deity. But He reveals what is vital for us to know, He reveals God as Father."

What Is Heaven?

W hen we pray to "Our Father, the One being in the heavens", we are led to the question, "Where is heaven [or 'the heavens', as the Greek text has it], and what is it?"

The Scriptures reveal that there are three kinds of "heavens." The first is the atmospheric heaven, the heaven of the clouds from which rain comes down. It is that area of our universe that God uses to create the atmospheric conditions necessary for life on this earth. It is what we see when we look up at what we call the "sky." Acts 14:17 says, "And [God] gave us rain from heaven, and fruitful seasons." But we mustn't limit our concept of even the physical heavens more than is necessary, for they contain not only that which we can see and observe but also much that is beyond our understanding.

Secondly, heaven is described in the Scriptures as the dwelling place of evil spirits. It is the spiritual place of a spiritual being called Satan. The Apostle Paul speaks of this heaven in Ephesians 6:12, "For we wrestle not against flesh and blood, but against principalities, against powers, against the rulers of the darkness of this world, against spiritual wickedness in high places." What is translated "high places" is actually "in the heavens," in the Greek text. The concept, again, is that of a place, or an area.

I can't give you any further details, for I can't describe it because my limitations are as great as yours. For me, a "place" is an area with very definite spatial limitations. However, a spiritual "place" is not limited in this way. So this "heaven," a spiritual place, is the area where a spiritual being by the name of Satan actually dwells. Because we can't do any differently, we have to describe these dwelling places of purely spiritual beings as "spiritual places."

There is another "heaven" that the Scriptures refer to as the "heaven of heavens." Nehemiah 9:6 says, "Thou, even thou, art Lord alone; thou hast made heaven, the heaven of heavens, with all their host, the earth, and all things that are therein, the seas, and all that is therein, and thou preservest them all; and the host of heaven worshippeth thee."

Sometimes this is also called the "third heaven," and it is designated as God's dwelling place and the site of his throne (see *Life After Death,* by Zodhiates, 1981:149). Again, here I have used words that accommodate themselves to the human mind and its limitations. When I speak of the throne of God I don't mean anything similar to any earthly throne, on which an earthly potentate sits. The terminology is just to accommodate our concept of rule by God.

When we speak of God's dwelling "place" we must immediately dismiss the concept that such a "place" has any limitations whatever. The word "heavens" means "the dwelling place of spiritual beings." It's the place or realm where God is and where He can be seen. It's the spiritual place or realm where our spirits go when they depart from our bodies. In Hebrews 8:1 we read, "We have such an high priest, who is set on the right hand of the throne of the Majesty in the heavens." It is a place above and beyond us, a realm of spiritual personalities.

2 Corinthians chapter twelve gives us Paul's experience in ascending to this place. As we look carefully at verses two and four we find that Paul calls the place where he went "the third heaven" and "paradise." The word "paradise" means "garden." That's the word used in Genesis for Eden, the dwelling place of Adam and Eve. A garden is a delightful place. In order to convey the idea of the place where Paul went, and where the spirits of departed believers go, as being a pleasant place, it is called "paradise," a "garden," Again, God is accommodating Himself to our understanding by describing the place where our spirits go when they depart from our bodies as a place of comfort, delight, and rejoicing, even as a garden is to our physical bodies.

This "third heaven" or "paradise" is the heaven in which there is great joy over a repenting sinner, such as we find described in Luke 15:7. Thus we see that heaven is a place beyond us, a place of spiritual personalities, the abode of God, and the abode of disembodied spirits that belong to God.

Luke chapter sixteen gives us the story of the rich man and the beggar Lazarus. The poor man died and was carried to "Abraham's bosom." It is called that because Abraham was the father of the faithful ones and this is the place or realm where the disembodied spirits of the faithful ones go at death. It is equivalent to the third heaven of 2 Corinthians chapter twelve.

But where did the rich man go at death? He was definitely an unbeliever, because no believer would behave so indifferently toward the desperate needs of a helpless creature such as Lazarus, who was most probably a leper. No one who sees the wounds of a leper and remains indifferent can claim faith in God.

The destiny of the rich man after death is called in Luke chapter sixteen "hell." This is an unfortunate translation; it should have been rendered "Hades." Hades, however, was the common dwelling place of the spirits of both believers and unbelievers prior to the resurrection of the Lord Jesus Christ (A full study of this is given in the book, *Life After Death* by Zodhiates). Hades is called the place of torment for this rich man. The Hades of the New Testament is the "Sheol" of the Old Testament. It is the place to which both believers and unbelievers went at death.

Hades is the place where the spirit of the Lord Jesus Christ descended when it separated itself from His body. We read, however, that Hades could not hold Him. How could Jesus Christ go to a place of torment, since He was "the righteous One"? He must have gone to the section of Hades reserved for the spirits of the righteous. It's interesting that after the resurrection of the Lord Jesus, believers are never mentioned as going to Hades. They are said to go to "paradise," or to "go to be with Christ." The Lord Jesus Christ by going to Hades must have liberated the believers who were there and transferred them to a place called "paradise" or "the third heaven."

When the Lord was dying on the cross, He said to the repentant thief who was being crucified with Him, "Today shalt thou be with me in paradise" (Luke 23:43). He did not say "in Hades." This paradise is the place where the spirits of present–day believers go, and where all the disembodied spirits of believers of previous ages now exist, waiting for their resurrection bodies. It is there that the departed spirits of believers are in fellowship with God. This, however, is not the final heaven where we shall dwell with God forever and ever in our resurrection bodies.

Why We Have No More
Details about Heaven

In the Lord's Prayer we have a whole compendium of theology. It touches upon many relationships and doctrines. For instance, in the phrase, "Our Father, the One in the heavens," the word "Father" refers to God and forces us to study the doctrine of God. The personal pronoun "our," being in the plural form, forces us to study human beings as belonging to one and the same community. When we read the word "heaven" or "heavens," immediately we have to study the world that constitutes the dwelling place of God—that world beyond this one in which we now live. In this single clause of the Lord's Prayer, therefore, we have the study of God, of humanity, and of heaven.

Where is heaven? You stand over the corpse of a person in a casket. If he was a believer, you say, "He is not here, he is in heaven." What do you mean? I wish I could tell you where heaven is. I wish I could describe it for you. There is a certain amount that we know about it, but for the most part we are ignorant of the details of the makeup and the life of heaven. There are many questions that we cannot now answer. We are ignorant of many of the facts about it, not because the Lord Jesus Christ was deficient in His revelation about heaven, but because in His wisdom

He gave us only a limited amount of information, at the level of our nature's ability to absorb and comprehend.

The mother of a girl who had been blind from infancy had vainly tried to describe to her the colors of the rainbow, the glory of the sunset, the beauty of the autumn leaves. One day the doctors, using newly developed surgical techniques, restored the girl's sight. When the bandages were removed and her eyes looked for the first time upon the glories of the world around her, she cried, "Oh Mother! Why didn't you tell me it was this beautiful?"

With tears in her eyes, the mother replied, "I tried! I tried! But there were just no words that could make you see."

As the colors and shapes and forms of the world around her could not be fully expressed to her in words, so our comprehension and understanding of heaven cannot be achieved through descriptive words. We will have to experience it before we can fully comprehend it.

If heaven is a spiritual place and ours is a material world, then there exists an incongruity of essence between the two. That is why it is impossible for us to understand that which is purely spiritual, because our nature is partly spiritual and partly material. Our time has not yet come for a full understanding of heaven. We must be transformed in our essential being and become totally spiritual beings ourselves before we will be able to understand heaven, which is a spiritual place.

We often find it difficult as parents to enable our children to understand certain things that seem to be quite simple to us. We know that eating vegetables is essential to the growth of the child, for example. But try to explain to a child why it is necessary for him or her to eat vegetables and you will find yourself in sympathy with God's difficulty in trying to explain the realities that are beyond us. The gulf that separates an adult from a child is far smaller than the gulf that separates an infinite and eternal God from the finite and temporal mind of the human.

In the Lord's Prayer we have the statement of fact. However, we have no explanation of that fact. We are told that God is our Father. We are told further that He is in heaven and that there has never been a time that God has not had heaven as His dwelling place. We really have no choice about accepting facts; they are facts whether we understand them or not.

We expect our children to accept us and the rules that we lay down simply because we know better than they what is good for them. We would be better off if we acted toward God as we expect our children to act toward us. Let us treat God as a Father who knows infinitely more than we do and always knows what is best for each of us and for all of us together. Let us regard ourselves as children who know so much less than an infinite and eternal Father.

Never think of heaven as a purely material place, with purely material enjoyments for material beings such as we presently are. Heaven is a spiritual place where God, the Spirit, lives and where we shall live as spirits, and will finally have spiritual bodies after our resurrection. Only then shall we know God even as He knows us. When a person leaves the body, the body remains in the casket. The spirit, being immaterial, goes to an immaterial world. So let me repeat: never think of heaven as a material place for material people, but as a spiritual place where God the Spirit dwells and where our spirits go.

Someone once asked me if there is any passage in the Scriptures which says that when we die we go to heaven. Actually there isn't, but it is clearly stated that when we die we go to be with Jesus.

2 Corinthians 5:8 says, "absent from the body . . . present with the Lord." The Lord God, our Heavenly Father, is in the spiritual heavens. Therefore our spirit, when it departs from the body, goes to a spiritual heaven. That is, of course, if we are believers in the Lord Jesus Christ.

If someone should ask me to describe heaven, I'd have to say, "I'm sorry, but I am unable to do so. It's not because I'm dumb, but rather that I'm limited by the very nature of my constitution, which consists of both spiritual and material elements." If I were pure spirit I could understand heaven. I believe that Jesus Christ could have made far clearer and more detailed the explanation had He been dealing with purely spiritual beings. However, He recognized our limitations. He would have been foolish to try to explain things beyond our understanding and constitutional make-up.

The day will come when we shall have spiritual bodies, as described in 1 Corinthians 15:44, which says, "It is sown a natural body; it is raised a spiritual body." What Paul meant by the term "spiritual body" was that, though our bodies will have an identifiable form, they will not then be governed by the soul (which we hold in common with the animal kingdom) but by the spirit only, which is the gift God gave only to man (See the author's book, *Conquering the Fear of Death,* 1970:576–753).

As a Heavenly Father He Knows All, So Why Pretend?

Thomas Edison was once asked if he thought an instrument could be invented that would enable us to read the thoughts and purposes of people. The great scientist replied that, even if such a contrivance could be produced, it wouldn't be tolerated. It's certainly true that if our minds could be scrutinized as openly as our faces there would be fearful conflicts and scandalous disclosures.

In fact, pretense would be the first order of the business of life, if God didn't know all about us. To others we pretend to be what we really aren't, because we consider what we are to be less than desirable. A life of pretense can be a life of torture, because it's a life of continuous hypocrisy.

If God weren't all–knowing, we'd treat Him the same way we treat our fellow humans. We would hardly ever tell Him the truth about ourselves and our real needs. Instead of prayer being the baring of our inner selves, it would become a recitation of how good we are. This was the fundamental mistake of the Pharisee who prayed in the Temple. He thought God didn't know how good or bad he and others were. "Lord," he said, "look how good I am!" You don't have to tell God how good you are in comparison to others, because He's omniscient.

His omniscience serves to cleanse the polluted fountain of our thoughts and to make our confession honest and our prayers sincere. Maybe that's why the Lord Jesus advised secrecy in prayer, because prayers that are heard by others can tend to become hypocritical. When we pray in private and only God hears, our thoughts are purified by the consciousness of God's omniscience.

Without God's omniscient light our souls would remain in darkness. When we open our mouths to pray, our words ought to express only the thoughts that occupy the heart. Others can hear only what we say when we pray, but God can read our hearts. The fact that our hearts are private domain imperils their purity. Prayer, being as private as the heart itself, purifies it, because it gives to the heart the consciousness that it is standing alone in the presence of a God who knows all. Such knowledge makes pretense in prayer ridiculous.

There would be gross confusion in our moral life, disregarded and undetected, if the glowing searchlight of God's omniscient vision were not turned upon it. The ancient Greeks thought that for a long span of time the earth was formless and chaotic. However, no one was aware of this confusion until eventually Aether, the mythological divinity of Light, and Hemera, the divinity of the day, began to reign. Just so, prayer would bring complacency in the face of our dark moral chaos if it weren't for the divine light of God's omniscience that reveals it to us. Sin would be at its maximum and shame at its minimum.

God is therefore fully justified in intruding into the secrecy of our thoughts. While we can be thankful there are no windows by which human eyes can peer into our secret hearts, God has provided Himself a skylight by which our secret thoughts lie open to Him, and prayer is the constant reminder of this fact. He teaches us to look for omniscient aid that we may realize we are observed by an omniscient eye.

Not that He would have us regard Him as an austere spectator whose vision is solely censorial and critical, like the legendary Greek figure, Asurodeus. While passing through the air, Asurodeus was able by his supernatural powers of sight to see all that was transpiring in the houses below him. He used this gift for his own capricious and malignant ends. But God only uses His infinite attributes, such as His omniscience, to befriend and aid us. The knowledge of His omniscience makes our prayers sincere and honest, and therefore remedial.

How would God otherwise secure true confession, which is the first step in the purification of the soul? Confessions to an earthly "father confessor" are seldom fully genuine. But there is genuine confession to our Heavenly Father, simply because He's omniscient. Therefore we know it's useless to try to hide things from Him as we might try to hide them from a "father confessor." Unless it contains the element of genuine confession, prayer becomes self–deception. And confession can only be genuine as it's addressed to an omniscient Father. Praying a lie harms the soul instead of helping it. When you pray to an omniscient God, you stand before a mirror that shows what you really are, sans make-up.

As J. R. Lowell says, "No man can produce great things who is not thoroughly sincere with himself." In this age of artificialities there is a grave peril of our so habitually acting a conventional part that we become strangers to our true selves. Prayer, which gives us the gift of seeing ourselves not merely as others see us but as God sees us, is a most salutary corrective, tearing off any masquerading falsities and presenting us with a candid, unembellished portrait of our character. In such a process, the recognition of the omniscience of the Hearer must be borne in mind as one prays.

Hallowed Be Thy Name

"**N**o intelligent creature approaches the dignity and the blessedness for which he was created further than he reveres God," said one eminent preacher of the past. In light of this statement, how many are attaining this dignity and blessedness in our society today?

In our study thus far we have learned that the God who eternally dwells in the heavens is also our Father. This is the ground of all true prayer, for we would never have dared approach the majestic Creator apart from this revelation of His compassionate Fatherhood toward us. He would remain ever unknown and unknowable.

But once having established the fact of His Fatherhood through Christ, and having entered into the enjoyment of this filial relationship, we are led to the next consideration: how shall we address this Father God in our prayers? Are we to conclude that, because He is our Father who loves us, we are therefore free to approach Him with a familiarity that ignores His exalted majesty and holiness?

The answer to this question is found in the first petition of the prayer, "Hallowed be thy name." The word translated "hallowed" is *hagiastheto* in the Greek text. It is the verb from which the word *hagios*, or "saint," is derived. The word *hagiazo* basically means "to set apart as something that is due all possible reverence." This shows us that the name of God is not something common, but something very special, to be reverenced and "set apart."

Nor is it the same as the common name "father"; that we give to our earthly fathers. However, this does not mean that even our earthly fathers are not due proper reverence and respect. Just as children owe this to their earthly fathers, the children of God owe Him special respect and reverence as their Heavenly Father. To know Him as such, and to call Him by such a name, is a tremendous privilege. Do you give Him the respect and reverence that is His due?

But in showing this respect and reverence, we must keep in mind that God is not someone who is unrelated to us, far off and remote. We only respect as "father" in an earthly sense the one who is related to us (or one who stands in his place). He is the one who shows his fatherly love and care for us at all times. So it is with our Heavenly Father. He is related to us through the Lord Jesus Christ and He loves us and cares for us because of this relationship.

He is to be set apart as a special Person, and His name is to be set apart as a special name in our life. Whenever we pray the Lord's Prayer, we should first seek to make ourselves conscious of the holiness of God, and to recognize that He is due a very special reverence that belongs only to Him as our Heavenly Father.

Prayer—Worship or Beggary?

The story is told of a benevolent and much–loved king who at certain times allowed his subjects to come directly to him with their petitions. They brought their problems, their needs, and their grievances week by week before him.

The king noticed one man, who although he came every week, never asked for anything, or even spoke, but stood as a silent spectator. One day the king said to the man, "I notice that you come here every week when I hold audience, but you never ask for anything. Why is this?"

"Sire," the man replied, "several years ago, as a young man, I was being led through the streets to the gallows. As I was being taken to my death, you rode by, and I cried to you for mercy. You listened patiently as I told you my story. Having heard me and being touched by my youth and by my tears, you said, 'I will help you.' You then gave me a pardon and commanded that I be freed.

"I come to ask nothing of you because you have already given me everything. You gave me life and pardon and the opportunity to serve you. These people come to beg something of you. I come to bring something—the homage of my life, the love of my heart, and the offer of myself as your loyal and devoted servant."

The king, much moved by these words, said, "One possessed of such gratitude, love, and devotion could ask nothing unworthy. You shall have whatever you desire of all my kingdom!"

God has given us everything—life, pardon, and the opportunity to serve him. Prayer should primarily be a coming into His presence to adore and worship Him—to offer Him the homage, love and devotion of our hearts.

Yet so often we come as the people came to this king, little noting His beauty of character and His graciousness to us, concerned only with bringing before Him our problems, needs, and grievances.

Actually, both of these are a part of the Lord's Prayer, and of all true prayer. It is legitimate to bring our needs and our desires to our Heavenly Father; He expects us to do so. However, if we regard prayer simply as the means of having our personal needs met, we have actually turned it into a glorified form of beggary.

The problem we face is that of keeping both of these aspects of prayer, worship and requests, in the proper perspective and proportion.

For this reason, the order of the petitions in the Lord's Prayer is highly significant. Don't ever think they "just happened" that way. They are placed as they are for a very important purpose.

The petition, "Hallowed be thy name," is placed first because the Lord wanted us to see that the primary thing we are to seek in our prayers is not the satisfaction of our personal needs, but the exhibition of God's holiness. *We must adore God in the inner man before we seek the supply of the needs of the outer man.*

Even the exercise of God's will toward us in the granting of our requests is meant to exhibit His holiness and thus to hallow His name. This is why we pray. God is immutable, and our prayers can't change His *character.* However, they can change His *actions.*

We have freedom, when we come to God in prayer, to ask for anything, whether for ourselves (supplication) or others (intercession) This freedom, however, is not an unbounded freedom, for prayer imposes upon us moral obligations. All we ask should be primarily aimed at the exhibition of God's holiness. Otherwise, prayer itself becomes an ignoble thing, for we are praying with a self-ish, unworthy motive.

We are not to serve God because it's profitable but because it's right and because we consciously desire that His name be hallowed in our own lives and the lives of others.

For instance, when we pray for food, as we should, the primary aim should not be the mere satisfaction of our hunger, but the exhibition of God's holiness as manifested in His faithfulness toward us. Our relationship with God must never be based merely upon the personal benefit we derive from it.

The fact that the petition for the hallowing of God's name stands first in the prayer also indicates that a right comprehension of God's character lies at the root of all true prayer. Where there is a wrong understanding of that char-acter, the spring of piety is corrupted at it's source.

There is an inexorable law, the law of assimilation, that we become like that which we worship. Spiritually speak-ing, man is "made in the image of his god," whatever that god may be. The character of our "god" is to each of us the ideal standard of perfection to which we shall seek, con-sciously or unconsciously, to conform ourselves.

Like the boy in Hawthorne's story, *The Great Stone Face,* who gazed upon the stone image of a noble face until he became a noble man himself, we become conformed to the image of that upon which we fasten the gaze of admiration and adoration (See 2 Cor. 3:18).

Our views of God and of prayer must inevitably shape our character and conduct. If God is merely a "force of nature"—and He is just that to many—if He is only an "influence" which keeps the systems of the universe working, but exercises no will, manifests no spontaneous emotions, and, in short, has none of the characteristics of a living Personality, then prayer is mere mockery. That is not the "Father" of the Lord's Prayer, whose name we pray to be hallowed— kept distinct and venerated—above every other name.

Too often, prayer has been regarded as a magical expedient whereby we become learned without study, good without discipline, and successful without effort. We must never think of God as an infinitely endowed convenience for the gratification of our insatiable whims. Prayer presupposes not so much the stifling of our desires as the sifting of them. That sifting should be done on the basis of God's holiness and with a view to the hallowing of His name.

SECTION III

Hallowed Be Thy Name

What's In a Name?

"What's in a name?" wrote Shakespeare in Romeo and Juliet, "A rose by any other name would smell as sweet." By this he intimated that the name of an object is not really too important, since the name by which we call things doesn't alter their character or essence. To call them by some other name would really make no essential difference. This may well be true of the names of objects, but when it comes to the names of persons, it is a different matter. Especially is this reasoning not true when it comes to the name of God.

We begin to realize the importance of that name when we consider that the Lord taught us to pray, "Hallowed be thy name." Why not, "May we hallow *Thee*?" It would help us to understand the reason for this petition if we first realize that God called Himself by various names in the Scriptures in order to reveal to us the nature of His character and attributes. These revelations were made for the purpose of instilling within us the proper concept of Him, and the proper attitude toward Him.

A name is the summary of a person. It is the catchword that supersedes the necessity of interminable descriptions and renders amplification needless by setting before us the whole person—his face, form, and properties. Its use instantly recalls to us the person, figure, and distinctive characteristics in one. In one sense, then, the name is the person. By it, the absent, distant, inaccessible man is made present and comprehensible to us. As with the use of the human name, so also is it with the name of God.

One of the first names by which God called Himself in the Old Testament, and the name by which He peculiarly revealed Himself to the Jews, was *Yahweh*. It is sometimes transliterated from the Hebrew in the form "Jehovah," but is often translated "LORD," using capital letters to distinguish it from another Hebrew word, *Adonai* also translated "Lord." Jehovah is the name of God most used in the Old Testament, occurring 6,283 times. The name Jehovah is derived from the Hebrew word *Hayah,* "to be," or "being." Thus the name signifies "the self–existent One," the One who in Himself possesses essential life, permanent existence. He is the "I AM."

Moses Maimonides, most noted Jewish commentator of the Middle Ages, said of this name, "All the names of God which occur in Scripture are derived from His works except one, and that is Jehovah; and this is called the plain name, because it teaches plainly and unequivocally of the substance of God."

Girdlestone, in his *Old Testament Synonyms,* wrote, "God's personal existence, the continuity of His dealings with man, the unchangeableness of His promises, and the whole revelation of His redeeming mercy gathers round the name of Jehovah."

God said of the patriarchs, "By my name Jehovah was I not known unto them" (Ex. 6:3). What does this statement mean, in view of the fact that the name of Jehovah is first used as early as Genesis 2:4, and that it is used many times throughout the whole book? The meaning is not that they had never heard the name, or "known" it in that sense but that they had not understood the significance of it.

In Exodus 33:18—34:7, we read of one particular occasion when God revealed Himself, His character, and His attributes through His name. In verse eighteen of this passage, Moses prayed, "I beseech thee, shew me thy glory." He was told that to see the face of God was impossible, but that he would be privileged to look upon God's "back" after He had passed by in all His glory. Exodus 34:5–7 says that the Lord descended, passed before him, and in answer to that prayer for a sight of His glory, "proclaimed the name of the Lord." What was that name? Was it the "Jehovah," the "I AM," of the original revelation? As we read verses six and seven, we see that the name of God as given here is actually the sum of God's attributes: "The Lord, the Lord God, merciful and gracious, longsuffering, and abundant in goodness and truth, keeping mercy for thousands, forgiving iniquity and transgression and sin, and that will by no means clear the guilty . . . ." God such as He is—in mercy and righteousness, in boundless compassion, and in just judgment—that is His "name."

One name cannot comprehensively describe, of course, the qualities, or even the chief quality, of a complex human character. How much less, then, can one name demonstrate the complex and incomprehensible character of God? And yet, there is one name that expresses to those of us who are God's children the highest and fullest comprehension of all His attributes and of His character. It is that name which brings Him nearer to us than any other, the name of "Father."

Who Can Hallow God's Name?

Would it surprise you to learn that not everyone can truly hallow God's name, or even truly pray, "hallowed be thy name"? Actually, "hallow" doesn't mean "to make holy," but "to exhibit as holy." The Greek word is *hagiastheto*, from *hagios*, which means "separated" or "saint." But it involves the idea of separation because of purity. There is a distinct moral connotation to the term. It's something that's set apart as different from that which is around it.

Our first concern in prayer is that everything which takes place contributes to the realization that God is pure, undefiled, and holy. He permits nothing in answer to prayer that will be a cause of the desecration of His character as it is observed by all His creation. Therefore, God will not answer our individual petitions for anything of which the end result is not the recognition by the whole universe of the holiness of God. God is essentially holy in His being. The idea is not that we are to make Him more holy—that would be impossible. It is rather that we recognize that holiness on our part and seek to exhibit it to all others.

"To hallow" also means "to treat as holy." The name of God—which stands for the character of God—must be treated as holy. The first petition certainly knocks down any temptation for us to treat God with vulgar familiarity just because He's our Father. Remember, our Lord didn't tell us just to say "Our Father," but "Our Father, the One being in the heavens."

True, there is the closest relationship between Himself and us, as a result of Christ's work on the cross. Nevertheless, He is still to be considered as being far above us. In order to enforce that concept of His utter superiority, the Lord gives us the first petition, so that our primary concern in prayer is immediately established: to preserve and exhibit His holiness among all people.

When the Lord said, "I will sanctify my great name" (Ezek. 36:23), He meant, "I will exhibit it and make it be seen in its true holiness." On the other hand, when we read, "They shall sanctify my name, and sanctify the Holy One of Jacob" (Is. 29:23), the meaning is, "They shall recognize Me as holy, and treat Me accordingly."

This twofold use of the word "hallow" may be illustrated by the corresponding twofold use of the word "glorify" (*doxazō*), though that's a word of lesser meaning, being applicable also to created beings and things, whereas to be hallowed or sanctified is peculiar to God. "To glorify" in Greek means "to recognize one for what he is." The verb *doxazō* is derived from *dokeō,* which means "to form an opinion." But it doesn't speak of the state of being. However, when the word "hallow" or "sanctify" (*hagiazō*) is used, there is an actual declaration of what God is. He is holy. That holiness ought to be recognized and exhibited to all.

Only God's children recognize holiness or moral perfection in the character of God. The inanimate universe speaks loudly of the majesty and glory of God, but never of His moral perfection. Both born–again and nominal Christians may sing "How Great Thou Art," but only the born–again can sing, "Holy, Holy, Holy" with any true appreciation of its sentiments and meaning.

Every flower by its fair hue, every leaf by its delicate tracery of veins, every insect by its wonderful structure, every star by its individual radiance, glorifies God—declares His glory and magnificence. As the Psalmist asserts, "The heavens declare the glory of God" the Creator: His power, His magnificence, His grandeur, His skill, His wisdom (See Psalm 19:1–19).

But the only mirror in which God's holiness is reflected is the hearts of His children. Their hearts and souls "venerate and adore Him, lie low before Him," in conscious homage. God's image is reproduced in the believer by Jesus Christ. "The new man," says Paul in Colossians 3:10, "is renewed in knowledge after the image of him that created him."

The petition "Hallowed be thy name," therefore, carries the idea of rational moral agents who have acquired—by virtue of creation, as in the case of the elect angels, and by virtue of redemption, as in the case of believers—a capacity to comprehend and appreciate the holiness of God. Only such can truly pray, "Hallowed be thy name." Looking directly and fixedly at God dazzles and bewilders human reason, even as looking directly and fixedly at the sun dazzles and disables the human eye. We simply cannot comprehend God or His holiness with the faculty of natural human reason. Reason will never be able to ascertain a moral, unified, perfect, holy purpose in the seeming hodgepodge of providential events in our lives. The poet Cowper, knowing this, wrote:

> Judge not the Lord by feeble sense,
> But trust Him for His grace;

Behind a frowning providence
He hides a smiling face.

Blind unbelief is sure to err,
And scan His work in vain:
God is His own interpreter,
And He will make it plain.

This is why purely nominal Christians never pray first that God's name be hallowed, even though they may repeat the words of the Lord's Prayer. Before they could pray in such a way, it would first be necessary for them to recognize His holiness. But such a recognition is impossible without help from God Himself. Just as your child can never understand your character as a father from your corrective actions, so we can't possibly understand God simply by judging Him from His actions in response to our selfish petitions. Someone once wisely wrote, "Judge not God's heart of Love by His hand of Providence." It takes a father's willingness to explain to his child in understandable language why he does what he does, in order for the child to learn to attribute kindness or moral perfection to the father.

This is exactly why God revealed His holiness to us through His unique Son who had always been in the bosom of the Father (John 1:18). This is why the Lord Jesus said, "He that hath seen me hath seen the Father" (John 14:9). *Understand* Jesus and you understand God's holiness. *Receive* Jesus and you receive His holiness. Only then can you *exhibit* God's holiness. The character of Christ is the character of God, reflected in the mirror of a redeemed humanity.

As God's Children We Bear His Name

My surname was inherited from my father; I didn't choose it. Much of my constitution, also, is not of my own making. It is inherited. To a certain extent, I am what my parents made me. I am known by their name. I bear a facial, and sometimes a behavioral, resemblance.

This bearing of my parental name involves a certain responsibility on my part. I must seek to honor my parents' name. I must not hold it unworthily. Either my behavior must be consistent with what my name stands for, or I must be responsible enough to change my name.

When we pray, "Hallowed be thy name," we don't pretend to claim the ability to make God's name and, consequently, God Himself holier than He is. We cannot, by virtue of what we are or what we do, add to or detract from God's holiness. He is holy in Himself, and His character is unchangeable. James states this categorically: ". . . the Father of lights, with whom is no variableness, neither shadow of turning" (James 1:17). This doesn't mean that He doesn't change His attitude toward us, or His administrative methods of dealing with His universe but that His moral character is unchangeable.

Throughout history, God has chosen to reveal Himself by different names in order to indicate a change in His methods of dealing with men. In the New Testament, Christ reveals Him as the Father of the individual believer. This was not God's attitude in the Old Testament. Then, though occasional reference was made to Him as Father, He was essentially and predominantly Jehovah! Now, though He hasn't ceased to be Jehovah, He is also known to us as the approachable, loving Father.

If He is your Father, you are His son or daughter and you bear His name. Others look upon you as God's child, and they expect to observe in you the same family characteristics they see in Him. At one time or another, we've all heard it said of someone, "He's just like his father." Ideally, that's what people should be able to say of us as God's children. His name has been transferred to us, not by virtue of our imitating God, but by virtue of our being reborn, and thus coming into His family through what Christ did on Calvary's cross. When, therefore, Christ taught us to pray, "Hallowed be thy name," it is as if He placed squarely upon us, as His disciples, the responsibility of hallowing the inherited name that we bear. We are "Christophers," which in Greek means "Christ–bearers." Prayer for the hallowing of God's name is a recognition of a personal responsibility to live holy lives worthy of that name.

While we recognize that this responsibility exists, it is also true that God has a responsibility toward us as His children. Every father has that. You can't turn to the state or your fellow man and expect them to relieve you of that responsibility toward those children who bear your name. If they are known by your name, you must care for them.

That's one way God honors His name—by being a trustworthy Father who never shirks His Fatherly responsibility toward us. He can't allow us to bear His name and not take the necessary care of us. What would my neighbors think of me if my children, known by my name; were going around half–naked, starved, unkempt, without educational and cultural opportunities? That would reflect badly upon me as a father.

However, though the Father may provide, there is always the danger that the child will not take advantage of the parental provision. Whatever may be our condition as God's children with regard to temporal and spiritual benefits, we must never assume that we are what we are, and behave the way we do, because of any lack of God's Fatherly care and provision for us. The first thing we must realize when we come to God in prayer is that He is holy, and therefore He will not in any way abdicate His responsibility toward His children.

That doesn't mean, of course, that He must treat all His children uniformly. Just as we earthly fathers treat all His children individually, so our Heavenly Father also treats each child of His individually in order to accomplish His eternal purpose and plan for each one. Although God is unchangeable, and with Him there is no variableness, His actions toward each of His created beings in His universe are far from uniform. Therefore, just because the temporal and spiritual benefits that come to you from your Father God are different from what He gives to others, you are never to conclude that He is not holy, or that He is being unjust or partial.

By teaching us that in our prayers we should first of all be conscious of God's holiness, Christ was seeking to deepen our comprehension and appreciation of God's perfect nature. Our prayers are not intended as a means of wringing benefits from God, as though He were a grudging miser. Nor are they meant to be a cunning utilization of persistence, as though sheer tenacity could overcome, irrespective of moral considerations, some fancied reluctance on God's part. Why try to foist our will upon Him, as though our well–being were not His first concern? Why "wrestle" with One who presents no resistance or antagonism? He is our Father!

Reverence Is Not Outward Solemnity and Formality, but Inward Respect

"In prayer let your first thought be that God is your Father, inspiring you with confidence; your second, blending with the first, that He is in heaven, far above you, inspiring you with reverence," said Dr. Woodworth in one of his sermons. But what is reverence? It is not something negative. It is not holding God far off from you and making Him unapproachable, nor is it mere outward solemnity. You do not express true reverence toward God by putting on a long, sad face. Self–imposed sadness is not really reverence, although we sometimes want others to think it is.

In Matthew chapter six the Lord Jesus gave us some examples of people who were mistaking outward solemnity for inward reverence. They were showing off to others the fact that they were engaged in religious exercises, such as giving alms, praying, and fasting. What, for instance, did the one who was fasting do? He made his face look "gloomy and sour and dreary" (Matt. 6:16, NASB) simply to impress others and to bring to their attention the fact that he was fasting.

Just so, we may become solemn when we want to impress others with our "reverence," or perhaps because we ourselves have mistaken ideas about what reverence really is. But solemnity is not the same thing as inward reverence. You do not hallow God's name by looking toward Him with a sad face. Nor are you expressing reverence for Him by doing so.

Again, you are not necessarily showing reverence for God by simply going to church and being silent while there. Your mouth may be silent, but your mind may be very actively engaged in thinking of material or worldly things. While you are sitting in church you may be thinking of the problems you are facing at work, or the preparation for Sunday dinner. Mere silence does not necessarily mean reverence, nor are you hallowing God's name just by being outwardly silent.

Now that we have looked at some of the things that reverence is not, let us look at some of the positive aspects that show what it truly is. It is first of all an inward state of being. It is the state of the heart, the mind. It is thinking of the highest and the best. To "reverence" is to honor and to love.

Reverence is not only a very important attitude toward God as a Father, it is also the most revealing aspect of one's character. It entitles its owner to a place among the spiritual aristocracy. It involves spiritual power. Consider how a child would act upon being introduced or brought into the presence of a famous personality. Suppose, for instance, that the president is to appear at a certain place. You are excited and thrilled at this opportunity to see the leader of your country, and you try to share this with your little child by pointing out the president to him. Not realizing what the title involves, he is not really interested.

Now that is the way that some people are. Like a child, they may show complete indifference to the greatness of the God before whom they stand. This is because of their ignorance of His greatness. You can thus tell whether a person is a mere child or a grownup, spiritually speaking, by his attitude toward God—by his respect or his lack of it.

Two men once stood in the hushed silence of the Lincoln Memorial, contemplating that great statue. One of them was an old man. As he stood there he was so moved by the remembrance of this great man's life that he slowly reached up and removed his hat, then stood with bowed head. The other occupied himself by writing obscene verses on the statue. After he finished his cigarette he ground it out on the base of the statue. By their actions, each showed what he was.

You, likewise, reveal your true character by the way that you treat God's name in your daily living. True reverence is not outward solemnity, nor is it outward formality, but it is a state of the heart which is a mark of character. The more respectful you are to God, the more you hallow and glorify His name.

God's Holiness and Our Divergent Wills

Here's a problem for you: Suppose two Christian schools have football teams that are rivals. Before the big game of the season, each team bows and prays that their side may win the championship. If you were God, how would you answer the prayers of both those teams? The answer is, you couldn't! Nor does God.

Have you ever asked yourself what God is supposed to do when two of His children ask for opposite things in a given situation? It's obvious in such a case that He can't possibly grant both their requests, since they are divergent. Yet both are praying to the God each considers his loving Heavenly Father. What is the solution to this dilemma? What determines God's answer to prayers in such a case?

There is an English word, criterion, which is a direct transliteration from the Greek word *kritērion,* which denotes "a means of judging." What is God's *kritērion* when it comes to deciding how to answer the requests of divergent wills?

It is this: He must always act in such a way that His holiness and perfection are manifested to all concerned, and to the whole universe, for that matter.

When we make our individual requests to God in prayer, we are rightly exercising our freedom to express our God–given faculty of will. However, we need to realize that other people have been given this same faculty and this same freedom to express their desires. We should never seek the satisfaction of our own desires at the expense of someone else's.

The important thing in prayer is not that our requests be granted by God, but that our life becomes attuned to God. Prayer is not so much an act as a process; not the presentation of a casual request but the prosecution of a campaign; not so much receptivity as reciprocity.

What is the goal toward which we are moving in prayer, anyway? That God's will be done and His holiness manifested to all.

One who is ignorant of God's designs in nature may assume that some forms of animal life have been brilliantly patterned or colored in order to make them individually conspicuous. Actually, just the opposite is true. Through the means of what naturalists call "protective coloration," those bright colors and patterns are meant to blend with their surroundings so that they may escape the detection of their natural enemies.

There are exotic looking insects and birds, for example, which look very conspicuous to us because they have been removed from their natural habitat. When they are placed in their ordinary surroundings, however, they can't even be seen. Thus they escape the notice of their enemies and survive.

At first glance, it may seem that the colors and figurations were given for the sake of the individual of the species, but actually they are all meant to blend together in such a harmonious whole that none stands out as distinct from the other forms of flora and fauna around it.

Just so, when we imagine that God through prayer endows us with the riches of grace merely that He might minister to our egotistic, individualistic importance, we mis-interpret the purpose of prayer.

He doesn't grant our requests in order to gratify our bla-tant individualism but in order that through these endow-ments of those we may be brought into harmony with the divine scheme of things which is the best for God's corpo-rate creation.

Just as those exotically marked birds and insects are meant to blend into the whole, so we are meant to blend into the harmonious whole of God's Plan.

It may be contended that if this interpretation be correct, prayer is a giving rather than a receiving. It is giving up our own desires, if necessary, so that the holiness and perfec-tion of God may be more fully manifested. But it is a recip-rocal giving, which results in our receiving far more than we give.

When we yield our personal wills to God, it's like the old–fashioned method of priming the pump, or "raising the water." A small quantity of water was first poured into the pump—something was given up to it. The result, however, was an abundant flow of water. That which was given enabled one to receive much *more* than he had given. But he had to give up a little water before he could receive a great quantity of it.

Just so, when we give up our little wills and desires to God and pray that His will be done and His holiness mani-fested, we always receive much more than we have given. If we follow such a pattern, even though we may not receive the granting of our own personal desires in each matter, we shall receive the far greater gift of becoming conformed to God's holiness and thus be better able to manifest it through our lives.

What is true prayer, then? *It is an assertion of our desires, through communion with God, which has as its aim the harmonization of our wills with His and the subjugation of our personal interests to the interests of His creation as a whole.*

To put it another way, prayer is the expression of communion in the form of petition and the direction of petition to the attainment of cooperation.

SECTION IV

Thy Kingdom Come

Thy Kingdom Come

"Hasten the day when grace shall make way for glory," was one writer's way of paraphrasing the portion of the Lord's Prayer that we shall now consider. Having been taught to pray for the hallowing of the divine name, the disciples were then taught to give expression to what should be the deepest desire of their hearts and ours—"Thy kingdom come."

What was it that our Lord wanted us to understand by this petition? First of all, that the kingdom of God is not yet fully established on earth, it has not yet come. God is not fully reigning on this earth yet, even though He is reigning in the hearts of those who believe in Him. There is someone else who is exercising rule, also. During this present age God is allowing the devil to exercise a limited rule in this world. God has a timetable by which He works, and His dealings with men are different at various times and stages in history. He manifests His power and His glory in different ways at different times and for different purposes. At this present time He has voluntarily restricted His sovereignty in the world, so that it is not being fully exercised.

Secondly, we should understand that God's kingdom will be fully established at a certain point of time in the future. The full and absolute rule and reign of the Lord

Jesus Christ has not yet come, but it is coming, it is on the way. When God's timetable reaches a certain point, His dealings with mankind will undergo a change. His power and glory will then be manifested in a different way from what it is during this age.

Thirdly, when we pray "Thy kingdom come" we acknowledge our utter dependence upon God. We recognize that there are many things we cannot change by our own human efforts. There are some people who think they can usher in the kingdom of God through their own efforts. But if we were able to accomplish this by ourselves, why pray "Thy kingdom come"? No, we cannot bring in the kingdom of God, for as Zechariah 4:6 says, "It is not by might, nor by power, but by my spirit, saith the Lord of hosts."

Fourthly, when we pray, "Thy kingdom come" we are acknowledging that we must do our part in making this kingdom a reality upon earth. And what is our part? It is to make His kingdom known, to proclaim the fact that He is the ruler of the universe, that He can rule now in the hearts of people who believe in Him, and that one day He is coming back to rule in absolute righteousness. "Thy kingdom come" is thus an acknowledgment that we are co–workers with God. We recognize that His kingdom will not come, apart from our cooperation through our proclamation of it, even as He commanded His disciples to proclaim it.

At prayer meeting, a man had prayed fervently for the cause of missions around the world. Then when the offering plate was passed he put in only a dime. The preacher, who was watching, said to him, "In the name of heaven, man, stop mocking God and prayer! Don't say 'Thy kingdom come' and then give Him a dime with which to accomplish it."

138

When we pray, "Thy kingdom come" we should lean upon God as if all our efforts were worthless; yet at the same time fling ourselves into the task of proclaiming the kingdom as if the whole responsibility rested upon our shoulders alone. We must allow God to do His part, which only He can do, but we must realize that we also have our part, which only we can do. Each has his own task and his own responsibility. We are not supposed to do God's work, and He is not supposed to do ours.

There are certain things that only God can do. What can you or I do, for instance, to save a soul? Actually, nothing. We can only expose people to the Gospel, not convict them of sin and convert them to God.

On the other hand, there are certain things that only we can do, not because God is unable to do them, but because He has seen fit to delegate these responsibilities to us. When you see a need you should say, "Lord, it will go unfulfilled unless I fulfill it. This Thy work will remain undone unless I do it." And He will then give the grace and power necessary for you to do your part. Yet apart from Him it will be useless. As the well–known saying goes; "Pray as if it all depended upon God, then work as if it all depended upon you." And that is very sound advice, isn't it?

William Woodworth, a learned minister of the past, illustrated this with the following words: "With what propriety, then, can he pray 'Thy kingdom come' who does not labor in the sphere that God has assigned to him? Let me illustrate this by a supposition which, though it seems violent, is suggested by the imagery of Jesus—'Ye are the light of the world.' Suppose, then, the sun, constituted by God the light of this solar system, to be an intelligent agent, endowed with power to dispense or withhold his beams at pleasure, and suppose that from some selfish motive he should withhold the whole, or the greater part, of his light. What mockery, then, for him to pray to the Father of lights that *He* would illumine the solar system! What sin, then, in his prayer, 'Father, pour light over this system of worlds!' Why, he was made and placed in the center of the system to do this very work, and it is a glorious work. Might not God reply, 'Wherefore criest thou unto me? Do thine own work.'

"Similar is the inconsistency of those who pray 'Thy kingdom come' and yet do not shine as lights in the world. God has assigned them a work to do, and their work they must do. God will not do that—He works in His own sphere—He sends down His Spirit, like the fertilizing shower, but He will not sow the seed which this rain makes to germinate. He gives the increase, but Paul must plant. He will not preach the gospel, as He once proclaimed the law from Sinai, with His own voice; nor distribute Bibles and tracts; nor exhibit before men the beauty of a Christian example. Men must do that. It is our work" (From *Sermons of Woodworth*).

Where Is God's Kingdom
to Be Established?

What is the sphere in which the kingdom of God is to come? The first place that the Lord wants to reign is in our hearts. When we pray "Thy Kingdom come," we are not praying solely for the work of foreign missions, although that is certainly included in the petition. First of all we are praying for ourselves. We are praying that God's rule may be absolute in our own hearts. As John Bunyan wrote in his Holy War, we want Him, "To lodge in the castle, with His mighty captains and men of war, to the joy of the town of Mansoul."

No other person, no power, no position, no possession, should be allowed to rule in our heart. God must be the absolute and uncontested Sovereign. For it is imperative that His kingdom come in our hearts before it can come to rule in the world at large. Heaven must be in us before we can be in heaven. God's kingdom must be in us before we can be in God's kingdom. It must begin in our hearts.

Thus when we pray this petition we are asking God to come and rule within our own hearts. Once He has come in, we must see to it that this rule is extended to every area of our lives. Whether it be the area of the spiritual or the physical; the mental or the emotional; the personal or the social; the vocational or the recreational—all must be subjugated to His kingly rule. We must be willing to say with Frances Havergal in her great hymn of consecration:

> Take my will and make it Thine,
> It shall be no longer mine.
> Take my heart, it is Thine own,
> It shall be Thy royal throne.

Can others really see the marks and the characteristics of the kingdom of God in our lives? Can they see that we are righteous, that we are just? Can they see in us the peace that passes understanding? Is the joy that fills our hearts evident to them? Yes, the initial sphere of the kingdom is first of all the individual heart.

But it is by no means limited to the heart, even though that is where is begins. It will ultimately be extended throughout the whole world. Therefore we are to pray, "Thy kingdom come," not only for ourselves and our immediate surroundings, but also for the places where God has never yet been known. Every time we pray the Lord's Prayer it should make us realize anew our responsibility to spread the Gospel everywhere. Not only our community, our country, our race, but all people need the dominion and the rule of Christ to be extended to them. We ought to be "Christian imperialists" in the best sense of the word, always seeking to extend the kingdom of God to the far corners of the earth.

> Jesus shall reign, where'er the sun
> Doth his successive journeys run;
> His kingdom spread from shore to shore,
> Till moons shall wax and wane no more.
>   —Isaac Watts

Not only do we need to know the sphere of the kingdom—where it will come—we also need to know how and in what manner it will come. It would help us to look first at the ways in which it cannot be established. First of all, it will not be brought in by force. All the great conquerors of history, such as Alexander, Caesar, Napoleon, established their kingdoms by force. But God's kingdom can only be established by love. Force may increase the numbers of a sect, but it cannot add one single person to the membership of the kingdom of God. The sword can compel a man to change his name, but it can never cause him to change his heart.

Nor can we establish God's kingdom on earth by giving people the name "Christian" when they have never been born again. We don't come into the kingdom of God by any external act or rite, we come into it as we open our hearts to the King and invite Him to enter, overthrow the forces of evil that have held sway there, and then rule as our Sovereign Lord.

May the Lord enable us to realize how dependent we are upon Him for the transformation of human hearts, and yet how dependent He is upon us for the proclamation of His saving power and of His kingdom.

> Thus onward still we press
> Through evil and through good,
> Through pain and poverty and want,
> Through peril and through blood:
> Still faithful to our God,
> And to our Captain true;
> We follow where He leads the way,
> THE KINGDOM IN OUR VIEW.
> —Author Unknown

SECTION V

Thy Will Be Done

Praying for God's Will
to Be Done

"The Lord's Prayer began with the acknowledgement of God's rights as our Father. Then followed the ascription of worship: 'Hallowed be Thy name.' Next came the recognition of sovereignty: 'Thy kingdom come'; and now succeeds the acknowledgement of service, as due the Parent, the God, and the King. This petition, then ['Thy will be done, in earth as it is in heaven,'] asks for grace to obey God's arrangements in His Providence, and His appointments in His revelation" (William R. Williams, *Lectures on the Lord's Prayer*).

Remember that the first three petitions concern God Himself. They have to do with His name, His kingdom, and His will. The name stands for God's character and revelation; the kingdom stands for God's sovereignty and rule; the will stands for the execution of His plan.

It is important for us to understand that although the Lord taught us to pray for His will to be done, He did not specifically reveal to us what that will is. Although God's will at times may not be revealed to or understood by us we are still to desire and seek it. We sometimes feel that if God's will were more perfectly known or understood by us, it would make it easier for us to pray, or at least to know more specifically what to ask in a given situation. We cannot trace His purposes and discern what He wants to do in the matter about which we are praying. These are the times when we must tell Him what is in our hearts, then simply leave the matter with Him, praying that His will may be done, yet not knowing ourselves what that will may be. It may not be the thing that we ourselves would have chosen if the choice had been left to us, but we know it will be the best in God's purpose, for He is all–knowing and all–wise.

Sometimes we pray for what seems like the logical or ideal solution to the matter about which we are concerned. But what seems good to us may not be God's will for us under the circumstances. We do not have the liberty to command God to do something merely because it seems good in our own eyes. William Gurnall, the well known Puritan preacher and writer, said, "We have not the liberty to pray at random for what we will."

Writing further on this matter, Williams says that God's will has two aspects: His will *of control* and His *will of command*. His will of control, according to him, is, "That sovereign and all–governing purpose, which foresees and uses all occurrences and all influences, and all resistances even, providing for the eruptions and the avalanches of our revolt, and of our sinful disregard of Him, and of our league with hell, and weaving even these into His wide plans. The great outlines and last results of this controlling and sovereign purpose He has made known; but its details and many of its relations are as yet inscrutable to our limited faculties."

He goes on to say that the will of command is that which God has made known more clearly to us, especially through His Word. "God's will of control is but partially known, as compared with His will of command."

Secondly, when we pray, "Thy will be done," we acknowledge that God's will is best. It may not always seem best to us, but that is because our knowledge and perspective are so limited.

Thirdly, we acknowledge that the voluntary acceptance of God's will makes us the conscious tools of His providence, by which His will is voluntarily accomplished through us as we put our entire dependence upon Him.

Recently I read a book in which the writer states that we should never pray that God's will may be done about a matter, but that we should ask and expect God to do what we already know assuredly to be His will. He claims that when we see a sick man we may assume that it is God's will for him to be healed. Therefore we must not only ask for God's healing for him, we must go a step further and "claim" it, as though that were the only possible direction which God's will could take in the matter.

That is absolutely wrong. Our knowledge is so limited that we cannot be absolutely sure of God's will in every situation. It would be far too easy for us to choose our own will and then try to force God to rubber–stamp it.

When the Lord taught us to pray, "Thy will be done on earth as it is in heaven," He wanted us to realize that it is impossible for us to know absolutely and in detail what the will of God is in every given situation. If we knew this absolutely and infallibly at all times, we would not be human, we would be little gods. So first of all we must accept the fact that we cannot always know what His will is.

Observe God's Operations in Nature as You Pray

"Have you had your daily miracle today?" one radio speaker asked his listening audience. That seems to be the way many people regard prayer, expecting a "miracle" every time they pray, feeling cheated if they don't get one, or becoming discouraged about the whole matter of prayer. The daily miracle seems to have become as much a necessity to some as the daily vitamin pill.

This is the wrong view of prayer. We mustn't regard it as a means of influencing God to alter those laws upon whose dependability we rest in our daily lives. It's essential that there be a recognition of the necessity of orderliness in God's operations in the universe. Apart from this order, science itself would be a sham, for it is based upon the proven existence of certain unchanging natural laws.

Although prayer shouldn't be construed as freedom to ask God to alter His normal methods or deviate from His usual procedures, that's the very thing we're often tempted to do. Satan tempted Jesus in this very way, suggesting that He turn the stones into bread, and that He jump from the pinnacle of the temple while relying on the angels to protect Him from the death.

The fact that God doesn't usually depart from His established providential laws doesn't mean He can't bypass them if He chooses. It's wrong, however, to feel that we can order Him to do so for our own personal benefit.

That God sometimes departed from His usual methods and procedures and bypassed His established natural laws in the past, destroying the regularity of His operations, is a fact of history. That He can do it again we must have no doubt. If He doesn't, let us not conclude it's because God has changed. Remember, *God doesn't always do what He is able to do, but what He chooses to do. His wisdom directs His omnipotence.* If our prayers could manipulate His omnipotence, He would cease to be God. Instead of our being the executors of His will, He would become the executor of ours. Can you imagine where we'd all be if God submitted His kingly omnipotence to our direction? Would you like another person to be able to influence God to act in your life as that person, with his limited knowledge and wisdom, believed best for you?

God practices no partiality in the exercise of His natural laws, He is holy and just toward all. If He exercised favoritism toward some and neglect toward others, He would be unholy. Christ told us that in the giving of His common graces the Father is strictly impartial. He allows the rain to fall on the righteous and the unrighteous. In the same manner, He allows life's calamities, such as sickness, disaster, and death, to happen to believer and unbeliever alike.

This isn't to say He isn't a Father in a different way to those who have chosen to live for Him than He is to those prodigals who refuse to acknowledge Him as their Father through Christ. He does exercise special providence toward those who call upon Him as His children. That's where prayer comes in. However, such special attention never contradicts His holiness. He is always a benevolent Father, perfect in His plan for each individual, and holy in the execution of that plan.

The father of the prodigal in Luke chapter fifteen wasn't showing favoritism to the elder brother who, by virtue of his choice to stay at the father's house, enjoyed all the privileges found there. The prodigal, in losing those privileges during his rejection of home ties, was merely reaping the consequences of his own choice.

Therefore, we who are God's children must never conclude that, because God decided to answer a particular prayer in a way that bypassed His usual and orderly operation through natural laws, He has abdicated the holiness He exhibits through such dependable orderliness. Nor should we conclude that we are always to seek in prayer God's miraculous intervention, as though He had made the extraordinary the ordinary.

For instance, our prayers for particular needs of provision and protection must not seem to imply that God is normally inclined to abandon everyone to a cruel fate, but that in answer to prayer He is influenced to exercise a little kindness in the case of a few favored ones. Nor should we imply that God could and would act as a protecting shield for all warriors or travelers if they were only the special objects of prayer.

It's certainly evident that most of the people and events in the world are not the subjects of prayerful intercession. But we can't conclude that a holy God leaves a multitude of people to their fate because they are not individually prayed for, while a few are rescued in answer to prayer. Such preferential treatment would be rank favoritism, partiality, injustice—not characteristic of our wise, loving, holy and just Heavenly Father!

There is one fundamental concept of prayer that must not be overlooked: man can only exercise his volitional power insofar as God wills that he should. He is a Father who loves everybody, but His love is governed and regulated by His sovereignty. As sovereign God, He gives us the ability to choose, in certain ways, our own course. However, He has already predetermined where that course will lead. The fact that it leads to suffering and perdition doesn't mean God isn't holy, or that He lost control. There are vast areas of human affairs that are carried on in contradiction to God's word. The greater proportion of them are not occasioned by the direction of God but by the sin of man.

When the brightness and warmth of the day pass from us, we use the expression, "the sun sets." This suggests that the fires of the sun have been blotted out, that its lamp is extinguished, that, at the least, it has forsaken us. But we know it isn't the sun that flickers out and deserts us. It's the earth that plunges us into darkness by turning away from the light of the sun.

So it is with the dark, benighting pall of sorrow and sin that has fallen upon the world. We realize that it isn't God who has withdrawn the light of safety and joy from us, it is humanity that forsakes Him and thereby plunges us into the darkness of sin and strife and suffering. Recognition of the fact that God is not the sole arbiter in regulating our experiences leads us to the conclusion that the scope of prayer is perhaps not so unlimited as we were first led to believe.

Can We Speak to God Without First Hearing Him?

Who is it who tends to speak the loudest? The one whose hearing is impaired usually does. The reason deaf people often make considerable noise when they talk is that they can't hear themselves, and they tend to think others can't hear them either. Just so, those who pray the loudest and are the most selfishly demanding are almost without exception those who are the deafest to God's voice. On the other hand, it's deafness that is the sole cause of many deaf mutes being unable to speak. If they could only hear, they would be able to speak normally.

This is true in the spiritual realm, also. Men can't pray aright when they haven't let God speak to them. And the less they hear, the more they try to compensate by speaking. Since what they say isn't a response to having heard God speak to them, it becomes only vain repetition. That's what our Lord meant when He said in Matthew 6:7, "But when ye pray, use not vain repetitions, as the heathen do: for they think that they shall be heard for their much speaking." The heathen hadn't received God's communication to them. Therefore, their prayers weren't a response to God's revelation. Like the deaf mutes, they had all the organs of spiritual "speech," but since they had never heard the sounds that result from God's speech, they were unable to address Him in a proper manner. Just so, if we don't learn to listen to God, we shall never learn to address Him in the proper way so that our prayers are heard and answered. If we're deaf when He speaks to us, we'll be dumb when we try to speak to Him.

Scientists tell us that in the natural world those insects and animals which have the most acute hearing are those who make almost no noise themselves. The volume of expression seems to be in inverse proportion to the capacity of hearing. Likewise, in the realm of prayer, those who learn to listen quietly to God speaking to them will make the least clamor and loud noise about prayer.

As the rain descends from the clouds and is afterwards drawn up heavenward again by the sun, prayer likewise is part of an unbroken circuit of receiving that which descends from heaven and then sending it heavenward again. Only as we understand this can we understand why Jesus taught us to pray for God's will to be done on earth as it is in heaven.

God gives us our desires that He may draw from us aspiration. He prompts our instincts that He may inspire our supplications. And for this reason we must be more eager to hear what God has to say to us than that He should hear what we have to say to Him.

The Psalmist knew how necessary it was to hear God before speaking to Him, for he said in Psalm 85:8, "I will hear what God the Lord will speak," God expects us to listen to Him and then to petition Him. In this way we know first not only what He is capable of doing, but what His plan is for us as individuals. His revelation is the basis of our petition. When Christ says that we shall receive what we ask for, the promise is always on the premise that our asking is within the delineation of His *revealed will to us*. Here are some of Christ's promises for answers to our prayers. Note how each promise is based on revelation:

John 15:7: "If ye abide in me, and my words abide in you, ye shall ask what ye will, and it shall be done to you." Observe that the "if ye abide in me and my words abide in you" is the basis of the promise. When we receive God's revelation in Christ, then we know what to ask for, and only if we ask for those things which are within God's purpose for us are we going to be heard.

Matthew 21:21, 22: "Verily I say unto you, if ye have faith, and doubt not, ye shall not only do this which is done to the fig tree, but also if ye shall say unto the mountain, Be thou removed and cast into the sea; it shall be done. And all those things, whatsoever ye shall ask in prayer, believing, ye shall receive." This isn't a limitless, reckless promise that God will give us whatever springs from our selfish desires. The element of faith is what prescribes the limitation of our petitions. "If ye have faith," the Master said. What is this faith? It's the God–given ability to receive God's revelation and appropriate it as part of our personality. To ask in faith or believing doesn't mean to ask without God's prescribed limitations, but to ask for what we desire within the context of what God has told us we can have or be. Faith is thus the most paradoxical element in the Christian life. It makes initial contact possible through Christ's revelation to us; then it's the authority by which we can continually ask and appropriate all that's available from God. But we don't know what's available from God unless He reveals it to us and by faith we accept that revelation.

John 14:13, 14 says: "And whatsoever ye shall ask in my name, that will I do, that the Father may be glorified in the Son. If ye shall ask anything in my name, I will do it." Again, observe that twice the expression, "in my name" is given in conjunction with the promise. What does that mean? Not simply the vain repetition of Christ's name at the end of our prayers, but the manifestation that our prayers are in response to Christ's revelation of the Father and His purposes for the world, others, and our individual lives. Furthermore, the phrase, "that the Father may be glorified in the Son" provides a definite limitation to our petitions. We must first receive God's revelation through Christ as to what will bring glory to our Heavenly Father. Apart from this, we will have no confidence that we'll receive what we ask.

Prayer therefore presupposes learning God's will in receptivity so that we may express that will in our petitions. If God didn't fully know us and our needs, He could never reveal Himself to us in the capacity of our understanding and His availability to us. That's exactly what Christ was referring to when He said in Matthew 6:8, "Your Father knoweth what things ye have need of, before ye ask him." He knows what He makes available to us through revelation. It's up to us to be receptive to the revelation and then to believe it's available to us.

In true prayer, it isn't only the lips that pray, but the soul. And the soul may express itself through inarticulate desires, pleading words, or an entreating attitude. Even an unexpressed longing can be a prayer. This is why James Montgomery said:

> Prayer is the soul's sincere desire,
> Unuttered or expressed.
> The motion of a hidden fire
> That trembles in the breast.

Feel Free to Express Your Desires, but Allow God to Determine What Is Good for You

A preacher had just received a call to a large and influential church, with a salary that was considerably larger than the one he was presently making. As he flew in the door of his home with the news, he shouted, "Honey, you go up and start packing, while I go in the study and pray about it." This little story makes us laugh because it is so apparent that he already had his mind made up, and the prayer was not going to influence his decision. He was not really seeking God's direction in the matter, he was going to do what he wanted to do about it, which was to accept the offer. Yet, don't we often do the same thing?

It is significant that this petition, "Thy will be done," comes before the petitions for personal blessings. The reason for this is that it is infinitely more important that God's will should be done than that we should have the things upon which we have set our hearts. So many times we do set our hearts upon someone or something, just as the preacher in the story did. We then do what we call "praying for God's will to be done," when what we are really doing is trying to get God to adapt His will to fit our desires in the matter.

For instance, a young woman may fall in love with a man and then begin to pray, "Lord, please give me this man for a husband." Or a businessman may set his sights upon a certain amount of money that he wants to make, and then begin to pray, "Lord, please let me achieve this. I am sure that it is Your will for my life." We must be extremely careful about praying like this, for prayer is not a matter of demanding that God do whatever we wish. God is not our servant, He is a king. This is why the petition, "Thy kingdom come," precedes "Thy will be done." Prayer is not bringing God into harmony with our desires, it is bringing ourselves into harmony with His.

However, this doesn't mean that it's wrong to tell God about our personal wishes and desires. Our children don't hesitate to ask us for what they want, but they don't really know what's good or bad for them. It's up to the parents to decide what to give them of all that they ask.

A little child may cry for the pretty bottle that he wants for a plaything. He doesn't understand why his parents are so cruel as to deny him his request, which to him is perfectly reasonable. It's pretty, and he wants to play with it. Why can't he have it, then? But the parents refuse not because they are selfish, or want to deprive the child of his toy or his enjoyment, but because on the side of the pretty bottle is a "skull and crossbones," which we know contains poison. Would the parents really be serving the child's best interest to give him the pretty bottle just because he cries for it? Of course not!

In just the same manner, God often denies us something that we think a good and desirable thing, because He knows that for us it would truly be "poison."

Or, look at the case of a child who is allergic to some type of food that he is really fond of. It is a wholesome food, but his parents will not allow him to eat it because they know that, though it is a good thing in itself, it will be harmful to him. Just so, God not only withholds what He knows would be positively bad for us, but also at times withholds things that are positively good in themselves, just because He knows that for us in our particular set of circumstances that thing would not be good.

The story is told of a very poor family during the middle ages who had a daughter who was very ill. Because of her physical problems the physicians had told her father that she could eat no heavy or sweet food whatever, only the very lightest of food and drink until she was well. At Christmas a wealthy person gave the father some rich cake for his family. He took the cake home, and explained to his little daughter that she should have the cake when she was well, but that she could not eat it then. At first the little girl was so disappointed that she cried, but she dried her eyes and insisted that the rest of the family eat their portion of the cake. She was able to watch them eat it without making a fuss, not because she understood fully why she could not have hers, but because she loved and trusted her father. She knew that if he denied her this treat it was for a good reason. She also knew that he would keep his word and give her the cake later when she was able to eat it.

Doesn't this illustrate the attitude that we should have when God as our loving Father deprives us of something we would very much like to have? It is not a matter of understanding why the request is not granted, it is a matter of trusting the love and wisdom of our Heavenly Father, who knows what is best for us at all times.

But just as the child is free to express his desires to his father, and just as there should be no reserve between the child and his father, there should also be no reserve between you and God, who is your Father. Tell Him your personal desires, but don't be determined at all costs to have your own way, because you don't always know whether your way is His will.

Sometimes it is God's will to send us the very things that we wish for, but sometimes He may choose to send us the things from which we would shrink. All of us are in reality but little children when it comes to spiritual things; we are ignorant and blind about what is best for us.

In this matter of praying for temporal gifts, we may often be praying to our own hurt without realizing it. We have not truly learned to pray at all until every petition is subjected to God's will. May He help us to conform to His will at all times, and to learn to pray, with Jesus, "Father . . . not my will, but thine, be done" (Luke 22:42).

Why Pray for Guidance When My Conscience can Guide Me?

"Just let your conscience be your guide" is the philosophy of many today, for people generally seem to think their conscience is God's guiding light in the decisions of life. Therefore, instead of praying for divine guidance and God's will, they simply follow their conscience.

The problem is, what the conscience of one permits him to do, the conscience of another forbids him. Many have the mistaken idea that our conscience has the inherent power to distinguish between good and evil, but actually our moral sense gains its discriminating faculty through education. An enlightened conscience isn't born, it's made. The tragedy of Christianity is that Christians have lost the consciousness of God's purpose and will and have developed a conscience all their own that often has little similarity to God's character. We think wrongly; therefore we act wrongly. Because we think our wrong thoughts of God are right, we justify our wrong acts. We have to think right if we are to do right.

Conscience is like the clock. It strikes twelve times just the same at midnight as at midday. But the one registers maximum darkness, the other maximum light. And when we recognize how grossly perverted our moral nature can be, we are made to see that, unless the pure light of heaven enlightens our judgment, our conscience will confirm us in error instead of establishing us in truth.

Conscience can also be likened to a compass. The principal compass on a ship is fixed in a position of special elevation so that its delicate poise won't be influenced by the ironwork of the vessel. Just so, the compass of one's moral judgment, having so many evil forces playing upon it, needs to be both established in a fixed position of truth and elevated to the highest spiritual concepts.

We should remember that our judgment is merely a dependent faculty. It decides what is right or wrong, but its edicts are based upon its concepts of the universal moral principles that are founded upon the nature of God.

Again, conscience is like our standards of measurement. When we measure the height of a mountain, we don't judge it by its relation to the land around it, or by any such variable standard. We measure it by that unvarying denominator—sea level. Likewise, in regulating our moral judgments or "measurements" we realize that human standards of measurement and judgment are variable. We are therefore impelled to base our personal standards upon God's character and law, which don't change.

This task is rendered peculiarly difficult, however, in that it's essentially individualistic. As moral responsibility is by its very nature a personal thing, every man is required in one sense to be his own lawmaker. No one—either God or man—can manufacture our moral standards for us, for if our moral decisions were imposed upon us from without, our personal responsibility would be at an end.

This means that our moral judgment has to be perpetually active. The Ten Commandments alone won't suffice for us; we need a fresh personal decalogue every day. How can our poor human capabilities achieve this, when our duties are often so conflicting, the difference between right and wrong frequently so vague, and our motives generally so mixed? We realize we are doomed to failure unless we can constantly consult the supreme Law-giver. The Mount of Prayer has to become our daily Sinai.

Thus our supreme need is for that divine enlightenment that will guide our moral deliberations aright. We need deliverance from the shallow thinking that leads to shallow living. And prayer is the means by which this deliverance is accomplished. To make anything a matter of prayer is inevitably to make it a matter of thought. Desire, the root of all moral activity, is scrutinized in the light of God's character and purpose.

Prayer is often likened to breathing, and one of the primary functions of respiration is the purification of the blood as the endless chain of pulsation passes through the lungs. Doesn't prayer serve a similar purpose? It cleanses our ever-recurring thoughts and motives and actions.

Prayer is a reiteration of utterance to God. Don't think you're not truly praying because you present to God the same old circle of requests day after day. True, you don't give God new information. Nevertheless, as in our physical life breathing is an essential repetition, prayer is spiritual respiration that cleanses the ever-circulating life currents of the soul.

Thus we see that what we need to guide us is not our fallible conscience but God's wisdom and counsel. Therefore God's omniscience is an inspiration for prayer rather than a deterrent to it. Our moral necessities impel us to cry out, in the words of the Psalmist, "Teach me, O Lord, the way of thy statutes; and I shall keep it unto the end" (Ps. 119:33).

God's Will May Involve Prosperity or Suffering

Lokman, the famous Oriental philosopher, while a slave, was presented by his master with a bitter melon and immediately ate it all. "How was it possible," asked his master, "for you to eat so nauseous a fruit?"

Lokman replied, "I have receive so many favors from you, it is no wonder I should, for once in my life, eat a bitter melon from your hand." This generous answer of the slave struck the master so forcibly that he immediately gave him his liberty.

"With such sentiments," says Bishop Horne, "should man receive his portion of sufferings at the hand of God."

In the matter of praying "Thy will be done," we come face to face with the problem of suffering as the will of God. When we pray, we sometimes do not know whether God wants us to enjoy health or to learn to rejoice in suffering. Therefore we must simply be resigned to His will. It is sometimes very hard and painful to conform our wills to the will of Christ.

There are those who teach that because God is good He will not permit anyone to suffer. But was God not good when He permitted His Son to suffer? Christ, we know, did suffer and through suffering He was "made perfect," or He "reached the goal" of redemption. God permitted Job to suffer in spite of the fact that he was a righteous man.

165

There was hardly ever a person who lived on this earth who was more saintly or self–sacrificing than the Apostle Paul. Yet read the Book of 2 Corinthians, chapter eleven and see what this dear saint of God went through.

The religious faddists who tell us that God's will always has to be prosperity, health, and abundance are not being scriptural. Some who teach this "prosperity" doctrine present John's Third Epistle, verse two, which literally translated from the Greek says: "Dear [Gaius] concerning all matters, I wish you welfare or prosperity and health, as thy soul desires." This is not a promise that God by virtue of His nature will necessarily bestow prosperity and health. That is expressed as Gaius' will, his desire, as all of us humans naturally desire prosperity and health. None of us pray God to make or keep us poor and sick. That is contrary to our sinful nature, which in its fallen humanity thinks that happiness is found in an abundance of material things and in the enjoyment of health. God may be glorified either through our joys or our sorrows. His glory is the object in view, or the goal toward which all is directed. When we speak of His "glory" we mean that we come to recognize God for all that He is. That sometimes is accomplished better through suffering than through health and abundance.

Doing God's will should be our primary consideration, for in this way He is glorified. We should not allow anyone or anything to hinder us from doing that will. The moment that we can sincerely say, "Thy will be done," we are surrendered Christians. We are not surrendered if, instead, we pray, "God grant my prayer, no matter what."

A simple farmer had a weather–vane on his barn which was inscribed with the words, "God is love." A scoffing neighbor, knowing of this man's devout faith in God, said, "Aren't you afraid that people will think your God is

166

changeable, that He is like the wind, by putting that on the weather–vane?" He thought the farmer would be upset by this and unable to make any reply, but he said calmly, "I meant it to show that God is love, whichever way the wind blows." The scoffer said no more. God's love doesn't change with circumstances. God is love whether you wake up in the morning with a headache, or whether you enjoy the fullest measure of health.

He loves us as a Father and He cannot permit anything to happen to us that is not an expression of His love. So don't be afraid to say, "Thy will be done." As we have said previously, He is not a despot whom we are forced to obey. He is our Father, but this Father is a king. We recognize this when we pray, "Thy Kingdom come." So as our Father and as our King we must respect and accept His rule in our lives. Since He is our Father, we must exercise trust and believe that He is trustworthy. We must have faith that His will is always better than ours, even if that will involves suffering and pain.

Consider the suffering of our Lord Jesus. It was agony for Him to drink the cup of suffering and sacrifice, and to be ridiculed by evil people. He felt so alone as they spat in His face and mocked Him. But His pain was alleviated by the realization that it was His Father's will.

Do you remember His words in John 18:11: "The cup which my Father hath given me, shall I not drink it?" This was in the Garden of Gethsemane, as He was facing the suffering of the cross. He did not say, "The cup which the king hath given me," but, "The cup which my Father hath given me." The cup of suffering came directly from the hand of a loving Father, but the will was difficult to accept in this case, as it sometimes is. However, Jesus recognized that His Father knew best, and so He said, "shall I not drink it?"

It was God's will that Jesus should die on the cross. He was thus manifesting His love to the world. Can you say with Christ, "The cup which my Father hath given me, shall I not drink it?" Drink it with joy, and the fullness of God will be your portion.

God Chooses the Means by Which to Accomplish His Purpose in Our Lives

A businessman had suffered heavy losses, as a result of which he began to have doubts about God's goodness and love. In his home hung a plaque that said, "His work is perfect." The man's little boy, knowing that his father was troubled, pointed to it and said, "Dad, doesn't that mean that God never makes a mistake?" The father, realizing that this was true, was recalled to his condition of trust in the wisdom and goodness of God.

However, even though we know it is true that God never makes a mistake, the word perfect actually has the meaning of "reaching the goal." God's work is perfect in that it has a purpose. This purpose, or goal, will eventually be reached by God. He never allows anything to happen without a purpose. His goal is that He shall be first in our lives. Whatever He permits in our lives is with this purpose and goal in mind.

Health and abundance may not always be the means through which He can accomplish this purpose. He is working toward the goal of a close relationship between Himself and us, and sometimes these things, instead of drawing us closer to Him, will actually draw us away from Him.

Not only does He have this goal, this purpose, for us, but He is also omniscient and all–loving. The tears that we are sometimes called upon to shed may serve to wash clear our eyes so that we may see and understand God more clearly. As the title of a song that we sometimes hear sung in church says, "He Washed My Eyes With Tears, That I Might See." We would all do well to remember the saying, "God is too wise to make a mistake, and too kind to be cruel."

Being a Christian doesn't mean that we shall never suffer or have losses or trials in our lives. But these are all working toward the purpose of God for us, to draw us closer to Him. When we pray for His will to be done, we have to realize that it will not always mean the pleasant and painless way.

Once as a woman was praying, "Thy will be done", so the story goes, the Savior appeared to her, holding in His right hand health and in His left hand sickness. He said, "Choose, my daughter, whichever you please." She replied, "Thy will, not mine, be done, my Lord." She knew that she was not wise enough to choose for herself, and so she left the choice to him.

> All those who journey soon or late
> Must pass within the garden's gate;
> Must kneel alone in darkness there;
> Battle with some fierce despair.
>
> God pity those who cannot say,
> 'Not mine, but Thine'; who only pray,
> 'Let the cup pass,' and cannot see
> The purpose in Gethsemane.
> —Author Unknown

Don't look upon your affliction as evil if it is God's will for you, and don't let others look upon it that way either. The height of holiness is reached when submission to God's will becomes not a painful thing, but a willingly and gladly accepted manifestation of His loving purpose for your life.

Doing God's Will Is More Than Passive Submission

Philip Melancthon, at the time of the death of Martin Luther's daughter, Magdalen, said, "Parental love is an image of the Divine love, impressed on the hearts of men; God does not love the beings He has created less than parents love their children."

We who are parents know how we plan and work to secure happy and prosperous lives for our children. Though the children prefer all play and pleasantness, we who are much wiser know that discipline and hardship are also a necessary part of their training. For instance, a schoolboy is prone to regard his studies as a hardship, something he would prefer not to have to do. But we know that these studies, though they require much work and time, are really for his good in the long run. In later years we as parents, and our grown children, will be thankful they didn't always have their way. Their ability to make a living, and their good training are a result of our parental discipline.

Sometimes we believers also act like little children. The experiences of life that God considers necessary for our training we consider hardships. Sometimes we want all sunshine and pleasantness in our lives, but He knows that we need the rain more than we need the sunshine. The Lord is working all things together for our good, but we have to understand that there will always be a mixture of the pleasant and the unpleasant, the joyful and the painful, in our lives.

Since it is the will of a loving Heavenly Father for which we are praying, and not the arbitrary will of some harsh despot who doesn't care anything about us, we can trust Him to give us that which will ultimately be for our benefit.

We should also understand that this prayer, "Thy will be done," is not simply a passive resignation to the will of God, but rather an active participation in it. It doesn't mean, "Lord, help us to suffer Thy will, and to bear it all." Of course, it does mean that at times, but it also involves much more. It should engage our active participation in accomplishing God's will in our lives. "Thy will be done" should mean "Lord, I'm ready to do Thy will actively. I want to cooperate actively with You in being what You want me to be and doing what You want me to do."

Suppose a farmer prays, "Thy will be done" concerning his need for food for his family, and asks that their needs be supplied by the Father. Can he then sit down at the table with folded hands and wait for God to set the supper on the table, so to speak? No, that would be stupid. He knows that he not only has to pray and ask for God's will to be done, and for His provision to be made, but also that he has to plow the field, plant the seed, cultivate it and then harvest it before that prayer is answered. God gave the sunshine, the soil, and the rain, as well as the health and strength to work, but he had his part to do also. That is an example of active involvement in the accomplishment of God's will, rather than passive resignation.

This, then, is what it means when we pray, "Thy will be done." It is saying, "Help me to discern Thy will, to know it, and then to participate actively in its execution."

SECTION VI

Give Us This Day Our Daily Bread

Give Us This Day Our Daily Bread

The petitions of the first part of the Lord's Prayer have to do with the end for which man lives—the glory, dominion, and service of His Creator. The last half of the prayer, beginning with the petition, "Give us this day our daily bread," has to do with the means by which we live, both the life of the body and of the soul.

In the first part of the prayer the Lord Jesus was bringing to our attention our duty toward God the Father. The purpose of life is to glorify God. It is not to have a healthy, prosperous, and pleasant time here on earth, but to show forth the reality of who and what God is.

In the second part of the prayer the Lord shows us that after our duty and obligation to God have been fulfilled, we can then expect God to fulfill His obligation to us. For since He has given us life, and since He is our Father, He has a Fatherly obligation for the maintenance of our physical and spiritual welfare.

The Lord Jesus was a realist. He realized that man is not only made up of an immaterial spirit and a soul, but also of a material body. The soul is the window toward our environment, the spirit is the window toward God. The body, of course, is that tangible element in which the soul and the spirit dwell.

Our souls and spirits are important, and they are provided for in this prayer, but they dwell in bodies that need physical nourishment if they are to continue to have life. We glorify God through our bodies as well as through our spirits. Hence the petition, "Give us this day our daily bread." It is obvious, isn't it, that without daily nourishment we cannot do God's will on earth, or fulfill our purpose of bringing glory to Him? Without nourishment we will die, and then we will no longer be on earth. Therefore nourishment is a basic and obvious need, without which we cannot even begin to glorify God. We must be careful, however, that we don't make the means become the end. This is the trouble with many people today. They make the earning of their daily bread the goal and purpose of their lives, when they should consider it only a means to the end of glorifying God.

Socrates said, "How many things there are that I do not need." You will be a satisfied person when you begin to think the same way. He who covets much is never content. The truth of the matter is if you think of all the things you want and don't have, you can never have enough to satisfy you. But if you think instead of how many of these things you don't really need, you will be a very thankful person. For you will realize how much more God has given you than you deserved or actually needed.

Someone has pointed out that the Lord's Prayer is eminently practical, there is nothing mystical about it. The petition we are now considering is for that most common of all needs—our daily bread. Bread is the substance of life; it is that by which life is maintained.

The first thing this petition teaches us is that we are to live our lives one day at a time. It really rebukes all inordinate anxiety about the future, just by the way it's worded. It doesn't say, "Lord, give me my bread for this year, for this month, for this week." No, it's "this day" and "daily bread."

When we realize that we're to live one day at a time and that this is the way God provides for our needs, we will begin to find satisfaction in life and will find anxiety disappearing.

The second thing this petition teaches is that we should cultivate simplicity in our lives. It's bread, or necessary food, that we're praying for. We don't pray, "Give us this day our daily cake," or "Give us this day a banquet." Most of our anxieties are not about the necessities of life, but about the unnecessary luxuries to which we cling. If we start worrying about the luxuries, we will never learn the secret of contentment with what God has given us, we will always be wanting more. And remember, God has not promised to supply all our wants, only our needs.

The third thing we learn from this prayer is that we are not to pray selfishly. It is not, "Give *me my* daily bread," it is, "Give *us our* daily bread." This petition includes all who struggle for the necessities of life. We shouldn't forget that there are those who don't even have their daily bread. They should always be included in our prayers. Whenever I pray over the food on the table, I say, "Lord, remember those who are still waiting for the answer to this prayer." We should also keep in mind that He may be waiting for us to help answer it by sharing what He has given us.

We usually have much more than the basic necessities of life, because God gives abundantly and freely. But if we have much or little we should take what God gives as from the hand of a Father. He knows how much is sufficient for His child. Very rarely can a child determine what is best for him and how much of certain foods he should eat. The parents are the ones who must determine this for him. Why should we not allow God to make the determination as to what is necessary for us day by day? May God help us to learn to trust Him in this way.

The Sanctity of the Body

D r. Charles Stanford said, "The God who made the body, shall He scorn to feed it?" Through this petition for daily bread the Lord teaches us what our attitude toward the body should be. First of all, we should realize that the body is a gift of God. It is the dwelling place of the soul and the spirit, and the Bible tells us that for the Christian it is even the temple of the Holy Spirit. Therefore we are not to despise it, but to honor it, take care of it, and treat it with dignity and respect.

The Lord wants us to be balanced people. Some people have become so "spiritual" and "holy" that they neglect or even abuse the body. In this way they think they can become even more spiritual. Yet this is really implying that the body is something evil or, at least, not as important as the soul and the spirit. We should understand that this is not true Christianity, it is asceticism, which teaches that we should deny, repress, or even abuse the body for the sake of so–called spiritual progress.

The beginning of the Lord's Prayer was concerned with glorifying God through our spirits. But we have to realize that we glorify God just as much through our bodies. They are holy and precious in the sight of God. Our Lord took on a human body when He came to earth, and He died physically. God does not love just our souls, He loves our bodies also.

Since our bodies are holy in His sight, how can we defile them through fornication or adultery, or with alcohol, smoke, drugs, or gluttony? No one who does such things can hope to "glorify God in [his] body," as Paul tells us to do. Do you treat your body with the respect and reverence that it deserves as the temple of the Holy Spirit? Do you recognize it as a gift of God, and are you acting as a good steward of what He has given you?

"We have no proof that the half of man's nature, though it be the lower half, is disowned by Him who made it. It is not 'counsel of perfection,' whatever ascetics teach, that our souls are to starve or trample out the instincts of our bodies. There was no neglect of the body in Paradise. No such neglect is taught by the theology of nature or by the standing lessons of 'seedtime and harvest.' He who made the body will not scorn to feed it. He who, though Lord of all, stooped under the lowly lintel of this, our 'cottage of clay,' and dwelt in a body like our own for more than thirty years; He who gave bread to the multitudes by the hand of a miracle; He who pronounced a blessing on bread before taking it with His disciples; He who has taught each believer that His body is a temple of the Holy Spirit; He who guards it in the darkling decay of the grave, so that no mystic atom, essential to its continuous identity, shall be lost and missing on the resurrection day—stoops to no degradation, and speaks in no way unlike Himself, by teaching us to pray for it, and we, the children of God, feel that any interpretation is quite unnatural as well as unscriptural which would deprive us of the great privilege of casting our bodily wants in simple prayer upon our heavenly Father" (Dr. Charles Stanford in *The Lord's Prayer*).

You Are Not Self–sufficient in Meeting the Needs of Your Body

A lazy man who depended upon his neighbors to provide his family with food, and did as little work as he could, was fond of saying piously, "God provides for birds and He will certainly provide for us, so why worry?" One of his longsuffering neighbors finally grew tired of this and said to him with exasperation, "Yes, but even the birds have to get out and scratch for it!"

The man's problem was one that afflicts many people—a lack of balance. He didn't balance his so–called trust with work. Actually, he had a false piety and a twisted view of the Scriptures. Balance counts for everything in the Christian life, for without it we not only fall short of reaching the stature of the fullness of Christ, but we are also open to all sorts of error and false doctrine. Everything must be viewed in its proper perspective, and the Word of God must not only be known but also "rightly divided."

Those who see the Christian life as one of asceticism and mystical contemplation have erred because of a lack of balance. They have divided life into compartments of "holy" and "secular," of "spiritual" and "not spiritual." They see the Christian as one who should not be concerned with the mundane things of life, such as work, money, bread, and so forth. They want to be completely isolated from the world and all its concerns, and they see the body as some-thing "unspiritual," which must be denied and repressed.

But this teaching is contrary to the teachings of our Lord and of New Testament Christianity. We are not to neglect the spiritual and place all the emphasis on the needs, appetites, and desires of the body, but neither are we to neglect the body and its needs in quest of some super "spirituality." If we should ever achieve that kind of so called spirituality we should then have elevated our-selves above our Lord and the Apostle Paul, for both of them taught the sanctity and dignity of the body as a cre-ation and a gift of God, to be held in the highest honor and used for his glory.

It is true, on the one hand, that our citizenship is in heaven, but the complementing truth which balances this is that our bodies are not in heaven, they are on the earth. Since they are here and a gift of God, and since they must be provided for, we should realize that we need God's help in taking care of them properly.

Sometimes we human beings tend to think that, because we can till the ground and raise our crops, we can be self–sufficient. But we are always dependent upon God, in spite of the fact that we have our part and our work to do. He provides the soil in which the crops grow, the sun-shine, the rain, protection from blight and insects, and all that is necessary for the growth of the crops that man has planted and cultivated and will eventually harvest. If it were not for the mercy of God, probably none of our crops would ever come to fruition. Remember that He is the One who gives life to the worker, and then gives him the strength to do his work and the intelligence and ability to perform his necessary tasks.

It is still the matter of balance, isn't it? God has His part, and without it we would have nothing to eat. Yet we also have our part, and God expects us to do that work which He has assigned to man.

Truly we must realize that we are not self–sufficient in this matter of providing our daily bread. All ultimately comes from God's hand.

How Does God Provide
Our Daily Bread?

"**D**o whatever is yours to do, then trust," said Dr. Charles Stanford. Fairbairn said, "The man who thinks Providence exists simply to make up for his lack of service, despises Providence."

How does God provide our daily bread? There are two ways by which He can work. One is through the natural laws that He has set into effect, which govern all of life on this earth, and the other is by way of the miraculous, which bypasses these natural processes. There are instances of both kinds of provision in the Bible. God is the one who chooses which way He will provide for our needs. It is not for us to dictate to Him the way that He shall work.

God provided miraculously for the children of Israel as they were traveling through the wilderness toward the Promised Land. When they needed bread He rained manna down from heaven upon them. This was certainly not a normal process.

But this method was never repeated. It was a unique provision for unique circumstances. Have you ever considered that the Israelites were on a journey, constantly moving through an arid wilderness area, and that they had neither the time nor the necessary conditions for growing their own food? Have you thought of the fact that it would have been impossible for them to carry enough provisions from Egypt to last throughout their long journey? Nor was there enough animal life in the desert to provide food for that many people for that long. The occasion called for a unique provision of God.

The other way in which God provides, and the usual way, is through natural processes. He wants us to respect and to use the natural laws that He has instituted. We do this through plowing, sowing, cultivating, and reaping. It is we who do the work, but it is God who gives the increase and causes the crops to grow.

God is sovereign, and we cannot command Him to work miracles for us just because we desire to see them done. When we pray, for instance, for the healing of our sickness, we must believe that God is able to answer our prayer, but we have to leave the means by which He answers it to Him. He can use the natural processes of healing that He has implanted in the human body, and speed these processes through the use of medicine, the doctor's skills, and surgery. But if He chooses to do so he can also heal directly and instantly, without any human intervention. However, we have no right to dictate to Him that He heal our sickness in a miraculous way, nor even that He heal it at all. But whatever method He may choose to use in healing sickness, all healing ultimately comes from Him.

We are never free to abdicate our responsibility of doing the work God has given us to do, and of obeying His natural laws. Do you remember what happened when the Children of Israel arrived in the land of Canaan? All the fields with the wheat and the barley were stretched out before them as they came into the fruitful land. As soon as they reached their destination, God caused the manna to cease. They no longer had a need for this miraculous provision. They were now able to produce their bread through cultivating the fields, but this work would be in cooperation with God, and in dependence upon Him. It would not be done independently of Him (see Josh. 5:11, 12).

God does not divorce His provision from our work, nor ought we divorce our work from His provision, believing that we can provide independently of Him. God very rarely chooses to use the miraculous way of providing our daily bread, but He can do so if the situation warrants it. He did it for the children of Israel, and for Elijah, and for the multitudes that Jesus fed with the loaves and fishes, and He has done it for many others who had no ordinary means of cooperating with him to produce their needed food. He provided bread miraculously in the Bible so often that we know He can do so, and that He will if necessary, yet not so often that we would think it was the normal way He provides. It is not the normal way, it is the abnormal. But whether by the natural process or by the miraculous, God is still thc One who provides our daily bread.

Will Prayer Make You Healthy and Wealthy?

"Healthy and wealthy!" That's the theme of some prominent and popular religious leaders of this day. A recently published book promoting this idea is actually theologically shocking. It reveals a highly immature concept of God's Fatherly care of His children, stating that the Christian ought to be completely free from physical sickness and financial want, since, as a loving Father, God can't possibly be willing for His children to suffer. The writer maintains that, as a Father, God is obligated to give us unbroken health and prosperity—in other words, to keep us "healthy and wealthy"!

Now, that's probably what we would do as earthly fathers, for we think of health and prosperity as the best our children can possibly have. But we wouldn't think like this if we were true spiritual fathers. As a father who is indwelt by God through Christ, the greatest good of which I can conceive for my children is that they have an intimate relationship with their Heavenly Father. I don't look upon my children as merely creatures of an earthly existence, but of the Spirit, and of an eternal existence beyond the physical body they now inhabit.

God never acts as though His children could live by bread alone. He will provide bread, even as we earthly fathers provide bread for our children, but never in quantities that would cause us to concentrate all our desires and aspirations on material benefits Of what value is physical health if that's going to result in neglect of the spiritual life? "What shall it profit a man, if he shall gain the whole world [including health and prosperity], and lose his own soul?" (Mark 8:36).

God apportions His earthly, physical benefits according to the influence they bear upon our eternal destiny. It's often the healthy and the prosperous who tend to forget God, and it's often the sick and the poor who tend to conclude that God knows best—in view of our eternal welfare—how to balance His distribution of material and bodily benefits.

Most earthly fathers consider only the temporal good of their children, as it's expressed within the confines of the immediate family. God, however, isn't limited by such an outlook. He's eternal and infinite. When He made us in His own image, He put within us the ability to choose, and planted eternity within our hearts. His life is eternal, and the life He imparts to His children is likewise eternal. Eternal life doesn't primarily refer to length of life, although that meaning is included. It refers essentially to the quality of life, to God's own life, and since God is eternal, He has no terminal point.

Therefore, when God acts toward us as our Father, His scope isn't that of an earthly father, concerned only with time and space and temporal benefits. He's concerned with our spiritual destiny. God exercises His Fatherly care toward us by deciding how long we shall live on this earth, rather than allowing us a choice in the matter. As long as He sees that we need additional time here for preparation for our eternal destiny, He will leave us here. Is it too much to presume that, when God removes us from this earth, it's in view of His knowledge of our intended choices as they will affect our eternal state?

For instance, when He decides to take an unbeliever from this earth at an early age, His motive can only be that of love. Knowing the person will never repent of his sin, but is simply by the extension of his life amassing greater eternal condemnation to himself, as well as endangering society in general, God cuts short his life for the sake of mitigating his eternal punishment.

On the other hand, if He takes an unbeliever late in life, it's because He wants him never to have any grounds for complaining that God never gave him adequate opportunity to repent. If God acts in the best possible eternal interest of the unbeliever, how much more does He do this for the believer! Whether He gives us a short or a long life, prosperity or privation, health or sickness, He never acts blindly or solely in the context of time and space as earthly fathers do.

Who can deny, then, that there is great advantage in having God as Father? He knows our soul far better than an earthly father, and He always acts in view of the eternal destiny of that soul, since He treats us with love and care as children in His family.

The Puritan, Abraham Wright, wrote: "I am mended by my sickness, enriched by my poverty, and strengthened by my weakness . . . . Thus was it with [King] Manasseh, when he was in affliction, 'He besought the Lord his God': even that king's iron was more precious to him than his gold, his jail a more happy lodging than his palace, Babylon a better school than Jerusalem. What fools are we, then, to frown upon our afflictions! These, how crabbed soever, are our best friends. They are not indeed for our pleasure, they are for our profit" (See 2 Chr. 33:11–13).

Thinking of the contrast of our momentary afflictions with our eternal glory (see 2 Cor. 4:17, 18), another of the Puritans, John Trapp, summed it up succinctly:

He that rides to be crowned
will not think much of a rainy day.

SECTION VII

**Forgive Us Our Debts as
We Forgive Our Debtors**

Forgiveness of Sins—a Necessity For Peace in the Soul

Our Lord was real. He had a body. He ate and drank to sustain His physical existence. He knew that material food was needed for the body, although He emphasized that "man shall not live by bread alone" (Matt. 4:4). And in His model prayer for us He told us to say, "Give us this day our daily bread." That is the recognition of our material need.

But immediately He added the fifth petition, which deals with the needs of the soul. "And forgive us our debts [or sins]," indicating that as bread is to the body, so is forgiveness to the soul.

Once man begins to see who God is he feels a sense of guilt and dread. People outside the influence of Christianity also have such a sense of guilt, as attested by human sacrifices and horrible self–tortures. Fear lies at the door of every man's heart. They try through self–torture and animal sacrifices to assuage God's anger. It must be horrible to live without the knowledge of the gospel and the hope of forgiveness of sins.

One of the greatest reasons for the tremendous response to AMG's gospel messages in the press, which are read by non–Christians such as Muslims, Hindus, and Buddhists, is that in their religions they have no Savior who can remove the guilt and power of sin. There is nothing more torturous to the inner peace of man than a feeling of guilt and the ignorance of any remedy for it.

How different is life in Christ! When we pray, our Lord taught us to say, "Forgive us our sins." Christ has not given us "The spirit of bondage . . . to fear, but . . . the Spirit of adoption, whereby we cry, Abba, Father" (Rom. 8:15). In Christ, "Perfect love casteth out fear: because fear hath torment" (1 John 4:18). No other religious leader ever taught that it is possible to be forgiven and to forgive. The one is as important to peace of soul as the other. It profits us nothing to be forgiven if we are unforgiving.

One of the attempts of Satan will be to persuade us that we neither need nor can obtain forgiveness of sins. Sinning, after all, is obeying Satan; so why shouldn't he try to persuade us that we do not need to feel guilty about obeying him? He presents sin to us as the means of fulfilling a need, especially taking advantage of an easily aroused lustful nature. How easily he leads us to call lust "love" so that we can find our own justification for sin, instead of finding God's justification for sin through Christ.

Satan says, in effect, "There can be no forgiveness of sins. Look around you. In the natural world there is no forgiveness. You have sinned against yourself. Can you get back the health wrecked by the dissipation of your youth? Can a man change the color of his skin? Can the leopard eliminate his spots? In sins against your neighbor, can you recall the poison of your evil example, of your whispered temptation, of your slanderous word? Try to stop the stone which you have rolled down the mountainside! Omnipotence itself cannot recall the word once uttered; cannot undo the deed once done." So Satan whispers to us, "You are mine. Resist no longer, for it is vain."

"Father, forgive us our trespasses." It is the Gospel, good news. It is a miracle. It is true that there is nothing like it in the world of nature or of man. It is avowedly supernatural. It is exclusively the gift of God. With man this forgiveness is impossible, but with God all things are possible. There has never been any miracle greater than the miracle of the forgiveness of our sins and that of our forgiveness toward those who trespass against us.

That is one of the "greater works" Christ promised to His disciples when He said, "He that believeth on me, the works that I do shall he do also, and greater works than these shall he do; because I go unto my Father" (John 14:12). There is absolutely no greater work that any of us can do than to proclaim God's forgiveness of sinful man and to practice such forgiveness in our daily lives.

There is no comparison between the miracles God performs in the physical world and those He performs in the spiritual. What physical miracles He performs always have a spiritual purpose. That is why they are called "signs." They point to a spiritual truth. God is Spirit. We are both spirit and body, but our spirit never ceases to be, whereas our body is temporary, which is a good thing. To roll back the Red Sea or the Jordan upon itself was easier for God to do than to forgive our sins. To accomplish forgiveness cost Him the sacrifice of His own precious Son. And because of its cost we ought to consider it as the most precious bestowment God can give us.

God declares through this prayer that He can undo the harm done by Adam and by us. He can cancel out our unpayable debt. For such a miracle the Lord teaches us to pray. He not only tells us that sin can be forgiven, but knowing that we come before Him as guilty creatures, He also bids us ask cleansing from our daily defilement that results from being in the body and in the world: "Father, remit, send away, our trespasses that are such a burden to us. Make them as if they had never been. We need this more than we need our daily bread."

When Satan would tempt us to disbelieve the efficacy of this prayer, let us confront him with Christ's whole Gospel. It all turns upon this—that sin can be forgiven always; can be forgiven utterly; supernaturally, not naturally; in Christ, not in ourselves. "Though your sins be as scarlet, they shall be as white as snow; though they be like crimson, they shall be as wool" (Is. 1:18). "Who is a God like unto thee, that pardoneth iniquity, and passeth by the transgression of the remnant of his heritage? he retaineth not his anger for ever, because he delighteth in mercy. He will turn again, he will have compassion upon us; he will subdue our iniquities; and thou wilt cast all their sins into the depths of the sea" (Mic. 7:18, 19).

That is casting or remitting our sins away from us (*aphesis*). "As far as the east is from the west, so far hath he removed our transgressions from us" (Ps. 103:12). As Augustine said, "Nothing is so much our own as our sins." But Christ has told us that they can be daily purged through the simple prayer, "Forgive us our trespasses." Does an inexorable justice require a penalty? Mercy triumphs over justice.

Go beyond the promises of God in confronting Satan. Go to those who have tested and found them true. Think of those who were bidden as wedding guests to the great king's table (Matt. 22:1ff.), to each of whom, soiled from the wayside and the hedges, was given a wedding garment. Think of all the prodigals who have come, so weary and footsore, so sick, so disgraced, so stained from the far land and the swine, to whom there has been given the best robe and the rejoicing welcome. Think of all those polluted souls who have washed their robes and made them white in the blood of the Lamb.

Think of poor cheating Jacob, who became Israel, a "prince with God" (Gen. 32:28). Think of David, the murderer and adulterer, to whom God yet restored the clean heart and the free spirit (Ps. 51:10). Think of cursing and swearing Peter. Think of savage, persecuting Paul, who yet became chief among the Apostles. Think of the penitent thief on the cross, the rough jailer of Philippi. Think of the ignoble, swindling publicans, who did not beat upon their breasts in vain. Think of the harlots whom He saved by His marvelous grace, transforming them into virtuous, saintly women.

These entered into the kingdom of heaven before priests and Pharisees, because it is the helpless, who know their helplessness, to whom Christ came. Much forgiven, they loved much. Think of all the converts, once fornicators, adulterers, effeminate, thieves, covetous, drunkards, revilers, extortioners; but afterwards saints of God and dear children, washed, cleansed, justified, sanctified. Think even of all the demoniacs, sitting at last at Christ's feet, clothed and in their right mind.

How Is Forgiveness of Sins Possible?

That forgiveness of sins is an even greater necessity than our daily bread has already been demonstrated. But how is forgiveness made possible? We could never have done anything ourselves to obtain this forgiveness. Because God knew that no effort of ours would avail, He provided the means. He sent His own Son into the world to procure it. Christ Himself bore for us the crushing burden, paid for us the immeasurable debt. He didn't have to for it was our own choice in Adam that incurred the debt. God's interest in us was neither a necessity for Him, nor was it a duty. It was only out of love. It was an act of utter mercy. Christ loved us so much, even while we were yet sinners; He thought our souls worth so much, sinful though they were, that He came down to earth to live for us as a sinless man and die for us as a hated malefactor. Otherwise our sins would be incurable.

It was the One who paid the penalty to make our forgiveness possible who taught us to pray, "Forgive us our trespasses." How can we have any doubt about His promise? He would never have asked us to pray for forgiveness if forgiveness were unavailable. If so many millions have found forgiveness possible and obtainable, why should it not be available to you? Only you can be blamed if you do not possess it. If you meet conditions prescribed for it, Christ will fulfill His promise that says, "Him that cometh to me I will in no wise cast out" (John 6:37). As far as He is concerned, His forgiveness is available to all at any time, even daily. He who was known as the Friend of sinners will never repudiate you.

The relationship that is revealed by the Lord between God and man is that of a Father and child. The forgiveness of our sins is therefore consistent in the exercise of concern by a father to a child. A child is absolutely dependent on the father, his initiative and provisions. That is the only way a child can continue to exist. Its life is derived from the father. The sustenance of life is something that the parent owes to the child. This notion, however, implies also that as long as the child draws his subsistence from the parental bounty, so long is he bound to be subject in all things to the paternal will.

These obligations are correlative. No one would think of interfering with a father's rights by transferring to himself the duty and obedience of the child, unless he also took upon himself the charge of its maintenance and support.

The same is true of our Heavenly Father, with some important additions. His Fatherly care of us in sending Christ to us and for us took place after our rejection of Him. Therefore His forgiveness and care for us is not a matter of obligation toward us, but a demonstration of mercy. Furthermore, we never get above the necessity of seeking our supplies at His hands. In our natural development as children we become independent of our parents, but never as children of God. And since we never become independent, we never get above the duty of filial obedience and submission to Him.

All the petitions of the Lord's Prayer are beautifully interrelated. He who tells us to pray, "Our Father," says also, "Ask for the full remission of your sins." He must mean that it is such a request as a child should make of a father, and one that a father could grant his child. He who teaches us to say, "Hallowed be thy name," bids us ask for this remission. He must mean that God's name is hallowed in our making the petition, and in His hearing it.

He who taught us to say, "Thy kingdom come," bids us to say, "Grant us the remission." He must mean that it is consistent with His royalty, part and proof of it, that we should desire and receive this release.

He who desired us to pray, "Thy will be done on earth as it is in heaven," tells us also to ask for the sending away of debts. He must mean that this is the will that is obeyed in heaven, and that in praying so, we are obeying it on earth.

He who taught us to look up to God as a Giver, not as an Exactor, and to pray for the bread which is needful for us, further commanded us to ask for this freedom. He must mean that rain and fruitful seasons are not a clearer sign to men of what He is, than remission; the one is at least as much needed by His creatures as the other; the one is as much an utterance of His disposition and purpose as the other.

He who came down to declare the name, the kingdom, the will of God, and to bring all good gifts to men, must have wished us to understand Him thus, or He could not have trained us to the use of a word so precise and yet so unlimited.

Christ wants us to understand one basic fact through this prayer. A God who offers us forgiveness is no longer a terrible God. That's what we should have expected with the utterance of the word "Father." He is a loving, forgiving Father. The effect of sin is to frighten us away from God, to make us hide ourselves from Him, as Adam and Eve did; to make us fly away from Him, as Jonah fled from the presence of the Lord to Tarshish.

Our Lord did not teach us to ask for peace, but for forgiveness. Why? Because peace is the result of forgiveness, both of our acceptance of forgiveness and our dispensing of it. "Therefore being justified by faith [which is equivalent to having received forgiveness of sins], we have peace with God through our Lord Jesus Christ" (Rom. 5:1). We cannot have peace with God unless we receive His forgiveness, and we cannot have peace with others unless we forgive them. We need God's forgiveness as much as others need our forgiveness.

Why Are We Sinners?

The first thing we confess through the petition, "Forgive us our sins," is that our very nature is corrupt. Few of us become notorious criminals, but all of us are sinners.

One of the greatest proofs of man's depravity is the aversion with which he naturally and spontaneously contemplates God, who in reality is man's greatest Benefactor. The result of that aversion is that man either seeks to avoid God or else cringes before Him in slavish fear.

We need forgiveness because we are sinners. We are sinners not simply because we personally sin, but because our representative, Adam, sinned. We are burdened with hereditary sin. Paul expressly states this in Romans 5:12: "By one man sin entered into the world, and death by sin; and so death passed upon all men, for that all have sinned."

There is therefore a connection between our present state and Adam's sin. We sin because we are sinners and vice versa. The universality of sin is a consequence of Adam's sin.

Death is a *consequence* of sin, but not always a *punishment*. I die because I must bear the consequences of Adam's sin, but the punishment in death was borne by the Lord Jesus who died for our sins.

Our nature, therefore, suffers from a hereditary taint of sin. We all get sick and we all ultimately die physically. Is this not enough proof of our depravity? If we are natural heirs to disease and death, which are the consequences of sin, we must also be heirs of what caused them in the first place—sin. Our nature by inheritance is sinful, but the degree to which we imitate Adam's sin varies.

Read carefully Romans 5:12–18 and you will see that Paul presents Adam and his disobedience to God's command as responsible for our sinful nature. But he also presents an act of reparation performed by Christ. These two acts he contrasts with each other, particularly as regards their respective effects on the destinies of the human race.

Christ's death served to undo, both universally and individually, that which was caused by Adam's disobedience. Whatever is universal in the disease is universal in the remedy. Thus, the whole race of man being tainted with hereditary sin by natural descent from Adam, the whole race of man receives full remission of that hereditary sinfulness in Christ.

"Christ", that is to say, "is the propitiation not for our sins only," who knowingly believe in Him, "but also for the sins of the whole world" (See 1 John 2:2). Not a single individual in the family of man is consigned to eternal perdition as a necessary consequence of his having sprung from Adam. Not a single individual of our race *must* perish because he inherits a corrupt nature. Salvation, insofar as it consists of a removal of the guilt of his inherited corruption, extends to every human creature. What Christ did was to pay the penalty for Adam's sin through the sacrifice of His life. Here are some statements that indicate the universal effect of Christ's death:

Romans 5:6: "Christ died for the ungodly." 2 Corinthians 5:14: "If one died for all, then were all dead." 2 Corinthians 5:15: "He died for all."

That basic verse, John 3:16, states it unequivocally: "For God so *loved the world,* that he gave his only begotten Son, that whosoever believeth in him should not perish, but have everlasting life." If Christ died only for a few, then it would be impossible for "whosoever believeth" to be saved.

Therefore, as Adam's disobedience made us all guilty, so Christ's obedience unto death liberated us all, or justified us before God, who is the Judge. Adam brought us under condemnation and Christ's death, having been accepted as adequate payment for Adam's sin, declared humanity "Not guilty," or justified us. This justification, however, is a judgment passed on man. It is not a work wrought within man, automatically transforming him and making him a child of God.

God has done His part, once and for all. It was once that Christ was offered to bear the sins of many (Heb. 9:28). Jesus Christ did not need, as Hebrews 7:27 tells us, "Daily, as those high priests, to offer up sacrifice, first for his own sins, and then for the people's: for this he did *once,* when he offered up himself." And as 1 Peter 3:18 says "For Christ also hath *once* suffered for sins, the just for the unjust, that he might bring us to God, being put to death in the flesh, but quickened by the Spirit."

On the other hand, what is partial in the disease is also partial in the remedy. I am sinful by nature, but the decision to sin and the extent to which I sin is my own particular decision. When I become old enough to know the difference, I have the choice of yielding to my sinful nature or of allowing Christ's atonement to transform me into a new creature.

The acts of Adam and of Christ extend respectively to every individual of our race: every human being has a sinful nature by natural descent from Adam, the first transgressor, the whole necessary effects of which are neutralized by Christ's atonement. This atonement, however, is of no practical value to us unless we appropriate it individually and allow it to become effective in our own lives. When it does become effective we are not only declared justified, we are actually made just or righteous.

What Is Sin?

In understanding the Lord's Prayer, we must determine the meaning of the word sin, or trespass. In Luke 11:4 our Lord taught us to pray, "And forgive us our sins." The word in the Greek is *hamartias* (accusative plural of *hamartia*). But in Matthew 6:12 it is another, entirely different Greek word that is used: *opheilēmata,* also in the accusative plural of the substantive *opheilēma,* derived from the basic verb *opheilō,* which means "to owe, to consider a duty." *Opheilēma* is a debt and it is correctly translated in the only other place it is used in the New Testament, Romans 4:4: "Now to him that worketh is the reward not reckoned of grace, but of debt [*opheilēma*]."

Paul here is arguing about Abraham's justification by God. It was not pay (*misthos*) for his good works, but was the result of God's grace. If you pay somebody for what he does, it is a reward he has earned. Therefore any justification which is pay for works is not of grace but is an indebtedness (*opheilēma*) for work accomplished.

Opheilēma is the actual debt—that which is due someone. The suffix *ma* at the end of *opheilē* indicates the result of owing, that is, the actual debt. In the same way, baptize (*baptizō*) refers to the act of baptizing, but the result of this act is called *baptisma* (baptism). Only in two places is the work *opheilēma* (singular in Rom. 4:4 and plural [*opheilē-*

mata] in Matt. 6:12) used in the New Testament, and we can easily see that what is spoken about in Matthew 6:12 is our debts toward God. "Forgive us our debts."

Debts are owed to someone, either to God or to fellow humans. Forgiveness is asked from the person to whom you owe something. In Matthew 6:12, we are asking God to forgive us our debts or, in other words, what we owe Him. And in Romans 4:4 Paul tells us that the justification which God offers to a human is not something God owes man for what man has done (*opheilēma*), but is *charisma,* the result of God's grace—it's a gift. And this is possible because of what Christ did on Calvary's cross.

Only in Matthew 6:12 is sin defined as *opheilēma,* "debt." The Lord uses the metaphor of the debtor to explain man's situation in relation to God. And this debt is so large that it is impossible for man to pay it on his own. This is demonstrated by the parable of the wicked servant in Matthew 18:23ff. The debt owed was 10,000 talents, the equivalent of fifteen million dollars. Why did the Lord teach us to pray for the forgiveness of our debts? Because they are so great that on our own we find it impossible to pay them off.

The Pharisees thought that they could pay off their debts through the performance of some good deeds. Their reasoning was something like this: I owe you fifteen million dollars. I don't have it to give you. But let me take you out to dinner and you forget the debt I owe you. That's the Pharisaic philosophy: I owe you much. I'll do a little bit for you and we'll call it even.

All the teaching of the Lord Jesus and of Paul is that divine remission of sins, of our debts, cannot be accomplished by what we do for God or for others, but only by accepting God's mercy toward us. Divine remission is inseparably connected with God's mercy. It is based upon it. If it were not for God's mercy there could be no forgive-ness.

The Lord Jesus does not ask His disciples to do any works to earn God's forgiveness, or to sacrifice a certain amount so that they can become worthy of it, or to fast for a certain period for it. He merely says, "When you pray, say, 'Forgive us our debts.' " It's just a matter of asking for it instead of working to earn it. If we could do anything toward the earning of our forgiveness, He would have made it easy for us by telling us what to do. Forgiveness is a matter of grace.

We must recognize facts in our relationship with God. First, that we owe God so much that it is impossible for us ever to pay our debts to Him on our own. These debts are not only those for which we are personally and directly responsible, but also those for which we are indirectly responsible. Adam's sin has made each of us personally indebted to God. The sin of all creation is also ours. The sins of our fellow humans are also our sins insofar as our sinful estate and practice have to some extent contributed to the sinfulness of the environment. This includes what each of us has done and what we have neglected to do.

Christ considered us debtors to God and others, but in none of His own prayers did He ever ask for forgiveness or express any notion of His indebtedness to the Father. Among all the prayers that He offered while on earth, we have no record of any that included any sort of confession of personal sin. Yet He taught us that we must confess our sins, we must ask for forgiveness, we must be possessed with an awesome feeling of indebtedness toward God and our fellow humans. He didn't practice what He preached, so to speak. Why? Because, though He was fully human He was also God's unique Son, one with the Father, (John

14:10), in whom "dwelleth all the fullness of the Godhead bodily" (Col. 2:9).

If He were only human, He would also have prayed, "Father, forgive *me,*" or, "forgive *us,*" equating Himself with mere humans. But He never did. On the contrary He boldly asked, "Which of you convinceth me of sin?" (John 8:46). His enemies never dared accuse Him of sin. They never took up the challenge.

In many other ways He asked us to imitate Him, but not in the confession of our sins and the asking of pardon. It was because He "Was in all points tempted like as we are, yet without sin" (Heb. 4:15). He didn't need God's mercy because He was not a debtor to God. But as far as we are concerned, we are commanded, "Let us therefore come boldly unto the throne of grace, that we may obtain mercy, and find grace to help in time of need" (Heb. 4:16).

The parable of the Pharisee and the publican in Luke 18:9–17 clearly teaches that no matter what we do, good though it may be, it is not enough to pay off our indebtedness to God. The Pharisee prayed. You may pray too. But if you do not pray, "Forgive us," it is as if you never prayed, because your prayers do not reach God's ear and will therefore result in nothing. After all, when we pray we want to move God to activity on our behalf. The Pharisee prayed thanking God that he was not as others—extortioners, unjust, adulterers. He wasn't lying either. He may have been honest, just, and moral. But his honesty, justice, and morality did not cause him to stand clear in the sight of God, without any debt toward Him.

Our debt toward God is so large that it cannot be paid off by the highest sense and life of honesty, justice, and morality.

On the other hand, all the publican did was to ask for forgiveness by saying, "God be merciful to me a sinner."

His indebtedness to God, in order to be wiped out, needed the exercise of God's mercy, not anything he himself could do, even if that may have included fasting twice a week and giving a tenth of all his belongings to God and charity as the Pharisee did. This proves that our indebtedness to God cannot be paid off either by the evil we avoid doing—extortion, injustice, and immorality—or by the good we do—fasting and charity. It is because there is nothing we can do to wipe out indebtedness to God that the Lord asked us to pray, "Forgive us our debts."

What is really implicit in Matthew 6:12, "Forgive us our debts," is that man, whether a believer or an unbeliever, owes something definite to God, but what God offers man, justification, is not anything God owes man. It is all of grace, and as such it cannot be purchased, but can be obtained only through faith, the belief that God will cancel the debt. That is justification.

Every time you pray the Lord's Prayer and say, "Forgive us our debts," you confess humanity's debt to God. Observe that what our Lord taught us to say was not, "Forgive me my debts to Thee," but "Forgive *us*," in the plural—*our* debts. This is recognition of the sinfulness of the entire human race. All humans are "debtors to God."

In what way is all humanity indebted to God? First of all, by virtue of God having created us all. "And God said, Let us make man in our image, after our likeness" (Gen. 1:26). "So God created man in his own image, in the image of God created he him; male and female created he them" (Gen. 1:27). We didn't create ourselves. We owe our very lives to God. That's our first indebtedness.

What do you owe your parents? Your very life. That's why we are commanded to honor them. We never cease to be debtors to our parents, and we never cease to be debtors to God, because in Himself He is a Father to us all.

Of course we have estranged ourselves from Him. We left His house and we have gone to a far country and have ceased to consider ourselves His children, but He has never abdicated His right of Fatherhood in regard to any of us. The father of the parable in Luke chapter fifteen considered himself a father both to the older son who stayed at home and to the younger prodigal who left home.

Lawlessness Is Sin

Besides *opheilēmata,* "debts," used in Matthew 6:12, and *hamartias,* "sins," used in Luke 11:4, there are several other Greek words that are indicative of an interference in man's relationship with God that need forgiveness or restoration.

One is *adikia,* meaning "behavior that does not conform to the moral norm, translated "iniquity" in Luke 13:27 and 2 Timothy 2:19. It is also translated "unrighteousness" in Luke 16:9; John 7:18; Romans 1:18, 29; 2:8; 3:5; 6:13; 9:14; 2 Thessalonians 2:10, 12; Hebrews 8:12; 2 Peter 2:13, 15; and 1 John 1:9; 5:17. Although it is a noun, it is mistakenly translated as an adjective, "unjust," in Luke 16:8 and 18:6. It is translated as "wrong" in 2 Corinthians 12:13, and as "iniquity" in Acts 1:18; 8:23; 1 Corinthians 13:6; 2 Timothy 2:19, and James 3:6.

The verb is *adikeō,* which means "to act unjustly, to harm others." In the passive form it means "to suffer injustice" and is always found in the context of relations between man and man (Acts 7:24; 1 Cor. 6:7; 2 Cor. 7:12).

Also, from the same stem comes *adikēma,* which is the result of wrong behavior or a criminal act. It occurs three times: in Acts 18:14; 24:20; and Revelation 18:5.

Adikia, "unrighteousness," is made up of the privative *a,* "without," *dikē,* which means "penalty or punishment, or justice personified as a goddess." It therefore means the

214

absence of punishment or justice. Injustice is possible only because truth and justice exist (see John 7:18). 1 John 5:17 says, "All unrighteousness is sin" ("unrighteousness" here is *adikia,* and "sin" is *hamartia,* "missing the mark"). Everything that violates God's truth is missing the mark God has set. The goal therefore that God has set is His revealed truth. If we don't fulfill that truth we are missing the mark. The verb *adikeō* means "to do wrong."

Further, there is the word *anomia,* meaning "lawlessness or contempt of law." It is made up of the privative *a* and the noun *nomos,* which means "law." *Anomia,* "lawlessness," sometimes signifies absolute estrangement from God's law (Matt. 24:12; 2 Thess. 2:7). It is translated "iniquity" in Matthew 7:23; 13:41; 23:28; 24:12; Romans 4:7; 6:19; 2 Thessalonians 2:7; Titus 2:14; Hebrews 1:9, 8:12; 10:17. It is translated "unrighteousness" in 2 Corinthians 6:14, and "transgression" in 1 John 3:4. It is set over against *dikaiosunē,* "righteousness," in 2 Corinthians 6:14. In 1 Corinthians 9:21 it is used negatively of a person "without law" or to whom a law has not been given. The Antichrist, the "Man of Sin," is called *anomos,* "that Wicked," literally "the Lawless One," in 2 Thessalonians 2:8.

Anomia, lawlessness, is never the condition of one living without law, but the condition of one who acts contrary to law, just as *anarchia,* "anarchy," is the condition, not of one who has no rule, ruler, or authority, but of one who acts contrary to authority.

Another derivative of *nomos,* "law," is *paranomia* (found only in 2 Pet. 2:16 and translated "iniquity"), with the preposition *para,* which means "besides, near, on the side." *Paranomia,* therefore, is something that is unlawful or besides the law. As a verb, it is used in Acts 23:3.

An important theological problem is solved when we understand the words *hamartia,* "sin, or missing the mark,"

215

adikia, "unrighteousness, the lack of justice," and *anomia,* "the condition of going contrary to the law." In Romans chapter five Paul discusses the whole problem of how sin and its consequences entered the world. "Wherefore, as by one man sin [*hē hamartia,* 'the sin'] entered into the world, and death by sin ['through—*dia*—the sin'—*tēs hamartias*]; and so death passed upon all men, for that all have sinned [*hēmarton*]" (Rom. 5:12). This means that Adam missed the mark of obeying God's commandment, was spiritually separated from God, and ultimately died physically, as all men do.

Then came the Law which God gave to Moses. "For until the law sin [*hamartia*] was in the world" (Rom. 5:13). That means sin can exist as *hamartia,* missing the mark, without any law having been given. The specific condition that goes contrary to the law is *anomia,* but if there is no law there can be no lawlessness. However, there can be a missing of the mark. Now observe the balance of the statement in Romans 5:13: "But sin [*hamartia,* 'missing the mark,'] is not imputed when there is no law." Those who lived prior to Moses missed the mark in Adam in that he disobeyed a specific command of God. Those after Moses, the Jews, could be charged with *hamartia,* "missing the mark," because God gave them the Law.

For those who lived without the law (*nomos*) prior to Moses, there could be no *anomia,* "lawlessness." 1 John 3:4 tells us, "Whosoever committeth sin [*hamartian,* 'misses the mark,' whatever the mark may be, either a direct command, revealed truth, or one's own inner voice of God] transgresseth also the law [commits *anomian,* 'lawlessness']. And the sin [*hamartia,* "missing the mark"], is the lawlessness [*anomia*]."

Whatever God's standard or goal is, be it a commandment not to eat of a particular tree, as it was to Adam, or to keep a set of rules as prescribed in the Law God delivered to Moses, or the words of the law written in one's own heart, it must be met or there is sin for which man is responsible. Therefore where there is no law (Rom. 5:13), there may be *hamartia* (sin), *adikia* (unrighteousness), but there can be no *anomia* (lawlessness). Thus the Gentiles, not having a law (Rom. 2:14), might be charged with sin; but they, sinning without law *(anomōs chōris nomon,* Rom. 2:12; 3:21), could not be charged with *anomia.*

No one is excusable from sin, because behind that Law of Moses, which the Gentiles never had, there is another law, the original law and revelation of the righteousness of God written in the hearts of all (Rom. 2:14, 15). As this revelation in the human heart is never obliterated altogether, all sin, even that of the darkest and most ignorant savage, must still in a secondary sense remain as *anomia,* "unrighteousness," a violation of the older law, in spite of the fact that it is partially obscured. Hence the truth proclaimed in 1 John 3:4: "Everyone doing the sin [*hamartian*] also does the unrighteousness [*anomian*], and the sin [*hamartia*] is the unrighteousness [*anomia*]" (literal translation).

Sin as Godlessness, Disobedience, and Error

Our attitude toward God can be wrong. When it is, then we sin toward God. In Greek this is called *asebeia,* "godlessness." The verb is *asebeō,* made up of the privative *a,* "without," and the verb *sebō,* which means "to render reverential fear or profound respect." In its adjectival form, found in Romans 4:5; 5:6; 1 Timothy 1:9; 1 Peter 4:18; 2 Peter 2:5; 3:7; and Jude 1:4, 15, 18, it means "ungodly," and it is consistently translated that way. The noun *asebeia* is also consistently translated "ungodliness" in Romans 1:18; 11:26; 2 Timothy 2:16; and Titus 2:12.

Asebia, "ungodliness," is synonymous with *adikia,* "unrighteousness." This refers to active opposition to God and deliberate withholding from God of all that belongs to Him in prayer and service. An ungodly man fights God openly. It is not a sin that a Christian can be accused of. It is the sin of an unbeliever who is also immoral. In the New Testament the *asebēs,* "ungodly," and the *dikaios,* "righteous," are constantly set over against one another, as the two wage the great warfare between light and darkness, right and wrong.

There is yet another word, *parakoē,* translated "disobedience" in all three instances in the New Testament: Romans 5:19; 2 Corinthians 10:6; and Hebrews 2:2. In reality, it is not disobedience but failure to hear. *Akoē* means "hearing,"

218

from which the English word "acoustic" is derived. The verb *parakouō* "to hear on the side, or to fail to hear," occurs only in Matthew 18:17 and is translated "neglect to hear." That's what *parakoē* is—failure to hear, or hearing amiss. Of course, if you neglect to hear what someone tells you, you will disobey him. If you don't listen, you don't do. If you listen amiss, you'll do amiss.

Adam's sin is called *hamartia* in Romans 5:12ff., *parabasis,* "transgression," in Romans 5:14; *paraptōma,* "offense," in Romans 5:15–18, 20. In Romans 5:19 it is called *parakoē,* "disobedience or failure to hear," "For as by one man's disobedience many were made sinners, so by the obedience [*hupakoē*] of one shall many be made righteous." One is pulling your hearing away from the voice speaking to you, and the other is submitting (*hupo,* "under") your ear to His voice. That's one way of disobeying—just not listening. How guilty we are of that! We pray, but we don't listen to God's voice. What we end up doing is our own will.

There is yet another word, *agnoēma,* which occurs only in Hebrews 9:7 and is translated "errors": "But into the second went the high priest alone once every year, not without blood, which he offered for himself, and for the errors [*agnoēmatōn,* plural genitive of *agnoēma*] of the people." This noun comes from the verb *agnoeō,* which means "not to recognize, not to know, to be unacquainted with." *Agnoēmata* are those acts that are not the result of previous conscious thought or the result of conscious opposition.

There are willful sins and non–willful. The willful sins are spoken of in Hebrews 10:26: "For if we sin willfully after that we have received the knowledge of the truth, there remaineth no more sacrifice for sins." But Hebrews 9:7 speaks of *agnoēmata* as unwillful sins, called errors. The word refers not only to unconscious sins, but generally

219

all sin wherein consciousness is passive—sin which perhaps may enter into consciousness, but which does not proceed from consciousness. How prone we Christians are to such sins. We commit them out of ignorance, but we must become conscious of them if we are to ask the Lord to forgive us our *agnoēmata,* unintentional errors.

Sin is called *agnoēma,* the result of ignorance, when it is desired to regard it in the mildest possible light. For instance, when Peter spoke to the Jews in Jerusalem concerning their having crucified the Lord Jesus, he said to them, "And now, brethren, I wot that through ignorance ye did it, as did also your rulers" (Acts 3:17). He tried to mitigate their evil. Of course there is always an element of ignorance in every human transgression, which makes it human and not devilish.

The Lord on the cross prayed for those who were crucifying Him, "Father, forgive them, for they know not what they do" (Luke 23:34). Paul, looking back on his days of persecuting the Christians, wrote, "I obtained mercy, because I did it ignorantly in unbelief" (1 Tim. 1:13). No man really understands the full implications and seriousness of his sin.

Deliberate sin, with a knowledge of the full implications of its consequences, is mentioned in the New Testament as "blasphemy against the Holy Ghost" (Matt. 12:31, 32, see also Mark 3:28; Luke 12:10), for which there is no remission, no forgiveness. Why is this? Because as long as one consciously attacks the Holy Spirit, who is the convicting power unto salvation and repentance, there is no chance of repentance. God will not forgive anybody automatically. The sinner first has to say, "Be merciful to me a sinner." But he will never recognize himself as a sinner as long as he consciously attacks and blasphemes the Holy Spirit who convicts the ungodly to recognize themselves as sinners.

The sin of the believer with which the fifth petition of the Lord's Prayer is particularly concerned is, in a greater or a lesser degree, *agnoēma,* the result of ignorance, an error. And the greater the ignorance, as opposed to the knowledge of willful sin (Heb. 10:26), the lesser the gravity of the sin.

The errors of the people referred to in Hebrews 9:7, for which the High Priest offered sacrifice on the great Day of Atonement, were not willful transgressions, "presumptuous sins" (Ps. 19:13), committed willfully and premeditatively against conscience and with a high hand against God. Those who committed such sins were cut off from the congregation, no provision having been made in the Levitical constitution for the forgiveness of them (Num. 15:30, 31): but [the sins referred to in Hebrews 9:7] were sins growing out of the weakness of the flesh, out of an imperfect insight into God's law, out of heedlessness and lack of due circumspection, committed involuntarily (Lev. 4:13; 5:15–19; Num. 15:22–29) and afterwards looked back on with shame and regret (Trench).

As we look upon the sins of others, perhaps they would be much easier to forgive if we considered them as mere *agnoēmata,* the products of their ignorance. Peter looked upon the heinous act of his fellow Jews in crucifying the Lord as *agnoēmata,* sins which resulted from ignorance. So did the Lord. Let us imitate Christ as we say, "Forgive us our sins as we forgive those who sin against us." Let us count our sins as the result of ignorance, and count the sins of others against us in the same way. This makes it easier to be forgiven and to forgive.

What Are Trespasses?

There is yet another specific sin—*paraptōma* in Greek which is rendered in various ways in the Authorized Version. It is translated "trespass" in Matthew 6:14, 15; 18:35; Mark 11:25, 26; 2 Corinthians 5:19; Colossians 2:13b. It is translated "offense" in Romans 4:25; 5:15–18, 20. It is translated "fall" in Romans 11:11, 12, and "fault" in Galatians 6:1 and James 5:16, and "sin" in Ephesians 1:7; 2:1, 5; and Colossians 2:13.

The translators were inconsistent in their rendering of this word, causing much confusion to the reader of the New Testament who has no recourse to the Greek text. The verb *parapiptō* occurs only in Hebrews 6:6. This is a compound verb made up of the preposition *para,* meaning "over, by the side of, near," and the verb *piptō,* occurring many times in the New Testament and meaning "to fall, to fall headlong, to prostrate oneself, to fall down, to fall to pieces." *Parapiptō,* therefore, means "to fall beside, to fall down." It denotes conscious (hidden) deceitful and faithless action. It is the blameworthy and willful carelessness of him who falls into sin and, more rarely, inadvertency or thoughtlessness in so doing. The compound *parapiptō* is more related to *piptō,* with more of its meaning being "to throw oneself headlong" rather than simply "to fall."

Observe the meaning of the verb in the only place it occurs in the New Testament, Hebrews 6:6: "If they shall fall [*parapesontas,* aorist participle] away, to renew them again unto repentance; seeing they crucify to themselves the Son of God afresh, and put him to an open shame." The Apostle here is speaking about the persons mentioned in verses four and five, "who were once enlightened, and have tasted of the heavenly gift, and were made partakers of the Holy Ghost, and have tasted the good word of God, and the powers of the world to come." That's certainly referring to saved people.

Now it does not say that these people can lose their salvation, but "if they "throw themselves headlong", if they outrightly reject this salvation as unworkable, ineffective, then it is impossible for them to renew (*anakainizēn*), meaning to have a qualitatively new and effective repentance. Why? Because to have a new kind of repentance it would be necessary to have the Lord Jesus recrucified, making His former crucifixion a shameful event because it proved ineffective.

The word *paraptōma* belongs to later Greek and was seldom used. It meant "fault" or "mistake," for instance, of a writer. In an ethical sense it meant offense, neglect, error. But in the New Testament it does not have this lax meaning. As in Hebrews 6:6, it means in its verbal form "to fall headlong," indicating an outright, conscious rejection of salvation. Thus the noun *paraptōma* refers to a man who, having reached an acknowledged pitch of godliness and virtue, falls back from, and out of this (Trench). *Paraptōma* is not mere trespass or fault, but is mortal sin. It is not sinning as a result of ignorance. It denotes sin as a missing and a violation of that which is right. It may be regarded as synonymous with *parabasis,* "transgression," which means "disobedience of a specific command singly given or contained in the law." As *parabasis,* "transgression," so *paraptōma,* "trespass," involves sin as the transgression of a known rule of life and it involves guilt.

These two words are used synonymously by Paul in Romans chapter five. In verse fourteen Paul says, "Nevertheless death reigned from Adam to Moses, even over them that had not sinned after the similitude of Adam's transgression." The word translated "transgression" is *parabasis,* which refers to the actual act of Adam's transgression. In verse fifteen Paul says, "But not as the offense, so also is the free gift. For if through the offense of one many be dead, much more the grace of God, and the gift by grace, which is by one man, Jesus Christ, hath abounded unto many." What is translated "offense" in Greek is *paraptōma,* meaning not the act of trespassing, but the result of it, that is, the fall. Paul is telling us in Romans 5:15 that we can't really compare what Christ did for us through the gift of His grace (*charisma*) with the result of Adam's fall.

"The *charisma,* the free gift not as the *paraptōma,* the result of the trespass, the fall" (literal translation). Why? Because when Adam disobeyed God he himself fell and with him he dragged down all mankind. But Christ's grace did nothing to Christ. He didn't need the result of His grace. He was sinless. But we needed it. It affected all of us. The *charisma,* or Christ's grace, in its effects, is far greater than the fall, *paraptōma.* Therefore the seriousness of the fall or trespass, *paraptōma,* can be measured from the extremely precious remedy for it, Christ's sacrifice of His blood. Really, it would be far better to translate *paraptōma* in its six occurrences in Romans chapter five as "fall" instead of merely "offense," which makes it appear something light, of not too great consequence.

It is interesting that of all the petitions Christ mentions in the Lord's Prayer the only one He elaborates on after He finishes the prayer is this matter of forgiveness, in Matthew 6:14, 15. We do not find this after the record of the Lord's Prayer in Luke. We read in Matthew 6:14,15: "For if ye forgive men their trespasses [*paraptōmata*], your heavenly Father will also forgive you: But if you forgive not men their trespasses [*paraptōmata*] neither will your Father forgive your trespasses [*paraptōmata*]."

The word *paraptōma* in the plural accusative occurs three times in Matthew 6:14, 15 and is translated "trespasses." These may seem inconsequential affronts or harm done to us, which are easy to forgive, but this is not so at all. They are just as serious as Adam's fall, which resulted in the sinfulness of mankind. It is the *parabasis,* the voluntary disobedience of Adam spoken of in Romans 5:14, and called *paraptōma,* "offense," in Romans 5:15–18, 20. Our forgiveness should include not only trivial offenses against us, but serious willful harm done to us by others. We are guilty of trespassing against God. If we expect His forgiveness for such serious trespasses, we should be willing to forgive the trespasses of others.

How Does a Trespass Differ from a Transgression?

I s there any difference between *parabasis,* "transgression," and *paraptōma,* "trespass"? Yes, a very important one. *Paraptōma,* "trespass," is not as strong a word as *parabasis,* "transgression," which is only used in Hebrews 9:15 in connection with salvation, and elsewhere only where imputation and punishment are spoken of (Heb. 2:2). On the other hand, *paraptōma,* used privatively by Paul and additionally only in Matthew 6:14, 15; Mark 11:25; and James 5:16, is often used where pardon is spoken of.

As an example, we can take Galatians 6:1: "Brethren, if a man be overtaken in a fault [*paraptōmati,* dative singular], ye which are spiritual, restore such an one in the spirit of meekness, considering thyself, lest thou also be tempted." Here a sin is meant which involves guilt. But it refers rather to a missing of the mark (*harmartia*) than to a *parabasis,* transgression of the law, or a disobedience of a particular commandment. The difference, then, between *parabasis,* transgression, and *paraptōma,* trespass, is that *parabasis* refers to sin objectively viewed as a violation of a known rule of life but while *paraptōma* refers to the subjective passivity and suffering of him who misses or falls short of the enjoined command. It is closely associated with the guilt that it creates in the perpetrator. It is the guilt created by all sin, even though unknown and unintentional (see Ps. 19:13; Gal. 6:1).

In Romans 5:16, it stands in opposition to *dikaiōma*, which is the result of justification or right. When I am under a *paraptōma*, trespass, I feel guilty. I don't dare to act as if I had a right borne of innocence. But when I am declared not guilty for the trespass of which I am accused, then I have a right (*dikaiōma*). "But the free gift [*charisma*] is of many offences [*paraptōmatōn*] unto justification [*dikaiōma*]. The word for "justification" is not the ordinary *dikaiosunē*, "righteousness," or *dikaiōsis*, "the act of justifying," but *dikaiōma*, which means "the product or result of justifying" (*dikaiōn*). It means "right, or legitimate claim." "As a result of Christ's grace [*charisma*] from many trespasses [*paraptōmatōn*] unto the right of relationship and communion with God" (literal translation).

What are the many trespasses or falls? Adam's and ours. Christ's grace has liberated us from the guilt produced by them, which is called *katakrima* in verse sixteen, and translated "condemnation." If a court of justice declared me condemned, I would have no right to walk out of the courtroom. But if the court declared me not guilty, then I would have the right to walk out a free man. That's what Christ as the antitype of Adam has done.

In reality, Paul argues in Romans chapter five with the "much more" (*pollō mallon*) phrase of verses fifteen and seventeen that we are in far better position in our justification by Christ than we would have been in innocence had Adam never fallen.

Therefore *paraptōma*, "trespass," is used synonymously with *hamartia*, "sin, or missing the mark," as the generic word as Romans 5:20 makes clear: "Moreover the law entered that the offense [*paraptōma*, "trespass"] might abound." The disobedience of a stated, known law makes the trespass more easily discernible and condemnable. And Paul continues, "but where sin [*hamartia,* "missing the mark"] abounded, grace did much more abound." Here *paraptōma,* "trespass," and *hamartia,* "sin" are presented as synonymous. The expression "much more" is not the *pollō mallon* of verses fifteen and seventeen, but the verb *epleonasen,* "abounded." Thus *paraptōma* includes both *parabasis* (v. 14), a voluntary disobedience of a specific commandment or law, and hamartia, missing of the mark.

When we sin we suffer guilt. We are deprived of the rights originally bestowed upon us in being created in the image of God. We need to be liberated and have the right to act as free people in Christ. The only way we can obtain this freedom is by accepting Christ's justifying act that declares us not guilty. As we desire the obtaining of our rights in Christ, we must be willing to act accordingly in the lives of others who are equally guilty because of the sins and transgressions against God and against us. When we pray, "Forgive us our sins," we must include "trespasses (*paraptōmata*)," our sense of guilt and slavery to sin that causes us suffering.

What Does "Forgive" Mean?

Before we conclude what the full meaning of this fifth petition is, we must examine the word "forgive." The word in Greek is *aphes,* from the verb *aphiēmi,* made up of the preposition *apo,* meaning "from," and *hiēmi,* meaning "to put in motion or send." In Homer it is used to indicate the voluntary release (*aphesis*) of a person or thing over which one has legal or actual control. The noun *aphesis,* then, means "discharge, setting free." The verb used with a personal object means, "to send forth or send away, to release somebody." With an impersonal object it means, "to let go or discharge." To forgive is to acquit, to let go without a sense of guilt, obligation, or punishment.

The verb *aphiēmi,* "forgive," occurs 142 times in the New Testament. The noun *aphesis* is synonymous with *paresis,* used only in Romans 3:25 and translated "remission." *Paresis* means literally "passing over" from *para,* meaning "near" or "by," and *hiēmi,* "to send." Letting something go unpunished is the meaning thus implied. Other synonyms are *kaluptō,* meaning "to cover," *airō,* "to take away" (John 1:29), and *apolouomai,* "to get oneself washed." In Paul's writing the idea is expressed in more precise theological terms by the word *dikaioō,* meaning "to justify," and *katalassō,* "to reconcile."

Man in his relationship to God is presented as a sinner, one who disobeyed God through Adam, and therefore is separated from God and estranged from Him. There is a broken relationship between the two. The only way this relationship may be restored is for man to be set free from the bondage and burden of sin. But sin cannot go unpunished. Christ therefore paid the penalty of death Himself and thus remitted or put away the guilt and bondage of Adam's sin. Forgiveness therefore is the putting away from us the sin which separates us from God. It is a work of God the Father through Jesus Christ.

The main purpose of Christ's death, however, was not merely to secure our acquittal, but also to restore our relationship with God the Father. "In whom [Christ] we have redemption through his blood, even the forgiveness of sins" (Eph. 1:7; Col. 1:14). It is not merely a declaration of "not guilty" but is also actual, effectual deliverance from the dominion and power of Satan and sin, and the creation of a new nature within man.

In order, however, for this forgiveness to become effective in the life of the individual, it is necessary that it be preceded by repentance (*metanoia,* "changing of one's mind by exercising hindsight"). Before God can forgive our sins through Christ, whether in salvation or consequent to salvation, we must ask His forgiveness through what we call "confession of sins." Salvation and forgiveness are not automatic. Christ has done His work once and for all. He purchased our redemption, but we must accept this forgiveness as a gift from Him if it is to result in our acquittal and new life in Christ. We must "repent and believe the gospel." (Mark 1:15). "If we confess our sins, he is faithful and just to forgive us our sins, and to cleanse us from all unrighteousness" (1 John 1:9, see also Acts 2:38; 5:31; Heb. 6:1, 6; James 5:16).

Forgiveness, therefore, is God setting man's sins away from him. When man repents and accepts God's offer of forgiveness, then God imputes the righteousness of Christ to him and Christ indwells him with His Spirit. This is what Paul calls *justification*. It is God not only *declaring* sinful man justified before God, but actually making man just in Christ. It is the "righteousness of God which is by faith of Jesus Christ unto all and upon all them that believe" (Rom. 3:22). It is available to all but it comes only upon those who believe.

This justification is followed by *reconciliation* of the sinner to God the Father through Christ. "For if, when we were enemies, we were reconciled to God by the death of his Son, much more, being reconciled, we shall be saved by his life" (Rom. 5:10). "And all things are of God, who hath reconciled us unto himself by Jesus Christ, and hath given to us the ministry of reconciliation" (2 Cor. 5:18, see also Rom. 5:10ff.; 11:15; 2 Cor. 5:19ff.) That is the center of the Gospel. Forgiveness takes place because God gives Himself completely in the sacrifice of His Son (Rom. 8:32; 2 Cor. 5:21) and so gives man a share in His own righteousness (Rom. 3:21–28). Thus "in Christ" man becomes a pardoned sinner (Rom. 8:1), and a "new creature" (2 Cor. 5:17).

In the Lord's Prayer, our Lord commanded that we pray the Father to "forgive us." That means that He knew that even after our initial repentance for the forgiveness of our past sins, for the purpose of being saved, we continue to be burdened by sins that tend to interfere with the closeness of the relationship of Father and child. It is for our sins as believers that Christ told us to pray, although it is through "forgiveness of sins" unto salvation that we were originally regenerated, or born–again.

What Is Not Meant by "Forgive Us Our Sins"

That we are all sinners because of Adam's disobedience, there is no doubt. That is declared in Romans 5:12: "Wherefore, as by one man [Adam] sin entered into the world, and death by sin; and so death passed upon all men, for that all have sinned."

In Romans 5:6, 8, 10, Paul stated the fact of our sinfulness: "For when we were yet without strength in due time Christ died for the ungodly" (v. 6). This lack of strength (*asthenōn*) was owing to our being sinners. "But God commendeth his love toward us, in that while we were yet sinners, Christ died for us" (v. 8.) And verse ten says, "For if, when we were enemies, we were reconciled to God by the death of his Son, much more, being reconciled, we shall be saved by his life." (5:10). We are without strength (*astheneis*), sinners (*hamartōloi*), enemies (*echthroi*). Why? He tells us in verse twelve: "Because of this, just as through one man the sin came into the world." That refers to Adam.

Verse twelve begins with two Greek words, *dia touto,* which are translated "wherefore." Why are we all sinners? Because of this— that sin came into the world "through one man" and automatically affected all humanity. This is not a progressive corruption of the human race, but an instantaneous effect. "*Because of this* we are without strength, sinners, and enemies of God"—that the sin

232

entered (*eiselthe*—aorist tense of *eiserchomai,* "come in"), indicating a once–for–all entrance. "And through the sin [the definite article appears in both instances before the word "sin" (*hamartia*)], the death; and likewise the death went through [*dielthen,* aorist of *dierchomai,* indicating once and for all passing through] to all men." The verb is the same for "entering" (*eiselthen*) and "went through" (*dielthen*). The only difference is in the preposition used as a prefix, *eis,* meaning "into," and *dia,* meaning "through."

Adam's one act in the Garden of Eden is responsible for sin's original entrance into the world and the passing on of a sinful nature to every human being thereafter. It is not only death as a consequence of Adam's sin that is passed on to all men, but also sin itself, as indicated by Paul's statement in Romans 5:12: "upon this [fact] all sinned" (literal translation). This was not personal sin, because in Romans 5:6, 8, 10 Paul used the first person plural when he speaks of being "without strength," "sinners," and "enemies." This sin of Adam passed on to Paul and all of us who were yet unborn.

Christ's death on the cross more than canceled the result of Adam's sin. That is the basis on which those who die as babies, and those who have no opportunity of personally sinning, are entitled to go to heaven and be with Christ. When we ask the Lord to forgive us, we are not asking for forgiveness of the condemnation brought upon us through Adam, but of our own sins. The Lord taught us to pray, "Forgive us our sins." Our hereditary sin is automatically cared for by Jesus' death, but not our personal sins.

It was His disciples whom the Lord taught to pray, "Forgive us our sins." Weren't they saved? Weren't they children of God? Of course they were. Wasn't their Adamic taint of a sinful nature redeemed by Christ's death? Of course it was. But they were not delivered from the actual presence of sin. The fact that the Lord taught His very own disciples to ask for forgiveness means that in this life they could not live apart from the presence of sin and the possibility of falling short of God's expectations of them. That is fundamentally the meaning of the word sin. No believer pursues sin as his goal. If he does he is not a believer. But sin pursues every believer. The possibility of sin is always with us because our sinful nature is not eradicated while we are in the body, although it is definitely subdued and can be overcome by the indwelling Spirit of God.

Physical death is the consequence of Adam's sin. We all die, whether we are unbelievers or believers. When a man believes on the Lord Jesus Christ and becomes born–again (John 3:5) a child of God (John 1:12), he does not thereby automatically become exempt from physical death. Thus we can conclude that the death of Christ as the antidote of Adam's sin does not cancel this physical consequence of Adam's sin. Nor does it exempt the believer from physical illness and weakness leading to physical death. The Bible reveals that death came upon man as God's curse, just as life was granted to him as God's gift. In Genesis 3:19, we read God's sentence on Adam: "In the sweat of thy face shalt thou eat bread, till thou return unto the ground; for out of it wast thou taken: for dust thou art, and unto dust shalt thou return." This verse refers to man's body, for only the body was taken from the earth, according to the Genesis narrative, and it is this alone that goes back to the earth.

The breath of life (Gen. 2:7), that spirit or soul that God breathed into man's body, was neither earthly nor taken from the earth. Therefore, since its origin was not from the earth, neither is its destiny to return to the earth. In every instance where Scripture refers to death as the end of man's life on earth, it is the death of the body that is spoken of, and not the soul. Wherever the soul is mentioned in connection with death, it means its separation from the body (See Gen. 25:8; 35:29; 1 Kgs. 17:20–22; Job 14:10; Eccl. 8:8; 12:7; Luke 8:55; 23:46; Acts 5:10; see also author's book, *Life After Death,* AMG Publishers, 1989:36–41).

Besides the physical consequences of Adam's sin, we also experience spiritual consequences. Sin affected man as a total personality. It affected his soul or spirit. Spiritual death came upon man. Death basically means separation. Physical death is the separation of the spirit from the body, the nonmaterial essence of man from his material being. But spiritual death is the separation of man's spirit from God, who is Spirit. God said to Adam in Genesis 2:17, "but of the tree of the knowledge of good and evil, thou shalt not eat of it: for in the day that thou eatest thereof thou shalt surely die." But Adam did not die physically that day, but spiritually. The fact that he and Eve tried to hide from the presence of God, shows that the immediate death which came upon them was separation from God (Gen. 3:8). What Ezekiel declares as the consequence of sin came upon them: "the soul that sinneth, it shall die" (Ezek. 18:4).

When Paul says "Wherefore, as by one man sin entered into the world, and death by sin; and so death passed upon all men, for *that all have sinned*" (Rom. 5:12), he refers to people that are considered sinners because individually they chose to continue in the general moral and spiritual corruption in which Adam's sin placed them. Accountability involves ability and opportunity to choose. While judgment is averted for those who believe, judgment comes upon those who do not believe. If we do not believe, it means that we have chosen to continue in the state of corruption into which Adam brought us.

But every man has God–given opportunity. Paul says in Romans 1:19, "Because that which may be known of

God is manifest in them; for God hath shewed it unto them." John 3:18 states: "He that believeth on him is not condemned: but he that believeth not is condemned already, because he has not believed in the name of the only begotten Son of God." The "not believing" is an act of personal decision just as the act of believing is. Therefore, as the responsibility of personal sinfulness is due to an individual decision to continue in Adam's sin and its spiritual consequences, so is individual justification or righteousness or salvation due to the personal decision to accept Christ's redemption for one's own self.

That initial forgiveness which transfers a person from Satan's kingdom of darkness to Christ's kingdom of light is *not* that is meant by the prayer, "Forgive us our sins." "And this is the condemnation, that light is come into the world, and men loved darkness rather than light, because their deeds were evil. For every one that doeth evil hateth the light, neither cometh to the light, lest his deeds should be reproved. But he that doeth truth cometh to the light, that his deeds may be made manifest, that they are wrought in God" (John 3:19–21).

That repentance is necessary for anyone to be effectually delivered from Adam's sin and its spiritual consequences in this life and ultimately, from the "humiliation" of our present bodies is demonstrated by the repentance of the prodigal son: "Father, I have sinned against heaven, and in thy sight, and am no more worthy to be called thy son" (Luke 15:21), and by the publican in Luke 18:13, who prayed, "God be merciful to me a sinner." Salvation or the new birth is the reign of Christ in one's heart instead of the reign of Satan. But the born–again Christian still needs to pray for the forgiveness of his sins, because he is not fully delivered from his sinful nature.

Can a Christian Sin?

Forgiveness is not automatic. It is something we must ask for. It involves confession on our part that we are sinners, that we are indebted to God. If it were automatic then the Lord would not have asked us to pray, "Forgive us."

Christ didn't ask us in the Lord's Prayer to detail our sins. But is there such a thing as pleading for forgiveness with God without a detailed catalogue of our trespasses? Is there any possibility of such a thing as a sense of shame, sharp and deep, without one description, or one rehearsal, or one express mention of a particular transgression?

All people are sinful, whether they are believers or unbelievers. The difference is that the believer is a saved sinner and the unbeliever is an unsaved sinner. When the unbeliever prays, "Forgive," he must pray like the publican, "God, be merciful to me a sinner." He must pray exclusively for himself. He must pray for forgiveness that leads unto salvation. When the prodigal returned to his father's house he said, "Father, I have sinned against heaven, and before thee, and am no more worthy to be called thy son: make me as one of thy hired servants" (Luke 15:18, 19). Observe that he didn't say "we," but "I." He didn't say, "You are not my father anymore," but "I am no more worthy to be called thy son." He had lost his sonship. His confession was for his personal sin.

The Psalmist addresses God by saying, "Against thee, thee only, have I sinned . . . wash *me* . . . cleanse *me* . . . purge *me* . . . fill *me* . . . create in *me* a clean heart . . . restore unto *me* the joy of thy salvation" (Ps. 51). Forgiveness is very personal; sin is not something separate from the sinner; forgiveness is the reconciliation of the sinner.

In the Scriptures, the salvation of the sinner involving the initial forgiveness of sins is indicated by various terms. In John chapter three, it is called being "born–again." Paul calls it "adoption" (Gal. 4:5; Eph. 1:5) or "justification" (Rom. 3:20, 26, 28, 30). Both result in a new creation (2 Cor. 5:17) of man through Christ.

Forgiveness, then, as far as unbelievers are concerned, is primarily a reconciliation of men to God and of God to men. Sin is not so much an "object" requiring removal as it is a personal condition of estrangement from God requiring a reconciliation. The conditions of forgiveness are still repentance and confession, but they are not acts that man can "do," as if to complete his part of the bargain. The whole act stands together as a single event. Forgiveness then is practically synonymous with salvation. Zacharias predicted of his as yet unborn son, John the Baptist, that he would "give knowledge of salvation unto his people by the remission of their sins" (Luke 1:77). Remission is synonymous with forgiveness, of course.

But in the Lord's Prayer we are taught to say, "Father, forgive us our debts." This prayer is not for unbelievers, but is for Christ's disciples. Therefore it is not for confession that leads to salvation but for the forgiveness of sin, of debts which a disciple has toward God. But someone may object, "I thought that Christians didn't sin." They don't, as a matter of course, but they are not immune to temptation.

The forgiveness of sins, like repentance and faith, is not something one receives in conversion and then is done with. It is a necessary component of all Christian experience. The unsaved person is not particularly sensitive to his sins prior to conversion, but he is afterwards. He rejoices in his new relationship to God and in the forgiveness of sins. But he often misses the mark God has set for him as an individual.

And here we come to the second word that is used in Luke 11:4 as the fifth petition in the Lord's Prayer. It is *hamartias* (plural accusative of *hamartia*). This is the most commonly used word for "sin" in the New Testament (173 occurrences, of which 64 are in Paul's writings—48 in Romans alone; 25 in Hebrews; and 17 in John's Gospel and epistles). *Hamartanō,* "to sin," occurs 42 times, including 7 each in Romans and 1 Corinthians, 10 times in John's epistles, and 3 times in his Gospel. The verb *hamartanō* is made up of the privative *a,* "without," and the verb *meiromai,* which means "to participate, to attain, to arrive at a goal." Therefore *hamartanō,* "to sin," means "not to participate in, not to attain, not to arrive at the goal; to miss the mark in shooting." It is the opposite of "succeed" (*tuchein*). It is to go wrong. In the Epistle to the Romans it stands as the opposite of *dikaiosunē,* "righteousness," which means "conformity to God, to His standard." Therefore the standard is set by God for all of us, and that is called His righteousness.

For the unbeliever, that standard is salvation, the new birth, becoming a new creature, transference from the kingdom of darkness to the kingdom of God. His righteousness for the believer is that goal He expects the believer to reach according to the endowments made and the opportunities given him. God's goal and standard for each believer is not the same. For every unbeliever, it is the same: reconciliation with God. When an individual believer misses the standard of God's will and goal in his life, he is a sinner. Not that he hasn't attained God's goal for all people, that of being saved, but he has failed to attain the goal of individual accomplishment within the body of Christ. If the eye fails to accomplish the purpose for which God placed it in the body, it misses its goal, it sins. If, therefore, any Christian misses the attainment of the purpose set by God, he is a sinner, although a saved sinner. There are sinners out of Christ and sinners who are in Christ.

What Does it Mean to "Walk in the Light"?

If it were impossible for Christians to miss the mark, to fail at times in their Christian experience, the Lord would never have asked us to pray, "Forgive us our sins." The First Epistle of John extensively discusses this subject. Let me literally translate the pertinent verses from the Greek text: "God is light and there is no darkness at all, or not one in him" (1:5). The word "darkness" is *skotia,* which refers to the consequence of sin. In other words, we cannot blame our suffering caused by our sinfulness on Him. "If we say that we have fellowship with him and we walk in darkness, we lie and we do not adhere to or perform the truth" (1:6). If we are related to God as Father, we cannot be in the darkness, in sin itself.

In the Greek text the word for "darkness" in 1 John 1:6 is not the same as in verse five. It is not *skotia,* which means "the consequences of sin," but *skotos (skotei,* dative of *skotos),* which means "darkness as sin itself." We do not walk in sin itself if we are born again. If there is no change in the one professing Christ, in the one who says that he has fellowship with God, he is not a true Christian. If he is in the light he cannot walk in sin, in the darkness itself. The one is exclusive of the other. A person who says he or she is a Christian, and does not consciously endeavor to please God, to attain God's standard, will, and goal for his life is a liar. He is not a Christian at all. He can't walk in the darkness, in sin, and say that he is in the light.

Now observe the two proofs that a person is truly in the light. In verse seven we read, "And if we walk in the light." What does that mean? If we behave as Christians, if we are truly born again. This is in opposition to the one who says he is in the light and walks in the darkness. Now observe what John says: "If we walk in the light, as he [God] is in the light." Not "as he *walks* in the light," but as "he *is* in the light." We *walk* in the light, but He *is* in the light. We need to walk in it. That means effort in the exercise of our will. As we walk we may stumble. But He is light. He is the light in which we walk. He produces the light that permits us to walk in it.

Walking in the light willingly is our responsibility. Being the light and in the light is His nature. When we become Christians we do not walk in darkness, we don't run after sin. We never try to shut our God's light from revealing the sinfulness of any action of ours. The Christian life is a different life, it is a life of illumination.

Now observe what is said immediately after: "And the blood of Jesus Christ his Son cleanseth us from all sin" (1:7b, the "all" here really refers to every individual sin and all of them put together.) That is, while we walk in the light, in the bright sunshine, so to speak, we may fail in some purpose that God has set for us. If we walk in darkness, we are not saved. If we are saved, while we walk in the light we may have some "misses" in our Christian life. But we are not to conclude that we have lost our relationship with the Father as a child of light.

In fact, what is sin for one Christian may not be for another. James says in 4:17: "To him that knoweth to do good, and doeth it not, to him it is sin." It is all a matter of knowledge, ability, and opportunity. The rich man in the story of Luke chapter sixteen simply neglected to pay any attention to the leprous beggar at his doorstep. If the beggar had not been so close to him, perhaps his punishment would have been less. The more closely we live to God the more sensitive we become to sin. One Christian may consider giving less than ten percent of his income to the Lord sinful. But a more dedicated Christian may consider giving less than fifty percent sinful.

Sin is reckoned according to the closeness of our relationship with God. A child who is close to his father will do much more for him than one who isn't as close. The one who is not close will do only what is absolutely necessary to maintain the father–child relationship, but the one who is close will do all he can to please him. It all depends on the degree of closeness of the child's identification with the father's purposes and aims in life.

Then in 1 John 1:8 we read, "If we say that we have no sin, we deceive ourselves, and the truth is not in us." "We have no sin" here means that we have never, or we may never, miss God's purposes in our Christian walk. Who can truly say that he has always helped everyone whom he could, as God expected him to? If he says that, he is a liar. Instead of saying that he never can miss reaching God's goals in his life, it is better to confess that he does, because 1 John 1:9 says, "If we confess our sins, he is faithful [dependable] and just to forgive [*aphē,* the same Greek verb used in the Lord's Prayer] us our sins [*hamartias,* 'misses'] and to cleanse us from all unrighteousness." And in verse ten John concludes, "If we say that we did not sin [miss the mark], we make him [God] a liar, and his word is not in us." In other words, if God says it is impossible for man always to hit the mark set by Him, and man says he never misses, God is made out to be a liar. And indeed, God would be a liar if Jesus His Son taught us to pray, "Forgive us our sins," when we as His disciples never have any sin!

Salvation Effects a Fundamental Change of Nature

As physical and spiritual death are the "wages of sin" (Rom. 6:23), so is life in Christ the gift of God. "Wages" here means something we could not attain on our own. It is what comes to us as a necessary consequence of Adam's sin. So it is also with the spiritual life in Christ, made possible for us in and through Christ—we cannot attain it by our own efforts.

Adam sinned, but that does not send us to perdition. We send ourselves, as we give ourselves up to follow Adam's sin. In the same way only they are saved who give themselves up to follow Christ's righteousness, throughout all the various degrees of ignorance and enlightenment. All the numberless individual cases of the family of man are comprised under the two great representative heads of that family. All are following the respective leadership of Adam or of Christ, whether they know them by name or not.

As Adam's sin is not imputed to his posterity, at least as far as its consequences are concerned (for if all die it is because all have sinned), so must Christ's righteousness not be merely imputed to His followers as far as its consequences for them are concerned. A fundamental change of nature occurs. Christ does not merely declare us righteous, but makes His righteousness effectual in us through our repentance. We are then not merely *considered* righteous but *made* righteous. We are not merely *considered* God's children but *made* so. We are not merely furnished with new motives but with new powers. It is not merely the guilt of sin from which we are freed but also the power of sin over us.

What is the nature of this change that the Savior calls being "born–again," and Paul in 2 Corinthians 5:17 calls a "new creation"? In our natural state brought about by Adam's sin, our will is perverted. It is estranged from God. We have no desire to please God, who is characterized as the source of holiness and goodness. We are selfish. We don't love our neighbor as we love ourself. When Christ's life becomes ours, our will is changed. The change in our deeds is the result of the change in our will.

Our knowledge is also changed. In our natural state we are not fully able to know the difference between right and wrong. We seldom attribute much seriousness to the sins of omission and disposition. Our knowledge is naturally defective in the moral realm. Many times we consider and avoid evil only because of the painful consequences if we are caught. But when Christ comes in He gives us the knowledge that the most important thing in life is not simply to avoid doing evil, but to do that which is good and helpful to others.

It is not so much the evil that men do, as the good they leave undone, that checks the progress of God's kingdom and delays the happiness of the world. It is the apathy of benevolence rather than the activity of malevolence that works the widest ruin. The road to hell is not paved so much with evil deeds as with good intentions. And this conception of the superior danger and mischief of those sins that men too generally hardly consider sin at all, is remarkably sanctioned by our Lord Himself.

For what crime is the wicked servant cast into outer darkness in Matthew 25:30? Not for dishonesty but for unprofitableness, for neglecting to use the one talent he had received from the Lord. It was not for squandering the talent or the pound entrusted to him (Luke 19:20ff.), but for not increasing it.

For what misdeeds are they who stand at the left hand of the Judge commanded to depart into everlasting fire, prepared originally not for the race of man, but for the devil and his angels? It is not for injuries inflicted, but for kindnesses omitted: not because they have wronged Christ's followers but because they have not benefited them (Matt. 25:31–46).

In this regard it is necessary to note two Greek words used in the Lord's Prayer. In Matthew 6:12 the word is *opheilēmata,* which means "debts," and in Luke 11:4 the word is *hamartias,* which means "sins," or "missings of the mark." In both cases it refers to sins of omission and not of commission, not doing for God and others what we know through Christ's indwelling that we ought to do.

Such knowledge of God's expectation of service comes only through a change of nature and character. What does the world generally consider sin? Not failing to help someone, but inflicting harm on others. To live harmfully is sin, and human law may punish it. But to live selfishly is the mode of natural life. Adam thrust us all into sin by wanting to receive something he wasn't supposed to have. And ever since, those who have been contaminated by Adam's sin (and that is all of us) prefer taking to giving.

But Christ's philosophy is that it is more blessed to give than to receive (Acts 20:35). When we become Christians that becomes intuitive knowledge. When we want to find out whether a person is in Adam or in Christ, we can test his knowledge of what constitutes sin. We will find that most unconverted people do not consider sin as selfishness, but only think of sin as wrongdoing that is punishable by human law.

On the other hand, a Christian, a righteous person, a just person, must be of an unselfish nature. If not, he is not a true Christian but is still in Adam's sin and giving it his full personal approbation. This is why Christ's concern is for us to know first what sin is, and to pray for forgiveness. The sin to which the believer is most liable is that of not *doing* what Christ would have done if He were in his place. After all, a Christian is one in whom Christ lives. Can we possibly imagine a selfish Christ walking the streets of our town?

Characteristics of a
Born–again Christian

The knowledge and discernment of what constitutes sin is the second basic characteristic of the nature of the justified believer, the first being a fundamental change of nature. This is illustrated by the actions of two men heading the department of a Christian organization trying to help establish television and radio stations for Christian groups. Suddenly they left to establish their own organization, and took with them the files of customers who belonged to the organization they were serving. They felt not a ripple of consciousness of sin in that act. Later it was discovered that while on the payroll of the Christian organization they had been personally trying to obtain part ownership in some of the stations they were establishing for various groups. They could see no evil or dishonesty in such behavior. One wonders whether they are still in Adam, with such lack of knowledge as to what constitutes sin.

When one can see no sinfulness in sin, he is not in Christ, he is still in Adam. What our Lord wanted us to recognize is the sinfulness of neglect, of not paying our debts to God and others, of not accomplishing what God expects us as individuals to do.

Those acts of daring and outrageous rebellion against God, to which men usually restrict the name of sins, are but the smallest portion of the weight that sinks men's souls into perdition. We are not to entertain a worldly estimate of sin, but to have instead the estimate of Christ. He presents the most fatal class of sins as those of omission. Of these sins, natural knowledge leaves us in the dark. We know generally pretty well what it is our duty to avoid; we hardly know what it is our duty to perform.

Again we must not delude ourselves into imagining that our duties are limited to the performance of those things that too generally merely lull the conscience. Let us not think that we cease to be guilty of the sins of omission when we give a pittance of our belongings, our talents, and our time to God and others. We do not discharge our liabilities by trifles. All our time, talents, health, and wealth ought to be devoted to effecting the greatest possible amount of good which the most systematic arrangement of our whole being to our Master's service can achieve. We can test our spiritual temperature by this simple rule: When we do a little, do we feel it is enough or even too much, or do we feel instead that when we have done our utmost it is not enough?

To recognize how indebted we are to God and to others is a proof of Christ's indwelling. The very first effect of the renewing of the mind adduced by the Apostle Paul is that it enables us to know, to prove, to ascertain, and to thoroughly appreciate what is God's will: "And be not conformed to this world: but be ye transformed *by the renewing of your mind* [that's the instrument of knowledge], that ye may prove what is that good, and acceptable, and perfect will of God" (Rom. 12:2).

Our being taught of God is one of the basic blessings of the new life in Christ. When He was on earth, Christ constantly taught His disciples. But in teaching the multitudes, those of the world, He often found they could not comprehend divine truth. They did not possess the necessary vehicle of knowledge.

And when our Lord was about to depart from the world, He promised His disciples the Holy Spirit. What was to be His function?—teaching. "When He, the Spirit of truth, is come, he will guide you into all truth: for he shall not speak of himself; but whatsoever he shall hear, that shall he speak: and he will shew you things to come" (John 16:13). And in 1 John 2:20 we read concerning the Holy Spirit, "But ye have an unction from the Holy One, and ye know all things?"—that is, all that is necessary to be known for our guidance in the disposition of our time and means. All the knowledge we require in order to perform the will of God in all its fullness in the everyday concerns of life is directly meant, not merely by implication, in these passages. The office of the Holy Spirit is to supply by His indwelling the wisdom we require in order to live wholly unto God.

Having the will and the knowledge to do what God expects of us is not enough, however. We need His power also. And we need this power because the implantation of the new nature in the regenerate heart does not at once destroy the old Adamic nature. The two natures exist together in the Christian. The struggle between them is not ended. The victory of the one over the other is not complete till death releases us from that body which is the very stronghold of our natural corruption.

Now the influence of our body is particularly felt in our actions, because they require its instrumentality. Our body limits our *power* of *performing* what is right much more than either our knowledge of it or our inclination or will for it.

What a struggle Paul had between the two natures coexisting in him and in every believer. Listen to his words:

"For I know that in me [that is, in my flesh], dwelleth no good thing: for to will is present with me; but how to perform that which is good I find not. For the good that I would, I do not: but the evil which I would not, that I do. Now if I do that I would not, it is no more I that do it, but sin that dwelleth in me" (Rom. 7:18–20).

This passage describes the state of man insofar as he is actually under the renewing influence of the Holy Spirit. This is indicated by what Paul says in verse twenty-two: "For I delight in the law of God after the inward man." The "inward man" is the new creature, the nature of Christ within the believer, the new regenerated will. Here we come to the basis and full meaning of the petition, "Forgive us our debts." It rests upon the fact that, though we are God's dear children in the Son of His eternal love, our adoption will not be completed until the redemption of our body. It means that for the present, while we are still in the body, two opposite principles are struggling in every Christian. The victory of the new nature, though assured, is slowly and painfully achieved.

The victory is not without struggle. That we often fail to win is confessed by the petition, "Forgive us our debts or sins." But let us be assured of the fact that Christ promises to be with us to the end. "He which hath begun a good work in you will perform it until the day of Jesus Christ" (Phil. 1:6). The day of Christ is the day when we shall no longer be in the present body. "If God be for us, who can be against us?" (Rom. 8:31). There is none to condemn us, since Christ has died, and now sits at the right hand of God, ever making intercession for us (see Rom. 8:34). All the sins of omission and commission that we incur during the struggle, provided only we truly and heartily repent, God engages to forgive by the very fact of the existence of that struggle.

But let us never construe that as sanctioning or excusing sin. Only they in whom their natural corruption is being slowly, but surely, subdued, have any right to expect pardon for its still remaining fruits. Only they who with their whole heart believe in the Lord Jesus Christ have any right to believe in the forgiveness of their sins. Only they who with Paul are tempted to burst into the despairing cry, "O wretched man that I am! who shall deliver me from the body of this death?" can with Paul in truth and soberness triumphantly rejoice, "I thank God through Jesus Christ our Lord" (Rom. 7:24, 25).

Prayer Is Asking with
A Personal Pledge

A superficial examination of the seven petitions of the Lord's Prayer would lead us to believe that only in one, the fifth, which deals with the forgiveness of our sins, is there a personal pledge: "as we forgive them that trespass against us."

But a more careful study of the other six petitions will show us that there is implicit in each one a personal pledge of responsibility. We ask God to do something, but at the same time there is a recognition on our part that we must fulfill what pertains to our sphere of responsibility. Every petition involves a duty and a vow. Not one of them is an idle prayer; each one of them requires a response on our part.

When we say, "Our Father," we acknowledge that we are His children and therefore pledge to behave worthily of His name and character.

When we add, "Who art in heaven," we recognize that we must not consider Him as a common Father, with limitations, but as a Heavenly Father, standing above and beyond all earthly relationships and therefore deserving our reverence and worship.

When we say, "Hallowed be thy name," we recognize that it is our duty to hate whatever dishonors His holy name in our daily lives, and actively to honor it by our words and deeds.

When we pray, "Thy kingdom come," we pledge ourselves against laziness in making Him known to others. How can His kingdom come unless we preach the Gospel, witness to all around us, and fight the evil in our environment?

When we pray, "Thy will be done," we pledge to strive more and more every day that our will may be one with God's will.

"As in heaven, so on earth" is our pledge of service that is ceaseless, vivid, hearty, and ungrudging, even as the service of those who do God's will in heaven.

"Give us this day our daily bread" implies our recognition that ultimately all good things come from God. But as we pray for our bread, we know that God will cooperate with us only if we do the task that is required of us—till the ground, plant the seed, and diligently and honestly work in our allotted sphere to produce bread for ourselves and others. It is a pledge of personal hard labor.

When we pray, "Forgive us as we forgive," the Lord does not merely imply our part but is most explicit about it. It is expressed clearly here because our Lord knows that it is the most difficult, though the most necessary, task in our lives to forgive. It points to the antecedent condition on which our prayer can be heard.

When we pray, "Lead us not into temptation," we pledge our careful behavior, that will not lead ourselves or others into sin.

When we pray, "Deliver us from evil," we make a personal pledge that we will not voluntarily do anything to cause us to fall slaves to Satan or to any evil habit or practice.

Thus we see that in all seven petitions there is a personal pledge of cooperation with God and others—explicit or implicit—to accomplish what we ask God to do for us.

In the matter of forgiveness of sins, the Lord was explicit in making our personal forgiveness conditional on our forgiveness of others because He wanted to impress us with the basic axiom that *the condition of all prayer is action*. Prayer, which seems so easy, which we often perform so perfunctorily, when it is real prayer becomes rather the passion of an effort, the wrestling of a lifetime.

The Lord's underlying law of prayer is that *an uncharitable heart cannot truly come to God, for God is Love*. Malice and uncharitableness are clouds that come between the soul and God, a closed door between the Father and His child. If, therefore, one with an unforgiving spirit seems to pray, he does not *truly* pray. He has not really come into the presence of his Father who is in heaven. The prayer of the uncharitable and unforgiving is not true prayer. It may be desire, and very earnest desire; but there is no prayer where there is not a filial relationship between the child and the Father; there is no such filial relationship when the child is unforgiving. This is not the only condition of prayer, but we can safely say that two of the most common reasons for unanswered prayer are an unforgiving heart toward man, and an unbelieving heart toward God.

(See "Forgiveness of Trespasses," by Archdeacon Farrar, in *The Christian World Pulpit,* Vol. 42:284. Also, "Prayer and Forgiveness," by Rev. Lyman Abbott, in *The Christian World Pulpit,* Vol. 34:158.)

Aren't Christians Supposed To Pay Their Debts?

Does the Lord's Prayer exempt Christians from meeting their obligations to other Christians in particular and other people in general? Is the doctrine of forgiveness an escape for the dishonest person? Suppose a Christian owes money to a fellow Christian and doesn't want to pay it. What is the creditor supposed to do? Is he bidden by Christ to allow the debtor to go scot–free and proceed to find another Christian to deceive so he can go on prospering, unworthily carrying the name of Christian while he defrauds his fellow humans who treat him so leniently? Is there no punishment for the Christian who fails to perform his duty in his interpersonal relationships? Is the Christian who wants to live according to the injunctions of Christ ever to allow himself to be defrauded? All these questions arise in connection with Christ's doctrine of forgiveness and our forgiveness of others.

Let us look at some basic considerations: Forgiveness, either God's or ours, should never be thought of as an opportunity to escape punishment for evildoing. If it were, the evildoer would never have an opportunity to realize his evil and would be emboldened to continue it. Let our society abolish law, justice, and the police and see what happens. We would have anarchy and the rule of crime and the criminal.

When God promised forgiveness, was it on the ground that the wrongdoer or sinner would still be allowed to continue in his sin, or on the basis of the work of declaring the sinner righteous because of the penalty having been paid by the Lord Jesus Christ? The penalty Christ paid was commensurate with the sin. The penalty was death. Jesus died both physically and spiritually on the cross. He cried to His Father, "Why hast thou forsaken me?" Because of Christ's death we are justified before God.

In order to be justified from our own sin it is necessary for us to repent and believe the Gospel, the good news that in and through Christ's death we may have eternal life, the life of God. That faith, however, doesn't simply free us from the penalty of sin, which is separation from God, but restores us to fellowship with God. It doesn't merely exempt us from the guilt of sin, but empowers us to live victoriously. If the second of these experiences doesn't occur, we have what James calls "dead faith," a mere profession without conversion. The person, therefore, who professes faith in Christ and doesn't endeavor to live in a Christian manner is none of His and should not be treated as such.

But is it possible for such people who deliberately defraud others to be in the Christian Church, in the circle of those who claim to be Christ's? Of course it is. Wasn't Judas among the Twelve? Did the Lord refuse the cup of communion at the Last Supper in the Upper Room to Judas Iscariot? We read in Mark 14:22, 23: "And as they did eat, Jesus took bread, and blessed, and brake it, and gave to them, and said, Take, eat: this is my body. And he took the cup, and when he had given thanks, he gave it to them: and they *all* drank of it." Observe, that "they *all* drank of it." That included Judas. Who would have believed that

Judas could get up after the Lord extended His cup to him, to betray Him? But he did.

Did the Lord compromise His cup? Or didn't He know that Judas was a betrayer? He knew it, but He wanted to give Judas every opportunity to repent right up to the last moment. The Lord never gives up on a sinner, but the sinner's ultimate destiny depends on his own choice, in the response he makes to the opportunity to repent. The Lord arranges things in such a way that none will be able to turn to Him in the Day of Judgment and say to Him, "You didn't give me an adequate opportunity to seek forgiveness."

Can there be Judases in the ministry, in the pews of our Christian churches, sitting around the Lord's Table? Of course. They are the people who systematically defraud others, and especially their softhearted brothers and sisters, because they know that they rarely resort to punitive measures. Did the Lord forgive Judas for what he had done? No. Why? Because Judas never repented (Matt. 27:3–5).

Think of the two thieves hanging on a cross on either side of the crucified Jesus. Which did Jesus forgive? Only the one who asked to be forgiven, the one who repented.

We're supposed to imitate Jesus in His spirit of dispensing forgiveness. In reality, the fifth petition can be read as "Forgive us our debts, so that we can forgive our debtors." His forgiveness must not be after our pattern, but our forgiveness after His. He forgives because we ask His forgiveness in penitence. And likewise we must forgive those who repent of wrong done to us.

But how about those who don't? As far as we're concerned, we must hold no malice or vengefulness toward those who harm us. If we do, we only harm ourselves. The unforgiving spirit is a disturbed spirit. Our attitude of forgiveness may not in any way change the object of our forgiveness. Our forgiveness must even go beyond the absence of malice and vengeance in us. It must project itself to whatever influence for good it can bear on the other person. What good would it have been if the only result of Christ's sacrifice for our sins was merely the satisfaction of God's justice without a change coming upon the sinner? Justifying the sinner is no good unless it simultaneously makes the sinner just.

When I forgive my debtor, what do I accomplish? By forgetting what he owes me I may not cause any change in him. He may think that I as a Christian am an easy mark and therefore he will do the same thing to another, and yet another. Forgiveness must be coupled with love. And love is not shown by bypassing the just punishment of an evil act. Does the parent who never punishes his child really love him? If forgiving his evil drives him deeper into it, it is not true forgiveness but a mere pushing him into further temptation and greater sinfulness.

Our Lord didn't say that we should forgive other people's debt, but "as we forgive our *debtors*." It is not the same as my remitting a debt due to me. It is the sinner that must be remitted, forgiven from his debt. Forgiving my debtor is seeking to enable my debtor to be remitted of his sin even as God seeks a change in me by remitting my sin from me. Therefore forgiving others doesn't mean simply forgetting their sin, but endeavoring either through kindness or punishment, to remit the sin *from* them.

Does Forgiveness Preclude Punishment?

Our Lord's teaching in regard to our duty of forgiveness toward those of the same church community is very clear in Matthew 18:15–17: "Moreover if thy brother shall trespass against thee [the Greek word is *hamartēsē,* "sin," referring to a particular act], go and tell him his fault between thee and him alone." Actually the Greek says, "Go and reprove him between you and him alone." Observe that the offended brother is supposed to discern the sin perpetrated against him. He isn't supposed to ignore it, but to bring it to the attention of the one who has wronged him. The Lord continues: "If he shall hear thee, thou hast gained thy brother." The purpose of confronting an offending brother is to bring him to the acknowledgment of his sin and repentance, resulting in a change in him.

Suppose he doesn't acknowledge and repent of his fault? The Lord says, "But if he will not hear thee, then take with thee one or two more, that in the mouth of two or three witnesses every word may be established." In other words, the offended party appoints two judges. If the offender doesn't listen to them, the Lord says, "And if he shall neglect to hear them, tell it unto the church: but if he neglect to hear the church, let him be unto thee as an heathen man and a publican." That is, you can go ahead and deliver him up to the law so that he may be dealt with, in order that he may not defraud others as he has defrauded you. Thus one who poses as a Christian brother can't forever go on being unpunished for his evil way. Delivering a sinner for necessary punishment is the duty of every Christian. If he doesn't fulfill this duty, then he doesn't really love the offender or care about turning him from his evil ways.

Almost immediately in verses twenty-one to thirty-five, we have the Parable of the Unforgiving Servant. The teaching here is that there should be no limit to the number of times we are to forgive.

The Lord is presented as a king to whom a certain man owed 10,000 talents. This would be between $15,000,000 and $20,000,000, an impossible sum to pay back. It is symbolic of that which we owe God, which is impossible to repay. If it is going to be cleared up it has to be written off, remitted. But observe that the forgiveness of the debtor came as a result of his seeking it: "The servant therefore fell down and worshipped him, saying, Lord, have patience with me, and I will pay thee all." He acknowledged his indebtedness. It is tantamount to confession. It was because of this that he was forgiven. "Then the lord of that servant was moved with compassion and loosed him, and forgave him the debt."

The forgiven debtor then went after one of his own debtors. It's apparent that the second debtor did acknowledge his indebtedness, but in spite of this, the first debtor put him in jail. His aim was the immediate payment of the debt owed him. His attitude was vindictive, full of malice, and he didn't dispense the same kind of forgiveness that he had experienced at the hand of his creditor. He should have given his debtor the opportunity to repay his debt. Depriving the sinner of the opportunity to repent and make good what he owes is what the Lord forbids.

The master of this servant therefore called him to him and said, "O thou wicked servant, I forgave thee all that debt, because thou desirest me [or because you asked me to]. Shouldest not thou also have had compassion on thy fellow servant, even as I had pity on thee?" It is implied that the debtor of the forgiven servant acted as he himself had, seeking forgiveness or at least acknowledging his debt. The lesson therefore is that whenever forgiveness is asked in sincerity it must be granted.

But when the master of the servant saw that the first debtor's repentance wasn't genuine, he didn't forgive him further. He condemned him. "And his lord was wroth, and delivered him to the tormentors, till he should pay all that was due unto him." So forgiveness is to be without end only if it results in the change of the forgiven one. If forgiveness were the granting of clemency without a change in the individual, then the Lord would never punish anybody.

And then comes the conclusion by our Lord: "So likewise shall my heavenly Father do also unto you." Do what? Punish you; deliver you to the tormentors; not forgive you. But only "if ye from your hearts forgive not everyone his brother their trespasses," which forgiveness is a proof that you have truly received forgiveness.

Forgiveness Seeks the Redemption of Others

How does Paul's teaching in 1 Corinthians chapter six fit in with Christ's teaching concerning a feud between Christians in regard to material differences? Paul doesn't state who is the one to dispense forgiveness and who is to seek it. Therefore the teaching in Matthew chapter eighteen is more definitive. Paul couldn't really teach anything different from what the Lord taught.

Both situations involve members of the local body of believers in each particular situation. Again, this refers to the local Corinthian church. So when a difference occurs between two or more members of the same local body of believers, the offended one must go first to the offender and try to get a confession from him and offer forgiveness, thus helping the offender to be remitted of his sin. He is to seek the restoration of a harmonious relationship with his offending brother. That's what real forgiveness means, not merely forgetting the offense but the restoration of fellowship between two people who worship together in the same church.

What Paul says is that they should not go to a court of law if they belong to the same church but should choose some of the most insignificant members of the church (1 Cor. 6:4) and allow them to sit as judges. That's also what Christ taught. But Paul doesn't go as far as the Lord does in detailing the final disposition of the matter. If the offended party is not asked for forgiveness, what is to be done about the offender? Is he to be allowed to stay in the church and continue in his sinful practices against the same brother and others? The Lord gives a verdict, whereas Paul doesn't see the case to its conclusion:

"Let him be unto thee as an heathen man and a publican" (Matt. 18:17). That is the treatment that the offended one is permitted, actually commanded, to proffer to the offender.

We must never justify or overlook sin in the lives of others, especially if it is a sin that affects us personally. Whether he repents or not we should never harbor any feeling of resentment toward the offender. On the other hand, we should do everything in our power to cause him to repent so that Christian fellowship may be restored between us. Our concern should not be for the injury we ourselves have received, but for the sin against God which the injury has involved.

We must not say, "Peace, peace; when there is no peace" (Jer. 8:11). We should never allow an offending and unrepenting brother to go on in his trespasses without remonstrance or reproof. If we treat him precisely as if he had not trespassed, or as if he had repented of his trespass, we are not demonstrating forgiveness but callous indifference toward his need of repentance. Forgiving our offenders excludes all feeling of resentment and all desire for retaliation, but it also excludes the hypocrisy of acting as though the offender had done no wrong. Thus, Scripture coincides with common sense. Ecclesiates 8:11 contains both God's wisdom and common sense when it states, "Because sentence against an evil work is not executed speedily, therefore the heart of the sons of men is fully set in them to do evil."

We must remember that God instituted laws that are inexorable in their consequences. The great principle by which God governs the world is that the consequences of sin serve to deter sin. The pain He permits is truly part of His economy of mercy. When we have sought pardon and found mercy, we may still have to suffer the consequences of past sin. Punishment is not incompatible with pardon. To forgive our debtor is not necessarily to permit him to escape the duties and responsibilities that are his.

Pardon really consists of two parts——the cessation of resentment and the removal of consequences. These two parts are not always concurrent. I may cease from anger, cease to feel resentment against my erring, disobedient child when he repents, yet may allow him to suffer the natural consequences of his wrongdoing in order to teach him that every evil act has its built–in consequence.

Ask God for Forgiveness
Of Your Explicit Sins

In the category of sin for which we must ask forgiveness from God there are several other Greek words of whose implications we must be aware.

One is *parabasis,* translated "transgression" in Romans 4:15; 5:14; Galatians 3:19; 1 Timothy 2:14 and Hebrews 9:15. It is translated "breaking" in Romans 2:23, and "disobedience" in Hebrews 2:2. The verb *parabainō* is consistently translated "transgress" in all four references of Matthew 15:2, 3; Acts 1:25; and 2 John 1:9. The noun *parabatēs* is translated "transgressor" in Galatians 2:18 and James 2:9, 11. It is translated "breaker of the law" in Romans 2:25. It is a compound verb, *parabainō,* made up of the preposition *para,* meaning "over, near, by the side of," and the verb *bainō,* "to walk, to go, to step." So *parabainō* means "to step over, out, near, to step on one side." It is "to transgress" or "to violate."

For anyone to become a transgressor (*parabatēs*), there must of necessity be something to transgress. In order to understand the peculiarity of *parabasis,* "transgress," we must look at Romans 5:14, which says, "Nevertheless death reigned from Adam to Moses, even over them that had not sinned after the similitude of Adam's transgression, who is the figure of him that was to come." The word translated "transgression" is *parabasis* (in the genitive singular, *parabaseōs*).

What did Adam transgress? God's specific commandment, given in Genesis 2:16, 17. As a result of Adam's transgression of that command, death, both spiritual and physical, came upon mankind.

But it cannot be said that all those from Adam to Moses died because of a transgression like Adam's. Adam transgressed directly. The others, and all of us, have transgressed indirectly: not in "the similitude of Adam's transgression."

The same is true for all who lived after Moses. They are considered sinners for the transgressions of the Law given to Moses, but not in the similitude of Adam's transgression. Their transgression, too, is indirect. What Paul says in these passages is that *parabasis,* being a direct stepping over, transgression, or disobedience of a specific commandment, is far more serious than *hamartia,* "missing the mark," that mark being more general—a life of obedience, holiness, and conformity to God's will.

When I as a father give a specific command to my child and it is disobeyed, I feel worse than I do about his nonconformity to the general principles for which I stand. And my child knows I do. Look at Romans 2:23: "Thou that makest thy boast of the law, through breaking the law dishonourest thou God?" You know the specific commandments of the law and yet you disobey them, says Paul. That is a direct affront and is dishonouring to God who gave those specific commandments.

In 1 Timothy 2:14, Paul puts the direct blame of disobedience and transgression not on Adam but on Eve. "And Adam was not deceived, but the woman being deceived was in the transgression [*parabasei,* dative singular]." (Hers was a direct transgression and Adam's was indirect). Eve transgressed (*parebē*) and Adam sinned (*hēmartēsen*). The sin of transgression (*parabasis*) is far more serious than the sin of hamartia, missing the mark.

We must watch, therefore, God's direct and specific commandments given to us through His Word and in the circumstances and opportunities He allows in our lives. Dishonoring God is a most serious charge. Take a look at James 2:9: "But if ye have respect to persons, ye commit sin [*hamartian*], and are convinced of the law as transgressors [*parabatai*]." That is a specific transgression against a specific commandment in the law—that we are not to discriminate against anyone. If we do, we are transgressing a specific commandment in the law and that is a most serious offense.

In other words, God is specific about what is important. Transgressing against His specific commandments is generally far more serious than disobeying rules not clearly expressed. Before the Law was given, men were reckoned only as sinners, with the exception of Adam and particularly Eve. After the Law there were not only sinners, but also transgressors. In other words—then, as well as today—there are those who disobey God's unwritten laws and those who deliberately disobey His written commandments. The punishment of the latter will be far greater. Remember this when you pray, "Forgive us our sins," and add, "especially my willful sins."

Does God's Forgiveness Depend Upon Our Forgiveness?

The fifth petition of the Lord's Prayer is the only one expressing the need for two objects. We ask for grace to be forgiven and for grace to forgive. The first is a prayer breathed by the spirit of repentance, and the second is the desire for a spirit of unity. We seek to deal with others as we would be dealt with by God.

There is a little difference in the way this petition is expressed by Matthew and Luke. In Matthew 6:12 we read: "And forgive us our debts [or the debts ours], as we also forgive the debtors ours" (author's literal translation). The Textus Receptus from which the Authorized Version is translated has the verb "forgive," in the clause "as we also forgive our debtors," in the present indicative, *aphiemen*. But the newest United Bible Societies' text has *aphēkamen,* which is in the first aorist tense indicating an act in the past, "as we forgave our debtors." Whether it is "forgive" or "forgave" doesn't really alter the meaning of the statement. If we take the aorist, "as we forgave," it refers to an act just completed. When we have the opportunity of granting forgiveness it gives us the consciousness that we have sins for which we need forgiveness.

The Greek proposition *hōs,* translated "as," is not casual. It doesn't denote the reason why God should forgive us. We don't ask Him to forgive us simply because we have

270

just forgiven our debtor, or we forgive our debtor. God forgives because it is His nature to forgive.

The second part of this petition doesn't make it a self–righteous prayer. We don't set the example for God by our own forgiveness. Our forgiving spirit is not something we develop for the purpose of deserving God's forgiveness. There is absolutely nothing we can do to deserve God's forgiveness. Our debt to Him, as the parable of the unmerciful servant makes clear, is beyond our ability to pay. Our righteousness is but "filthy rags" in His sight. The Pharisee in Luke chapter eighteen tried to tell God that he deserved His mercy because of what he was doing. Consequently the Lord never granted him forgiveness through His mercy. But He granted it to the publican who came with nothing but the confession of his need for mercy.

What we mean, therefore, when we say, "As we forgive our debtors," is that it is our duty to forgive, following the example of the Lord toward us. We confess that if we don't try to fulfill the condition of forgiving, our prayer to be forgiven is a sham, it is in vain.

Nor do we mean that God's forgiveness to us should be after the pattern and measure of our own forgiveness of others. What we have to forgive is infinitesimal compared to what God forgives. Let us never ask God to treat us even as we treat others, for we shall be sorry indeed. What is the hundred pence due to us compared to the ten thousand we owe God? The "as we forgive" implies "not equality in the degree, but only conformity." We recognize how generous God is with us, therefore we must measure up to His generosity when we deal with others. He forgives freely, and so must we. Let us not for one moment think that we can set ourselves up as an example to God. He doesn't need to imitate us, but we need to imitate Him.

The Lord asked us to say, "as we forgive our debtors" to remind us of a difficult duty we are apt to forget. We can live in the luxury of His bountiful mercy with little thought that mercy not shared loses its full influence on us. Christ doesn't seek people in whom to deposit His forgiveness but people by whom His mercy can be used. He wants us to be channels of His forgiveness to others. No blessing is fully enjoyed that is not shared. He gives us our daily bread that we may share it.

Whatever we keep tightly closed in our hands makes us its slave. Whatever passes through our hands makes itself our servant in showing Christ–likeness. If we try to clench something in our fists for a long time, it will actually harm our hand. God made the hand capable of receiving and giving. The health of the hand depends on fulfilling both functions.

There is a fundamental difference between the first and second statement of this fifth petition. In the first we ask for forgiveness, which is tantamount to confession and repentance. When we pray, "Father, forgive us our debts," we recognize our indebtedness, our sinfulness. Then we confess that our sin is against God, and therefore forgiveness must come from Him if it is going to come at all. God in Christ has forgiven us all of our original sin in Adam. But this is not primarily what we ask in the Lord's Prayer. Even for forgiveness at the time of salvation there must be confession of one's own personal sinfulness. And the same is also true for the sins of our walk in Christ. There is no forgiveness without repentance and confession.

Now the second statement is quite different. It says, "As we also forgive our debtors." Does that presuppose confession on their part as it does in the instance of our forgiveness at the hand of God? No. We ask God to forgive us. Since there is personal desire for forgiveness, God works in us, changes us, makes us conscious of His work of grace. There is a change in us when we ask for forgiveness. But we must forgive our debtors whether they confess their indebtedness toward us or not. We cannot force our forgiveness on anybody. If I go and tell someone, "You have harmed me, but I forgive you," his reaction may be, "Thank you, I appreciate it," if he recognizes that he has indeed done something that was harmful to me. But if he doesn't recognize it, he will turn to me and say, "Whoever said that I did any harm to you, and that I owe you anything? Who do you think you are anyway to pronounce forgiveness on me—God Almighty?" That's not the attitude of the repentant sinner toward God.

Then am I supposed to withhold forgiveness from my debtors simply because they don't acknowledge their indebtedness? Of course not. I am to forgive whether they are willing to accept it or not. The Lord is concerned with our relationships with others and how they affect us as His followers. He knows we cannot always change the attitudes of others. We must offer mercy whether it is accepted or not. In the Beatitude on mercifulness our Lord said, "Blessed are the merciful for they shall obtain mercy" (Matt. 5:7). He didn't say "Blessed are those whose mercy will not be rejected by those to whom it is offered, for they shall obtain mercy." The reward of our mercifulness is in the giving of it, not necessarily in its acceptance. As far as the debtor is concerned, he is only blessed if he accepts the forgiveness we offer him and that we feel we owe him.

Personal Sin Affects Others

Why did the Lord teach us to pray, "Forgive us our debts" and not "Forgive me my debts"? Because, in all these petitions of the Lord's Prayer, we as God's children are expected to be praying together. We say, "Our Father, give us our bread; forgive us our debts; lead us not into temptation; deliver us from evil." We pray to one God as we say "Thy," but we realize we, many of us, are His children. He expects us to be sharing, as far as we can, each other's burdens. We must recognize our personal share in the evil that exists in the world. The world is what it is not simply because of what others have done, but because I also have contributed to its present condition.

Oh, for the willingness to share the burden of our world, our nation, our community, our church, our family! I, too, need some of the forgiveness, along with others. The Pharisee would hasten to say, "God, I thank thee that I am not as other men" (Luke 18:11). But the Christian prays, "Father, forgive us: I am one of them!" Man's first reaction to the sin prevailing all around him, especially as the results of it become evident, is to blame it all on others. Remember Adam? He laid the blame on God Himself and on Eve: "The woman *whom thou gavest* to be with me, *she gave me* of the tree, and I did eat" (Gen. 3:12). We commit an immoral act and then blame God for having given us the desire. An overweight person might say, "I wish God wouldn't give me such a voracious appetite, then I wouldn't be such a glutton." We must be careful about blaming God, the environment, or our fellow human beings for our own sins.

We are the doers of our own deeds, the utterers of our own words, and the thinkers of our own thoughts. In fact, before we say, "Forgive *us*," we must say, "Lord, forgive *me*." David, in Psalm 51:1–3, said: "Blot out *my* transgressions. Wash *me* thoroughly from mine iniquity, and cleanse *me* from *my* sin. For I acknowledge *my* transgressions: and *my* sin is ever before *me*." He acknowledged that all the guilt was his and that the burden of the penalty was due to him alone.

We must hate sin not only for the effect it has upon us, but also for the effect it has on others, for personal sin never affects ourselves only. "My" sin soon becomes "our" sin. A father who drinks will most likely have children who will drink, or who will suffer in other ways because of his destructive habit. None of us can say, "What I do is my business." The cigarette smoke that a person exhales, others have to breathe.

Every man lowers the moral tone of those around him when he does wrong even as he benevolently affects his environment when he does right. In praying "Forgive us," we must be conscious that we are praying also for those whom our weakness has made weak, our extravagance has made foolish, our selfishness has made bad, our anger has made hard. If only our wrongdoing could end with ourselves! Perhaps one of the most awful revelations of the future will be the knowledge of the evil we have done to others. This thought should make us pray for those who, but for us, would have escaped some particular evil.

Many years ago, in a five–story building in Boston, someone left a faucet running from Saturday to Monday morning in a photographic studio on the top floor. The water ran for thirty–six hours, and by Monday morning it had seeped all the way down to the first floor, damaging extensively a millinery shop, a shoe store, and a restaurant. The damage to all parties amounted to thousands of dollars, just because one careless worker forgot to turn off a faucet.

The writer, in commenting on this incident, said, "Ah, brothers, sisters! We are all living in tiers; one above another, one below another —individuals, families, neighborhoods, towns, states, countries! Life is a vast office building, extending so far into the clouds as to make the Empire State Building green with envy. Half the time you do not know who is just above you, or who is immediately below. But though you do not know the other folks, even those on the next floor, you know that they are there, and they know that you are there. Folks, folks, folks, packed in tiers, layer upon layer, layer below layer, endlessly.

"Therefore, turn off the faucets! Therefore, be careful how you live! Therefore, take heed of what you fail to do as well as of what you do! A little heedlessness, how it accumulates! How soon it becomes a flood! And then— drip, drip, drip—how soon and how far it leaks through! The life below, the life below that, and the life below that— why, no one knows when and where it will stop!

"Your bad–temper faucet, running not water but acid. Oh, shut it off! There are delicate fabrics below, lovely colors, beautiful bits of character that cost months to fashion, and your flood of bad temper will spoil it all.

"Your worry faucet, a black stream, a stream of ink. Your base–thought faucet, running mud, and evil–smelling mud. Your malice faucet, giving forth hot water, blistering, scalding. Shut them off! Seal them up tight!

"You don't care for the old carpets in your room of life? You don't mind living in a mess from a running faucet? There are folks on the floor below. They mind, if you do not. No one liveth to himself, that is, no one lives on the ground floor. And you would be shocked if you realized who is suffering from your open faucet. Your child, perhaps, or your 'best friend.'

"Get over this idea that you are living in a little bungalow, a one–storied affair, in the center of a ten–acre lot. Nonsense! You are in the Empire State Building of the universe, and you are on the ten thousand, three hundred and forty–first floor!"

SECTION VIII

Lead Us Not Into Temptation

Lead Us Not into Temptation

Immediately following the petition for forgiveness comes the petition, "Lead us not into temptation." We know that temptation is any enticement to do wrong. This petition brings to our consciousness the fact that we are surrounded at all times by evil, which tempts us and can cause us to fall.

This petition comes right after the one for forgiveness, because it is after we have experienced the cleansing that forgiveness brings that Satan tries so hard to get us to fall into sin again. He can't stand to see someone with a clean, pure heart, so he goes to work immediately after we have been forgiven to try to get us back into a state of sin.

He is like the neighborhood bully who couldn't stand to see the little neighborhood children all clean and neat, because he was so dirty and unkempt himself. Therefore he led them down to the barnyard where there was a muddy hogpen. He watched with glee as the children whom he forced to walk through the muddy mess became soiled and besmirched by the filth. Just so, Satan delights to watch as others become besmirched and contaminated by the filth of sin.

It is interesting to note that one of the French translations renders this, "Abandon us not in temptation." It might be paraphrased, "Don't leave us in the place where temptation will naturally come to us, but help us to overcome it. We want to be conquerors."

We must understand that God never tempts or influences His children to do evil. Christ taught His disciples this prayer after He had passed through the fearful struggle of His own temptation in the wilderness. He was tempted with essentially the same temptations we all face as human beings. The Bible does say that "He was led up of the Spirit into the wilderness," but it then goes on to say, "To be tempted *of the devil*" (Matt. 4:1). God led Him into the arena, so to speak, but He was not the antagonist or the opponent, Satan was.

It was necessary for all—God, Christ, Satan, the angels, the universe, and ourselves—that Christ be led to this confrontation with the Tempter. But though it was God who led Him into the "arena" of the test, it was not He who tempted Him. So even though God may permit us to come into confrontation with the Tempter, this does not mean that the temptation comes from Him. He never tempts anyone to sin, for by so doing He would be contradicting His own holy character.

The Greek word for "temptation" is *peirasmos* which is derived from the word *peira,* which means "experience." In order for a soldier to be experienced, he has to fight, there has to be some battle in which he is engaged. And in order for us to be experienced, for our endurance to be tested, we must also engage in a battle, and that "battle" is temptation.

If we seek to know the Lord, to love Him, and to walk closely to Him, we won't be fearful when we are called upon to face temptation. When a father takes his child by the hand to lead him through the dark woods, the response of the child may be fear, and he may not want to go that way. But that may be the only path by which they can reach their home. The fact that his father is holding his hand will give the child the courage that he needs.

As children of God we hate sin and evil, and have no desire to come into contact with them. Yet in life we must meet sin daily, though we find it most unpleasant to have to do this. We fear temptation, for we know its strength, and the forgiven soul fears to be led into sin. Our Lord doesn't lead us into sin, but He allows us to face temptation for the purpose of making us victorious Christians, who have been strengthened through our encounters with the enemy. Remember that the only road to heaven leads through the valley of temptation and therefore the Lord has to allow us to go through it. But this is only in order to test us and make us worthy soldiers.

When we pray, "Lead us not into temptation," we are asking God not to withdraw His guiding and protecting hand from us. We are saying in effect, "Do not lead us into temptation and there abandon us, or leave us alone. Lead us, yes, but come along with us." Hebrews 4:15 is helpful to remember in this connection: "For we have not a high priest which cannot be touched with the feeling of our infirmities; but was in all points tempted like as we are, yet without sin." If Jesus goes with us, we need not be afraid to go anywhere—even into confrontation with the enemy. We should be so yielded to His leadership that we will be glad to follow wherever He may choose to lead us, knowing that He will not abandon us or leave us alone.

No One Is Exempt
from Temptation

The fact that Jesus was teaching this prayer to those who were His disciples and His followers shows us that no one is exempt from temptation. Not even born–again believers can escape it. In fact, they will probably be tempted to an even greater degree than those who have never believed in Christ. All are tempted, even as our Lord was tempted. We must never think we are beyond Satan's reach. He will tempt us, no matter who we are, where we may go, or what we may do. This world is full of his allurements. There is no place we can go where we cannot be assaulted by temptations at any time.

We live in a world where of necessity we are surrounded by evil influences. You may be working every day with people who curse the name of Jesus, or with people who are deliberately trying to lead you into temptation by the way they dress or talk. By the way, be careful lest you lead others into temptation by the way you dress and behave. Always recognize and be aware of man's basic weakness and propensity for sin. Women, don't increase your chance of being raped by the way you dress. Dress decently and modestly at all times. Woe unto a Christian who becomes a source of temptation to others, or causes them to stumble or to fall into sin!

How well I know that it is hard to be unworldly in a world of conformity such as ours. We are all naturally prone to sin. There is much within us which, if not restrained, will cause us to yield to this bent toward sin. This is why it is imperative that we dedicate ourselves wholly to the Lord and seek to keep close to Him, for this greatly lessens our chances of falling into sin.

But there is no way that we can escape or avoid temptation. We may be able to escape some of it, but never all. Escape from the world is not escape from temptation. At one time I visited a monastery on the island of Corfu in Greece. It was situated high on a hill, and below it was a beach with a public swimming area. There was a monk there who was trying to get one of the visitors to take some of his money and buy him a pair of binoculars so that he could watch the people on the beach. It is pretty certain that his observation was to be concentrated on those of the opposite sex. He was a monk, he was isolated in a monastery, but still within him he had the desires of the flesh.

None of us are free from temptation, not even a child of God, but we must not equate temptation with sin, for they are not the same thing. The Lord will never lead us into sin, but He will allow us to be tempted so that He can test us and strengthen us. The Christian life is a continuous resisting of temptation, but we have the assurance of victory through the help of God.

There are some vocations where the danger of being tempted is much greater than in others. For instance, think of those who work in restaurants or places where they must constantly deal with the public. They meet all kinds of people. Sometimes they can't help it if their lusts are aroused, because of the indecent and immodest way some people dress. Another example would be that of a Christian lifeguard who has to be out on the beach all day long, day after day. The Lord can keep him, of course, but it is a tough job and one in which temptations abound. We need to pray for people who have to make their living in an environment that is full of temptations, because it isn't easy.

If you have to choose between two jobs, one that gives you less money or one with more money but correspondingly greater temptations, by all means choose the one that gives you less money. While it is true that we live in a complex world, in which it is futile to try to avoid all temptation, why choose to try to navigate a sea of temptation that may well drown you? And what good is all the money if, in the process of making it, you lose your own soul?

When God Himself permits us to be tempted, He is certain to bring us out of it safely. But when we deliberately walk into it or are pulled into it by the allurement of the world, the danger of defeat is far greater. The Lord never leads us into a trap, He leads us into victory through the experience of temptation and struggle.

Luther said, "We cannot prevent the birds from flying over our heads, but we can keep them from building nests in our hair." It is folly to raise and fondle evil thoughts as if we found pleasure in them and then pray not to be led into temptation. What we pray to God to do for us we should strive to do for ourselves. We dare not play with temptation of any sort, for in so doing we let down the drawbridge of our soul's castle. As we pray that He will not lead us into temptation, we must fly from it as Lot did from Sodom.

Watch Your Achilles' Heel!

Greek mythology tells of Achilles, a hero of the Trojan War. When he was a child, his mother, Thetis, thought of a way by which she could see that her son was protected from injury and death. She held him by the heel and dipped his whole body into the Styx River, thereby rendering every part of his body invulnerable except for the heel by which she held him. As a result, Achilles for many years escaped unhurt. But at last Paris, son of King Priam of Troy, wounded Achilles' heel with a poisoned arrow, thereby inflicting a death wound. Of course that was the end of the mighty Achilles!

Each of us has an Achilles' heel. We have a weak spot, and we never know when the dart of the wicked one will hit us there. Temptations and sins all around us appeal to our inclination, passions, and lusts. They have a way of finding the weak spot. I know that I have one, and if you examine your heart you will surely know what yours is. You don't have to tell others, but confess it to yourself and to the Lord, and say, "Lord, I have to be very careful, lest I allow sin to hit me at my Achilles' heel."

Only Christ was foolproof against giving into temptation. Yet the devil tempted even Him, because he didn't believe that He was invulnerable. Peter was not foolproof against temptation. He was the man who said that, though all others might forsake the Lord, he never would. But he did!

One of the most interesting experiences a person can have in the Holy Land is to visit the church on Mt. Zion, in the heart of Jerusalem, called "St. Peter in Galigantu" (St. Peter and the cock–crow). This church is built on the previous site of the palace of Caiaphas the High Priest (You may recall that the first trial of Jesus was here, before Annas and Caiaphas). During the trial Peter was out in the courtyard, warming himself by the servants' fire. Out of cowardice and fear he denied that he even knew Jesus. When I am with a group in that place and I read that portion of Scripture aloud it makes us all weep. What had happened was that the enemy had found Peter's weak spot and had taken advantage of it. The sad thing was that Peter was not even aware that he had a weak spot, so he was totally unprepared for the attack. Thus he fell.

What a warning to each of us! We must be very careful about our weak spot, and very watchful against temptation, lest the same thing happen to us.

The Folly of Over–confidence
When Facing Temptation

When the Lord taught us to pray, "Lead us not into temptation," He was giving us a warning against over–confidence. We saw previously that we are not to cower in fear of a confrontation with the enemy if God leads us into this experience, but to be over–confident to the point that we have no fear or dread of falling into sin is to be foolhardy.

If a man's country calls him into war and he is brought into conflict with the enemy through the choice of those in authority over him, he is expected to face with courage whatever may lie ahead of him. If he goes to perform his duty in such a manner and shows such courage, he is considered a hero. But if the same man takes it upon himself to engage the enemy in battle without being authorized or commanded to do so by his superiors, he is not considered a hero; he is only thought to be a fool!

An example of this kind of over–confidence occurred in the life of David, the great king of Judah. He was over-confident as he stood there and looked at Uriah's wife, Bath–sheba. Probably he was thinking, even though it may have been subconsciously, "There is no danger in merely looking." Well, we all know what happened. He became an adulterer and a murderer. Who? A saint of God such as David? How could that happen?

The Bible says "Pride goeth before destruction" (Prov. 16:18). When you think you are so strong you could never possibly fall, that's the time to be careful. The temptation you are playing with may become your downfall. The Lord taught us to pray, "Lead us not into temptation" to keep us humble and to remind us to, "Let him that thinketh he standeth take heed lest he fall" (1 Cor. 10:12).

It is the knowledge of our own weakness that makes us fearful of temptation; without that knowledge we shall be overtaken. It is the person who knows he is weak who seeks to become strong. He realizes that the enemy is not fooling around but is out to get him.

It is not a mark of courage to throw yourself into temptation, it is a mark of foolhardiness. As Shakespeare said, "The better part of valor is discretion." To deliberately throw yourself into a place of temptation, and trust yourself not to fall is as foolish as thrusting your hand into the fire and trusting you won't be burned. You may not go that far, but perhaps you just try to see how close you can get without being burned.

You are being over–confident and foolhardy when you seek out immoral company. Many a child from a good Christian home has gone astray simply because he chose the wrong companions. You will learn to drink if you keep company with those who drink. You will learn to smoke if you keep company with those who smoke. You will learn to be an adulterer if you keep company with those who take pleasure in adultery. You will learn to curse if you keep company with those who use foul language. If you have a barrel of good apples with a few rotten ones mixed in, you will find that the good apples do not transfer their goodness and soundness to the bad apples. It's the other way around. That's why we say, "One bad apple spoils the barrel."

We must recognize our vulnerability and keep away from potentially harmful allurements. Don't buy foul literature. Don't look at pictures that may arouse your lusts. "Lead us not into temptation" is a recognition that we might fall, that we are weak. The Lord may permit us the experience of temptation, but He will never cause us to fall. We have only ourselves to blame for that, and sometimes it happens because we are over–confident.

For instance, any minister who does counseling with a woman in his office, without someone else being present, is making himself susceptible to temptation, or at least to suspicion in the eyes of others. It is my policy not to close my door at any time when there is a woman in my office. I have seen many, many preachers take the wrong moral path by exposing themselves to this sort of temptation. I have no right to ask the Lord not to lead me into temptation if I am doing something to lead myself into it.

Perhaps you feel you are so strong that you can go into tempting situations without being harmed. Don't be too sure of yourself. How often have you found yourself among sinful people and remaining silent when something evil is done or said? As someone has put it, you "just fade into the wallpaper." You don't protest what is going on. The one thing we "Protestants" don't protest enough is sin. We just keep our mouths shut and don't say anything. But we don't have the option or the right to remain silent in the face of evil. It is cowardly, and is the first step in giving in to temptation. Edmund Burke said, "All that is necessary for evil to triumph is that good men do nothing." As has been noted, "Sometimes silence isn't 'golden,' it's just plain yellow!" The silent acquiescence in evil is the first step toward full participation in it.

SECTION IX

Deliver Us from Evil

Recognizing the Presence of Evil
And the Need for Deliverance

In the old English wars between the king and Parliament, the town of Taunton, attacked by Lord Goring and defended by Robert Blake, sustained a long siege. Food rose to twenty times its market value. Half the houses were blown down by a storm of fire, and many of the people perished from hunger. Through all of this, the townsfolk had been accustomed to meet in St. Mary's Church to pray, and we may be sure that the burden of their daily prayers to the Father was, "Deliver us!" One day as they were assembled for this purpose, hoping to hear that the enemy had at last retreated, a trusty messenger came to the church door and spoke but one word, "Deliverance!" In a moment the magic word flew through the vast assembly, and all shouted with one voice, "Deliverance!"

We can all identify with their feelings, for who has not experienced the need for deliverance many times over in our own lives? The Lord Jesus, recognizing this constant human dependence upon the Heavenly Father for aid, intervention, and protection, taught His disciples the petition we shall now consider, "Deliver us from evil."

In order to pray sincerely for deliverance, we first have to recognize the presence of evil in the world around us. If we don't, we shall certainly suffer the consequences of ignoring it.

Man, since he has been corrupted by the Fall, is intrinsically evil. Even the natural world around us bears upon it the impression of evil, for it has been subjected to the curse because of man's sin. The proof of this is seen in the violence, the ruthlessness, and the constant suffering and death entailed upon the whole animal creation. Many animals prey upon other animals, or even upon human beings, in order to satisfy their need for food.

Even the weather and the climate show the results of sin and evil in this world, killing thousands every year with cataclysmic upheavals such as cyclones, monsoons, blizzards, floods, earthquakes, and other such catastrophic outbursts.

Of course, we know that nature was not like this in the beginning. What has changed it from the Paradise of Eden to the chaos it is today? What has changed society from what it was in the primeval days of Creation, fresh from the hand of the Creator? One thing has done it all—the presence of evil in the world.

There is no way, therefore, that we can ever hope to escape the presence of evil while living on this earth. The time when we shall no longer need to pray, "Deliver us from evil" will not come until our souls and spirits have left this body and its present sinful environment. Someday, the Bible tells us, God is going to create a new earth, "wherein dwelleth righteousness" (2 Pet. 3:13). In that new earth this prayer for deliverance from evil will never again be needed. But in this present earth, it certainly is!

We are in constant peril from the assaults of the evil all around us. We need to be aroused from a life of sin, selfishness, and deadness of conscience. We must be alert, for Scripture tells us that our life is a warfare that calls for constant vigilance on our part. It is also described as a "wrestling." Ephesians 6:12 says, "For we wrestle not against flesh and blood, but against principalities, against powers, against the rulers of the darkness of this world, against spiritual wickedness in high places."

The Christian is further represented by the figure of an athlete who has to undergo constant discipline and self–denial. Life is shown as a brief journey through a great and terrible wilderness. We are sojourners upon this earth, and we have to fight our way through it. The words of a well–known and well–loved old hymn express it aptly:

> Must I be carried to the skies
> On flowery beds of ease,
> While others fought to win the prize,
> And sailed through bloody seas?
>
> Are there no foes for me to face?
> Must I not stem the flood?
> Is this vile world a friend to grace,
> To help me on to God?
>
> Sure I must fight, if I would reign;
> Increase my courage, Lord;
> I'll bear the toil, endure the pain,
> Supported by Thy Word."
>   —Isaac Watts

We must not be blind to spiritual peril. There is also physical danger all around us, the outgrowth of moral evil, and we shall do well to recognize it. No one is exempt from the need of praying this prayer. Evil is everywhere. It is present with the one who sits in a solitary cell, it is present in a crowd. It is in the pew as well as in the pulpit.

The more keenly aware we are of our personal peril because of evil, the more prepared we will be to defeat it.

It is God's desire that we be victorious. That is why Christ taught us to pray, "Deliver us from evil."

The Devil Tries to Get Between You and God

In the Greek, this petition of the Lord's Prayer, "Deliver us from evil," means not only from abstract evil but also from a person, "the evil one," which is one of the names given to Satan. There are two Greek words that are translated "evil" in English, *kakos* and *poneros*. *Kakos* means one who is evil in himself, but does not necessarily try to propagate that evil. However, *poneros,* which is one of the Greek names given to Satan, means one who is not only intrinsically evil, but who also seeks to propagate evil. That is the word that is used in the Lord's Prayer. "Deliver us from evil," then, includes deliverance from the evil one, Satan.

The Lord Jesus Christ knew very well how real Satan was. After all, as God He created him! Of course we know that He didn't originally create him as an evil being. Satan became the evil one by his own choice, when he sinned and rebelled against God. Jesus also confronted Satan and was attacked by him during His wilderness temptation. He wants to make it very clear to us that Satan does exist.

In the Scriptures Satan is called by several names and titles, such as "tempter," "accuser," "destroyer" (which in the Greek is *apolluon*). *Diabolos,* "the devil," means "one who is a false accuser." *Diaballo,* the Greek verb derived from the same root, means "to put something through or in between." It is made up of the preposition *dia,* "through," and the verb *ballō* meaning "throw." The devil delights in putting something between us and God.

Therefore it is imperative that we not only recognize the existence of Satan, but that we also do everything we can to resist him. Jesus called Satan "the father of lies," and "a murderer from the beginning." He creeps up on us like a poisonous serpent, to take us unawares. The most dangerous thing we can do is to ignore him and his activity in the world around us and in our own lives.

Satan is "the deceiver," and there are two basic ways that he is deceiving people today about himself. The first is by causing people to believe that he doesn't really exist. He has been very successful in this tactic, which is why so many people will laugh at the suggestion that there is a personal "devil." He is thought by many to be only a character out of folklore, a figment of someone's imagination, or just a symbolical way of referring to abstract evil. One of his greatest stratagems is to get people to think he is not real, for then they will never recognize what he is doing in their lives and in the world around them.

The second way he is deceiving people today is by building up a caricature of himself in their minds. He gets people to laugh at him as a creature in a red suit, with a forked tail, hooves, and horns, carrying a pitchfork. He makes them think he is a subject for humor. Or else he gets them to believe that he is ugly and repulsive. The danger of this is that people do not know that the Bible says Satan can transform himself into an angel of light. Therefore they don't realize he can appear in the guise of that which is beautiful, attractive, and glamorous. They are completely deceived by the false picture he presents of himself.

We as Christians should never allow ourselves to be deceived in any of these ways. We should not only know that he is real, we should also have a healthy respect for his power. But at the same time we must exercise faith in Christ. The Bible says, "greater is he that is in you, than he that is in the world" (1 John 4:4b). Believe that He can deliver you, for though Satan is far stronger and more powerful than we human beings, he is no match for the Lord Jesus Christ.

We are never safe from temptation in this world because the devil is here and is constantly active. We need God's presence and help constantly in the fight against evil. Let us beware that Satan does not succeed in getting between us and God.

The Only Real Harm the Evil One Can Cause Us Is to Make Us Sin

Does deliverance from evil mean that God will remove the very presence of evil? Well, consider the case of Daniel. He was a man of God, who lived among people who hated God and hated his people, the Jews. Daniel was also a man who prevailed with God in prayer, and undoubtedly he must have prayed for deliverance from evil. Yet God permitted him to be thrown into a den of lions. While this was going on, Daniel was no doubt praying earnestly for deliverance.

But what did God do? He didn't stop the enemies of Daniel. Instead, He allowed them to throw Daniel into the den with the starving lions. However, God delivered Daniel by being with him and protecting him while he was there, by stopping the mouths of the lions so that they could not devour him. God allowed this to happen for a purpose.

We cannot dictate to God the way that He will deliver us, or to what extent He is going to allow us to be thrust at the mercy of evil men and the evil elements of nature. God is sovereign. He allows the devil to tempt us, even as He allowed the devil to tempt Christ. But the devil can never tempt us or cause any harm to come to us unless God permits him to do so.

Another example of this is one mentioned earlier, that of the three Jews who, during the time of the Babylonian

Captivity, were thrown into the fiery furnace for refusing to bow down to the idol statue of the Babylonian king. Could God have prevented them from being cast into the furnace? Of course He could. But instead He allowed them to be bound and thrown into the flames.

While they were there, however, a fourth Person was seen walking in the midst of the flames with them. This was the Lord Jesus Christ, in one of His bodily, pre–incarnate appearances recorded in the Old Testament that we call a "Christophany." The evil that surrounded them so closely, in this instance in the form of fire, could not harm them because He was with them and His presence gave them protection.

These young men did not dictate to God how He should deliver them. They knew that the greater evil from which they needed to be delivered was that of committing the sin of idolatry. They were more concerned about being delivered from this sin than being delivered from the fiery furnace. They were willing to die rather than be coerced into sin.

The prayer, "Deliver us from evil," in this instance could be paraphrased, "God, whatever Your will may be, I welcome it. What You will to bring to pass in my life, I shall accept and not refuse. My desire is that You be glorified through whatever comes, of good or ill." That is true deliverance from evil.

The sting of death, and the sting of all evil that befalls us, is sin. We may be afflicted by the evil one, Satan, but as long as he cannot induce us to sin he has gained no victory over us. God is providing, therefore, the deliverance He has promised, for He is delivering us from sin, which is the sting of evil. It is possible for us to be surrounded by all sorts of evil circumstances and yet not be harmed by them if we do not allow them to induce us to sin. The evil, apart from sin, has no "sting" for us.

We find that to suffer with Christ is not suffering in one sense, for if the affliction is permitted by Him there is always the joy of the Holy Spirit within our hearts. In Philippians 3:7, 8, Paul wrote: "But what things were gain to me, those I counted loss for Christ. Yea doubtless, and I count all things but loss for the excellency of the knowledge of Christ Jesus my Lord: for whom I have suffered the loss of all things, and do count them but dung, that I may win Christ."

What if you do lose your wealth, if that will lead you to the excellency of the knowledge of Christ? What if you lose your health, if that is going to draw you closer to Christ? Paul knew that the first and most important thing in life for the Christian is to know Christ. This is worth suffering, and worth the loss of all material things.

Paul was a man who could have been rich, yet he chose to be poor. He could have moved in the circles of the great, the educated, the famous, yet he chose to be forsaken, persecuted, and maligned. Yes, Paul counted them all but refuse in order that he might win Christ. What a tremendous attitude!

In A.D. 203, a young Christian mother named Perpetua was imprisoned at Carthage. She knew that unless she recanted and denied her Christian faith she would be put to death.

"Have pity on thy babe," they said to her. "Have pity on the white hairs of thy father and the infancy of thy child."

She replied, "I will not."

"Art thou then a Christian?" they said.

And Perpetua answered, "Yes, I am a Christian." She later said, "Then were we condemned to the wild beasts, and with hearts full of joy we returned to our prison."

That is what Christ does. He delivers from evil many times by delivering us from the sting of sin. The words of Luther are indeed timeless: "O my most dear God, I thank Thee that Thou hast made me a poor beggar upon earth. O my God, punish me far rather with pestilence, with all the terrible sicknesses of earth, with war, with anything rather than that Thou be silent to me." Luther knew that the greatest calamity that can come to a Christian is for him to cease to hear the voice of God. That is why in every evil that befalls us we should continually pray for deliverance from sin, the greatest evil of all.

The Evil One Cannot Touch Us Without God's Permission

To what extent does suffering and affliction come from Satan? To what extent does he control all the evil things that come to us? Let us look at one of the most enlightening verses in the Bible on this matter of "who's in control". Deuteronomy 32:39 says, "See now that I, even I, am he, and there is no god with me: I kill, and I make alive; I wound, and I heal: neither is there any that can deliver out of my hand."

There is none equal with God. No one is able to affect God's actions. Not Satan, nor any person can cause anything to happen without God permitting it to take place (Lam. 3:37).

But even in our individual lives we find that God permits things that we consider evil. For instance, He says, "I kill, and I make alive." When a person dies it is because it is God's will for him to die. It is also God who gives life, for He says, "I make alive." Every child who is born into this world is brought into it by the will of God. Not only does He give us life when we are born into this world, it is also God who will give us life in the future resurrection.

This verse continues, "I wound, and I heal [notice that it is God who does both]: neither is there any that can deliver out of my hand." God is a sovereign God. If you forget that, you will come to the conclusion that the devil is doing whatever he pleases in this world.

The story of Job, recorded in the Old Testament, shows us that Satan's power is limited by God, for he couldn't do a single thing to Job until God gave him specific permission. And it is the same way with us. Someone has said that before any evil can reach the child of God it is first "filtered through fingers of Love." God has set a hedge around about every one of His children, as Satan well knows, and nothing can pass through that hedge until He permits it. By the time it reaches us it has become His will for us. That is why we can say that "Disappointments are 'His appointments.' "

If you want to read an interesting case in point, look up the account of David and Shimei in 2 Samuel 16:5–13. Shimei was cursing David and casting stones at him. The men who were with David wanted to kill Shimei for this insolence to their king. But David restrained them with a highly unusual command. "Let him alone," he said, "and let him curse; for the Lord hath bidden him" (v. 11). Did he mean that the Lord had caused Shimei to curse? No, but He allowed him to do so, and David recognized this.

Psalm 147:3 says, "He [God] healeth the broken in heart, and bindeth up their wounds." One translation has it, "He giveth medicine to heal their sickness." It's good to know that even our medicine is given by God. Sometimes medicine is the way God chooses to answer our prayer for deliverance from evil, for it is often the method He uses to heal our sicknesses.

Psalm 34:19 says, "Many are the afflictions of the righteous: but the Lord delivereth him out of them all." Can God deliver us from evil, then? Of course He can! But the deliverance is always according to His sovereign will, and sometimes that will is to give grace in the trial, instead of

307

removing the trial from us. But whether He chooses to grant deliverance "from" or "in" it, what a blessed comfort to know that Satan can never touch us in any way without God's permission!

Is a Christian Exempt from the Consequences of Evil?

Some people today will tell you that if you become a Christian you will no longer be bothered by evil and its consequences. This is not so, for evil is all around us. We must be realists. Some of the most faithful children of God have faced evil. Even the Lord Jesus Christ Himself faced Satan. In fact, He was actually referring to Satan, the evil one, in this prayer for deliverance from evil. He was attacked by the evil one, and so are we all.

In a recent book I came across this statement: "If you live totally in the presence of God you will never get sick and you will never die." This does not agree with the Word of God. In refutation of this another author said, "Those people who are always talking about God's promises and always quoting them as a supposed source of protection against every unpleasant or hurtful experience of life should remember that this also is a promise: 'In the world ye shall have tribulation.' And as they themselves say, 'God always keeps His promises!' " Of course, the verse goes on to say, "But be of good cheer, I have overcome the world" (John 16:33b). His promise is that we will have trouble, but that we can overcome it, instead of letting it overcome us.

Suffering, poverty, disease and other forms of evil have always been a source of immense perplexity to many children of God, such as the ancient patriarchs, the Psalmist, and others whose experiences are recorded in the Bible. It is true that Christ provides a means of deliverance, but this does not mean that the trouble is always removed. God didn't deliver the three Hebrew children out of the fiery furnace. He delivered them and preserved them "through it" by being with them and giving them the grace and the protection they needed.

For unbelievers, evil and its consequences present a horrible and hopeless prospect. Since they have no resources outside themselves, they succumb to the circumstances and are thereby shattered or destroyed. Christians, however, have a different attitude. As they face the evils that are common to both unbelievers and believers, the righteous are strengthened by grace and illuminated by hope.

Paul says in Romans 8:18, "For I reckon that the sufferings of this present time are not worthy to be compared with the glory which shall be revealed in us." Then in 2 Corinthians 4:17,18 he says: "For our light affliction, which is but for a moment, worketh for us a far more exceeding and eternal weight of glory; while we look not at the things which are seen, but at the things which are not seen: for the things which are seen are temporal; but the things which are not seen are eternal."

When we experience sickness and trouble and other forms of evil in our lives, we are tempted to look at them simply from the temporal point of view. We view things from the here and now, while God acts in the context of the eternal and the infinite. Would you really want God to act only for your temporal good, or do you also want Him to act for your eternal good?

Consider your attitude as a parent toward your child. Suppose, because he is tired, he wants to shirk the performance of a duty, such as studying. What attitude do you take? As a responsible, mature person, you should think not only of pleasing your child at that particular moment, but also think of what will ultimately be for his good.

One definition of maturity is: "the ability and the willingness to forego present gratification or enjoyment for the sake of future gain or profit." Because you want your child to achieve this kind of maturity, you explain to him that, though he may be tired, it is necessary for him to study. His studying will work for his good throughout his entire life on earth. On the other hand, if he doesn't study, although he may experience temporary relief from fatigue, he may thereby be forming habits of avoiding work and shirking his duty, that will be detrimental to him throughout life.

Is God any less wise or responsible than we earthly parents? Of course not! On the contrary, He is much wiser than we will ever be. We must seek to understand the principles of God's dealings with us. We pray, "Deliver us from evil," but it does not necessarily follow that this will cause God to take away the sickness or the adversity from which we are suffering. If He doesn't take it away, it is because He has a purpose in allowing it. It may be that through our sickness, adversity or poverty we will achieve or accomplish things we would never have been able to do otherwise.

Annie Johnson Flint dedicated her life to the Lord at an early age. She planned to serve Him in the field of music, at which she was very talented, and was training for a career as a concert pianist. However, while still a young woman, she was stricken with a crippling and painful disease, and after a time she had to give up the piano completely, because her fingers had become so gnarled and twisted that she could no longer play. At first it seemed to Annie that her life was all over. But finally she reached up in faith and took the hand of her loving Heavenly Father and said, "Thy will be done."

Through the long, agonizing years of being a bedridden invalid, she poured out a constant stream of some of the most beautiful hymns and poems that have ever been used to bless a suffering world. What a blessing her life became!

Would she have ever written those beautiful songs and poems if this evil had not come into her life? It's very doubtful. Her piano concerts would have blessed a few thousands at the most, but her poems and songs of hope and comfort have blessed millions around the world.

The following poem was written by a woman who, while still a young girl, was tragically taken from her family, who remain to this day in a communist country that won't permit them to leave. Out of the darkness of her suffering she has mined these precious thoughts:

> There are many tears shed
> There are many burdens
> Along our path.
> There are many sufferings
> And reasons for grief.

> Perhaps all the sorrows,
> All the tears that are shed,
> Are doors through which we can behold
> Another person's sorrows.
> Perhaps all the miseries and burdens
> Are the most beautiful experience
> Through which we can know
> Some of the sufferings of the One
> Who, alone, mocked, and rejected,

> Walked along the cruel path
> To the cruel Cross!
>   —Maria Herrera

God acts within the context of the eternal, while we want Him to act within the context of the here and now. Remember that God's view of things is different from ours. God's desires are carried out in dimensions different from ours. Therefore when we pray, "Deliver us from evil," we should remember that God is far more interested in saving us from the eternal evil than from the temporal. He sometimes permits temporal suffering in order to save us from eternal torment. God knows what He's doing!

The Epicurean, Stoic, and Christian Views of Evil

Among the philosophers in the days of Christ and Paul were a group called Epicureans. Their philosophy identified any discomfort as "evil," and whatever was pleasurable as "good." They made the cultivation of personal pleasure and the avoidance of personal pain the end and goal of their life. This is why we call a very satisfying and pleasurable meal an "Epicurean" feast. It's a meal that will please and delight the bodily appetites and senses and give pleasure to those who partake of it.

The Epicureans made self–interest the basis of identifying good and evil. It was also the basis of determining right or wrong. If their interest was served and they received pleasure from it, that made it right. If their interest was not served, it was wrong. The Epicurean philosophy, of course, is contrary to Christianity. It is actually the philosophy of millions in the affluent countries of the world today, although it may not be called by that name. It is still the same old evil of Epicureanism taking a little different form.

The man who tries to play hide and seek with things disagreeable and to avoid his duty because it is painful or unpleasant does not thereby escape his responsibilities and obligations. Have you ever done something like that? For instance, have you ever avoided something unpleasant simply because you were tired? That is evil, and you should ask the Lord to liberate you from it. "Deliver me from evil" means, among other things, "Deliver me from laziness." We need to be delivered from the desire to be paid full wages while not doing a good day's or hour's work. That is evil. I'm afraid many of us Christians fall into the evil of Epicureanism.

Another popular philosophy prevalent in Paul's day was called Stoicism. In contrast to the Epicureans who tried to avoid suffering, Stoicism taught that obedience to the moral law was the end of life, and that nothing else was important or could compare with it. Their motto was "Obey and suffer."

Pushing their view to extremes, the Stoics tried to persuade themselves that pain is not evil and that earthly happiness is not good. They maintained a kind of indifference toward both pleasure and suffering. Their protest against the moral disorder and wickedness of the world was heroic.

We speak today of a stoic attitude toward suffering. That means looking upon suffering without any display of emotion. This philosophy was ineffective. The Stoics could inspire fortitude but not joy. In contrast, when the Christian faces difficulties, it is not with a grim sense of fatalism but with hope in the Lord. The Stoics demonstrated courage, but not hope; resignation, but not peace.

The Christian, however, says, "Thy will be done, Lord," and that brings peace. The Christian attitude is not that of the Stoic. The Stoics make believe that pain and sickness are not evils. Thus, they put too great a strain upon human nature. Such a belief could only be arrived at by crushing out some of man's sweetest emotions and tearing away some of his finest instincts.

Christianity is not Epicureanism, with its selfish indulgence and its avoidance of all hardship and suffering. Neither is it Stoicism, which merely endures suffering without showing any emotion. No, Christianity is a religion that recognizes and allows for the full range of human emotions. Christianity does not fall into either Epicurean or Stoic error. It recognizes evil things as evil, but it lays no check on the natural movements of human feelings.

Christ wept aloud over fallen Jerusalem. He shed tears over the grave of Lazarus. He sighed deeply when He witnessed the disabilities of the afflicted. He groaned with indignation for the hardness of men's hearts. That is certainly the expression of feeling!

Don't worry if you find yourself weeping in the face of the evil around you. Don't worry, either, if at times you find yourself rejoicing over the good things God gives you to enjoy. Christians are supposed to have feelings. As Christians we are neither Epicureans nor Stoics. We recognize evil and fight it, and we rejoice in the victory that Jesus Christ gives.

"Deliver us from evil" presupposes the acknowledgment of evil, the possibility of victory over it, and the joy that ensues. Christianity is a religion of feeling and emotion, both toward evil and the deliverance from it.

Your Attitude toward Evil and Its Consequences Spells Victory or Defeat

Your attitude toward evil and your deliverance from it helps or hinders you in acquiring joy in your life. Christianity is not a "pie in the sky" religion; it is very realistic. It recognizes that this world of ours is a sinful place. There is evil in it. We must face it, Satan goes about "as a roaring lion . . . seeking whom he may devour" (1 Pet. 5:8). He is a fallen angel, the destroyer, the one who is responsible for the existence of evil in the world. We had better face him and fight him. Our Lord taught us this by His own example. Yes, disease, pain and suffering are evil, but we can be victorious over them. Jesus Christ is the One who can deliver us.

But how are we delivered? Sometimes the evil is not taken away, but the Lord gives victory in bearing the evil. The Lord wanted us to see the connection between the evil that is in the world and its source, which is sin and wickedness. The nature of evil is sin. The beginning of evil is sin. When we say, "Lord, deliver us from evil," it is the same as saying, "Deliver us from sin." Evil in its ultimate sense is transgression. It is alienation from God.

If tribulation is not recognized as the product of sin, it may lead to crime. If a person blames his suffering on another person, he may resent him and try to harm him. God does not always deliver us from the presence of evil, but He does deliver us from sin and its power. And since evil is the child of sin, He can deliver us from the evil also if He so chooses.

For instance, if disease comes to you and you don't see the hand of God in it, but instead resist it, you may come to the point of cursing God. This was what Satan tempted Job to do, through the suggestion of Job's own wife.

It is not a sin to suffer calamity. The entrance of sin into this world brought with it evil consequences and suffering that are the common lot of all. When we pray, "Deliver us from evil," we must pray that God will give victory in facing these consequences of sin which come to the whole human race.

Evil in the form of pain, bereavement, sickness, loss, heartache, and disappointment comes to every one of us, without exception. Whether we are believers or unbelievers, these evils are unavoidable.

It makes a difference, however, how we behave in the presence of evil. If we allow these things that are really the consequences of sin in the world to have a devastating effect upon our lives, we will be defeated. But if you are able to accept the deliverance the Lord can give from these consequences of evil, we will be victorious. The thing to be concerned about is that we not sin as we fight the presence of evil all around us.

Deliverance From the
Corruption of Our Own Hearts

Before we can intelligently pray for deliverance from evil, it is necessary for us to know what Christ considered evil. As He was in the world, so are we. In fact, the world today seems to be more evil than ever. One reason for that is that today we have the means of becoming more quickly and fully informed of the evil that is taking place, not just in our own town, or our own country, but all over the world. The fact that people consider evil so newsworthy is a mark of the depravity of man's heart.

Since the first sin of Adam and Eve in the Garden of Eden, man has always been sinful and this has been an evil world. We as Christians must realize that we are always surrounded by evil.

We must always be ready to defend ourselves, for evil can attack us at any time, and it often happens when we are not looking for it. We also must realize that we cannot deliver ourselves, although there are a great many things that we can do to help in the process of deliverance. The ultimate deliverance from evil is a matter that must be left with God Himself. Sometimes the evil seems overwhelming, but He that is within us, Jesus Christ, is greater than the evil.

To Christ, evil did not primarily mean the sorrows, calamities, sicknesses, accidents and unpleasant events that the world commonly calls evil. Isn't that what we generally mean when we speak about evil? Unpleasant circumstances and afflictions we shall always have, but what concerned Christ more than anything else was hatred and malice and the wicked devices of men that cause pain to others. His concern was not primarily evil in the abstract, but the evil that exists in the heart of man.

He was deeply concerned about the sinful people in the world around Him. He wanted to see them repent and come to God and be forgiven. He was concerned lest they perish in their sins. How much pain and concern do sinful people around us arouse in our hearts? Enough to try to do something about it?

We are not to fear evil people and what they may do to us, for the Lord told us, "Be not afraid of them that kill the body and after that have no more that they can do" (Luke 12:4). The evil that we are to fear is the corruption of the human heart, whether it is our own heart or someone else's.

There is sin all around us, but the evil which is greater than the sin itself is the callousness of our own hearts toward it. The sinfulness of our neighbor is not as great an evil as our indifference toward the eternal destiny of that neighbor. The corruption of our own hearts and the degradation of our own spirits are evils that we must pray to be delivered from, day by day and moment by moment. When we pray, "Deliver us from evil," let us recognize that this means, "Deliver me from the corruption of my own heart."

Deliverance from the Evil of the Darkening of Our Conscience

Another evil from which we need to be delivered is darkening of our conscience. Conscience is the "monitor" or "sensor" which God has placed within us to make us aware of the approach of evil and to enable us to distinguish between right and wrong.

We are all familiar with the alarms used in the homes and public buildings of our day that are sensitive to heat and smoke. When smoke or excessive heat passes through the atmosphere, the sensor picks it up and the alarm is immediately sounded. These alarms have saved many lives, for without them people are often overcome by smoke or fumes, or else trapped in the flames, before they are even aware of the presence of fire. The purpose of the alarm is to alert people to the danger so that they can escape, instead of perishing in the flames.

Conscience is the "alarm" that God has given us, not for the purpose of making us miserable but to alert us to the danger of sin and to enable us to escape spiritual harm or even death. If our conscience is sensitive and alert it can save us from being taken unaware by the approach of sin, for it will warn us of its presence.

If a person had a smoke alarm in his home and heard it go off in the middle of the night, he would be a fool to ignore it and go back to sleep. He would know that the alarm is sounding because something is wrong, and if he had any sense at all he would investigate the problem immediately.

People who would never think of ignoring an alarm of this sort will regularly ignore and stifle the voice of the conscience–alarm that God has placed within them. Yet it is far more foolish to ignore this alarm than to ignore one that merely alerts us to physical danger, for the alarm of conscience is placed within us to warn of spiritual peril, which is far more deadly. It is far worse to lose one's eternal soul than to lose one's physical life, which is so short in comparison to eternity.

It is only as we recognize evil for what it is that we are able to turn away from it or to repent of it. This is the function of the conscience, to keep us sensitive to sin so that we can avoid it and not be harmed by it. It also approves and commends what is right in ourselves and in the world around us.

But if we allow our conscience to become insensitive and darkened, we will try to justify and rationalize that which is evil, both in ourselves and in others around us.

For instance, many people today justify the telling of what they call "little white lies." They protest that you can't live without resorting to such devices. Others justify such things as cheating on their income tax, or falsifying their expense accounts by saying that "everybody is doing it," and that they can't live without going along with the majority. They insist that in order to get along today one has to compromise with the evil that is permeating society.

Or they may see someone in need, or hear about the millions of souls who have never heard the Gospel. When they are asked to give something to help them, their reaction is often, "I don't like this begging all the time for money. I have enough to do to support my own family.

322

Besides doesn't everyone know that 'Charity begins at home?' "

As they respond to good and evil in these ways, and as they resort to these subterfuges, their conscience gets harder and harder. They are stifling the voice of conscience in regard to that which is the Christian's common duty—to help those who are in need.

Beware of trifling with your conscience! That is a very dangerous thing to do. The Bible tells us that one of the signs of the last days is this darkening of the conscience. 1 Timothy 4:2 speaks of those who depart from the faith and give heed to false doctrines as "having their conscience seared with a hot iron." The result of searing some part of the body with a hot iron is to cause a loss of feeling in that area, at least after the initial burn has healed.

Titus 1:15 speaks of those whose conscience is "defiled." Those who have defiled their consciences have lost even the capacity to discern between right and wrong, or to know good from evil. They have abused their conscience until it is no longer reliable as a guide to what is right. Verse sixteen connects this defilement of conscience with a profession of faith in God that is nullified by an evil life. That is something to beware of. These passages seem to indicate that, before one can become a deliberate hypocrite, he first has to get his conscience out of the way, and that he can do this either by deadening it completely or by defiling it so that it no longer is accurate in its judgments and perceptions.

Do you realize what is happening when you can sit down and eat three meals a day without ever giving a thought to the two–thirds of the world's population who go to bed hungry every night? When you dress your child in beautiful clothing and never think of the millions of children in the world who are naked, with not even one piece of clothing to put on their backs? What is happening is that your conscience is becoming dulled and darkened.

What a dangerous thing this is! The Lord wanted us to be aware of this danger and to pray, "Deliver us from the evil of a darkened conscience."

Guard Against the Lowering
Of Your Upward Look

We must always be on guard against what I call "the lowering of our upward look." When we become Christians and are born–again from above, we receive a heavenly vision. We have a new perspective, and our eyes are lifted from the things of this earth to things that are heavenly. We become aware of the fact that the things of this world, the things that money can buy, are not the most precious things in life.

As children of God we know that the things that sustain our bodies, such as food, clothing, and shelter, are temporal and will soon pass away. We no longer regard these as of primary importance, for we realize that the soul and the spirit are of far greater value, since they are the means by which we have access to God and are able to enjoy fellowship with Him.

We need to guard against the evil of being conformed to the world around us by adopting its values and priorities. As Wordsworth has well said: "The world is too much with us; late and soon, getting and spending, we lay waste our powers." We need to be careful to maintain a right sense of values and priorities, and to realize that our attitude toward God is of paramount importance.

The moment that we lose our sense of priorities, we lose our balance, and then we can't walk straight. We must be able to tell the difference between what is precious, what is important, and what is merely incidental or trivial. For instance, if you get your values so twisted that money becomes the most important thing in life to you, and then lose that money, you may commit suicide. If you consider your husband, wife, or children to be your most precious possession, then if you lose them you will be hopelessly depressed.

It is evil to place first priority on things or relationships that are earthly and temporal, rather than on things and relationships that are heavenly and eternal. The Bible says in Colossians 3:1, 2: "If ye then be risen with Christ, seek those things which are above, where Christ sitteth on the right hand of God. Set your affection on things above, not on things on the earth." Then 2 Corinthians 4:18 says, "We look not at the things which are seen, but at the things which are not seen: for the things which are seen are temporal; but the things which are not seen are eternal."

The Lord Jesus Christ Himself should always be the most precious possession of our lives. The comfort and assurance of His presence should mean more to us than all the earthly and material things, which are merely temporary. These are the things with which the world around us is occupied, but the legacy that Jesus left to His disciples and to us is this: "Lo, I am with you always." To allow anything or anyone to come between the Lord Jesus Christ and ourselves is to lower our sights from heavenly things and fix them on earthly things.

Deliverance from Degrading Of Our Ideals, Deviation from Rectitude, and Defiling of Our Purity

Among the evils from which we need deliverance are the evils of degrading our ideals, deviating from rectitude, and the defiling of our purity. Let us look first at the evil of degrading our ideals. Webster's dictionary defines an "ideal" as "a standard of perfection, beauty, or excellence." Ideals are things that are higher than the material, mundane things that we can perceive with our five senses.

A person who has no ideals is a person who never strives to ascend the road of holiness and Christ–likeness. For instance, if your life consists only of eating three times a day, going to work and coming home, it is evident that you have made no place in it for ideals. If you are only interested in material or physical matters then you have allowed your ideals to be degraded.

An ideal would involve setting goals for such things as reaching a certain number of souls with the gospel each month or each year, or memorizing a certain number of Scripture verses, or seeking to read and to comprehend the Word of God, or to earn a certain amount of money to give to the Lord's work. Have you placed Christian ideals in your life?

Then we must also pray to be delivered from the evil of any deviation from rectitude. "Rectitude" means "that which is straight." It has to do with moral uprightness and with adherence to moral standards as well as correctness of judgment or procedure. So many things are happening today to cause us to deviate from the straight path and to take a bypass. We tend to deviate at times from what we know to be right. So we need to pray that the Lord will deliver us from this evil.

We also need to pray for deliverance from the defiling of our purity. God's desire for every Christian is that his life be pure and holy. The Bible is full of exhortations to holiness, and it sets before us the ideal of God's holiness. But we live in such a filthy environment. We have to mix and mingle with people who are so morally filthy that just rubbing elbows with them seems to defile us.

That in itself is bad enough, but what is even worse is to be defiled and not be able to recognize it. Not everyone has the same standard of inner purity, just as all people have not the same standard of physical cleanliness. For instance, some people think it sufficient to bathe once a week, and they feel that they are clean if they have done so. Others, who are accustomed to bathing every day, feel that they are dirty if they have to miss a day for some reason. There are degrees of physical cleanliness, and there are degrees of moral purity. Some people's standards are higher than others. The standard of purity for the Christian ought to be the purity of the Lord Jesus Christ. If it is not, then we have become defiled by the world and we need to pray for deliverance from this evil.

Deliverance from the Loss of Faith and the Vulgarization of Our Sentiments

A s we continue to look at some of the evils from which we need deliverance, we would do well to consider the evils of the loss of faith and the vulgarization of our sentiments. It is easy to lose faith. For instance, when we make specific requests of the Lord and then do not see them answered as we had thought they would be, we tend to lose faith. We say, "Lord, I prayed for this, and You didn't give it to me. What is wrong?"

We forget that while we pray in the context of the here and now, God answers our prayers in the context of eternity. He doesn't have in mind only the few years that we live here on this earth, He is concerned with our eternal destiny and welfare. Many people have prayed for healing for themselves or their loved ones, for the sake of a few more years down here, but God has not seen fit to answer their prayers. Therefore they have been tempted to lose faith in prayer and in God.

It is so easy for us to lose faith when we don't get our way. We're just like little children in that respect. If a child asks his parents for something and they don't give it to him he will often pout and sulk. He temporarily loses faith in his parents' goodness and love, and not until he gets over his pouting will he be restored to his normal state of confidence in them. We sometimes act the same way toward God.

God doesn't always act just as we desire. Our knowledge of what is best for us in the context of eternity is very limited, to say the least. However, He has all knowledge and all wisdom, so He always knows what will be for the best.

Let us also keep in mind that God is not dealing with just one isolated person, He has to consider all who are involved, and how each fits into the execution of His plan for all of humanity. Just because our understanding of God and of how He works is limited, we need to pray for deliverance from the evil of losing faith.

Then there is the evil of the vulgarization of our sentiments. The word "vulgar" is defined by the dictionary as "boorish, offensive to good taste or refined feelings; coarse." We have certain sentiments and feelings toward our loved ones and friends. We should see to it that these sentiments are always gentle, kind, and considerate. If we become demanding, rude, or ungrateful toward others, then we have allowed our sentiments to be vulgarized. For instance, I always thank my wife for every little thing she does for me, whether it is preparing a meal, washing my clothes, or mending my socks. I do not take it for granted that she owes me these things. My sentiments toward her are gentle, and hers toward me are the same. When I allow my sentiments toward my wife to become vulgar, then there is trouble ahead.

These sentiments and feelings, toward God and toward our fellow human beings, are very important. Our dealings with others should always be characterized by gentleness, kindness, and consideration. This is the true refinement of character that God desires to see in each of us. Can we be Christlike without it? No, for these characteristics were always present in His dealings with others. He who acts toward others in a coarse, rude, demanding or domineering way and yet calls himself a Christian, will be denounced by the world as a phony and a hypocrite. He also becomes an offense and a stumblingblock to other Christians who have to associate with him.

Deliverance from the Chilling
Of Spiritual Fervor

There is yet another evil from which we need deliverance, and that is the chilling of spiritual fervor. According to a recent Associated Press dispatch, young people today are fed up with the sermons they hear from the pulpits. Do you know why? There is no spiritual fervor in them, they are only theoretical.

A church that had stood for many years in a certain community was just about as dead as it could get. Very few people attended its services. One night the church caught fire, and as they heard the sirens and saw the flashing lights and the flames billowing from the church, scores of people began to gather. Within a short time there was a large crowd, all watching the fire. One man turned to his friend and said, "That just goes to prove that when the church gets on fire the world will come to watch it burn."

The reason people are not attracted to many churches today is that they are not "on fire." They are cold and lifeless. They have seen to it that their congregations become "hearers of the word," but they have not been concerned that they learn how to be "doers of the word."

Preacher, don't just leave your people out in the cold with theories. Give them something practical to do. When you preach that they should love their neighbor, show them how they can put that into practice. Tell them of some people who are in the hospital who need a visit. Tell them of the need for bandages for the four million leprosy patients of India. Tell them of the support that is needed for the work that is being done by faithful missionary organizations. Don't just talk theoretically about love, give them an opportunity to practice it.

Not only should you suggest to them practical ways to express love and compassion, you yourself must set the example for them. By your own fervor, earnestness, and zeal you must show that you practice what you preach. As someone has said, "I'd rather see a sermon, than hear one, any day." Don't be one of those who say, "Do as I say, and not as I do." Be fervent and zealous and enthusiastic about the Lord's work.

This is what we need from our pulpits today, for people are tired of meaningless clichés, and bored by theoretical sermons. How true it is that "The world is not looking for a clearer definition of love, it is looking for a clearer demonstration of it." Perhaps most of us can remember the time when we couldn't wait for an opportunity to do something for the Lord. Then gradually our zeal lessened and we became more interested in satisfying our own desires.

As Christians, our greatest concern should be spiritual growth, but many of us give priority to the things that concern the body rather than those that concern the soul and spirit. We would rather seek out a place of amusement than a place where the Word of God is taught. We may spend hours in physical exercise or in the preparation of our food, but we have little time for spiritual exercise.

Are we really on fire for the Lord? Do we find the Word of God and spiritual truths exciting? If not, something is wrong. Our spiritual appetite has been lessened and the evil of spiritual coldness is taking its place. We must pray that the Lord will deliver us from this evil of the cooling of our spiritual fervor.

The Moral Fall, a Sin Against God and Man

What do you consider your greatest treasure on earth? Is it your little "nest egg" in the bank? Is it your health, your family? Or is the most important thing in your life the salvation that you have in Jesus Christ, and the peace that passes all understanding? Has your evaluation of what is most precious changed or diminished since you first became a Christian? Through our prayer for deliverance from evil, we express our concern lest we lose the best that God has given us.

We may understandably wish to be spared poverty and pain. However, above all things our cry should be, "Lord, save us from the disgrace and ruin of a moral fall." Of what benefit is the gain of wealth, fame, or position if it brings with it the loss of morality or uprightness? "For what is a man profited, if he shall gain the whole world, and lose his own soul?" (Matt. 16:26).

When we pray, "Deliver us from evil," we should not think only of ourselves. We should be concerned lest we become a bad example or a stumbling block to others. Sometimes we may wonder why the Scriptures do not have any strict delineation of the duties of a Christian, when it comes to things that he is to do or not to do. Is he permitted to drink or smoke, or should he not? Should he attend the theater, or should he not? In seeking the answers to these questions, we must not only consider what effect any given action would have on ourselves, but also what possible effect it might have on others.

Romans chapter fourteen gives us guidelines in these areas by laying down the principles of consideration for our weak brother in Christ. It admonishes us to avoid anything that would cause our brother to stumble.

It is of utmost importance that we consider others and how we can best be a help and a blessing to them. We certainly should not want to do anything that would make us an offense or a stumblingblock to others. So in praying for deliverance from evil we should not only seek to be delivered from the sins that separate us from God, but also from those things that destroy our witness for the Lord and bring harm to other people.

Deliverance from the Loss of Consciousness of God's Presence

In praying for deliverance from evil we are often prone to think only of troubles, afflictions and problems that we face in this world. But the thing we ought to fear most is the loss of the sense of God's presence with us. God is always with us, for He has promised that He will never leave us nor forsake us, but it is possible to lose the consciousness of His presence. It is a lonely and frightening experience to live in this world without the realization that God is in you and around you, and that He is holding you up in His "everlasting arms." You need to know that Someone stronger than yourself is protecting you.

Another reason we need a sense of the presence of God is that this will keep us from transgressing His laws. After all, when is a little child most careful to be very good and obedient? Is it when he feels he is out of sight and hearing of his mother, or when he knows that she is near and is observing him? Of course he is going to be on his best behavior when he has a keen sense of her presence. It is the same way with us in our relationship with God. If we are conscious that He is always with us, that He is aware of all that we are doing, we will be much more apt to be careful not to do anything to offend or grieve Him. If we lose the sense of His presence, it becomes much easier to go astray and do the things we ought not to do.

The sense of the presence of God is a blessed comfort to us in times of sickness, sorrow, and suffering. In 2 Corinthians 1:3 Paul says, "Blessed be God, even the Father of our Lord Jesus Christ, the Father of mercies, and the God of all comfort." The word translated "blessed" here is *eulogētos,* one of two Greek words commonly translated "blessed." The other is *makarioi,* which is used in the Beatitudes. *Eulogētos* means "worthy to be well spoken of."

Note that this verse is speaking of suffering. When Paul says, "Blessed be God," he is saying, "God is worthy to be well spoken of." In other words, in spite of the fact that God may permit suffering in our lives, He is still worthy to be well spoken of. Why does this verse refer to God as "The God of all comfort"? Because Jesus Christ was the Man of suffering. He endured the agonies of the cross, and the Bible says that He was made "perfect through sufferings" (Heb. 2:10b).

Yet the Father of the Lord Jesus Christ is an omnipotent God. Could He not have delivered Him from all evil? Of course He could have, but He did not choose to do so. Yet if we are sure of one thing, it is that the presence of God was always with our Lord Jesus. The only time He ever lost the sense or consciousness of that presence was when He was hanging on the cross, bearing the sins of the world, and God turned away from Him because He had become the substitute for sinners. This was when He cried, "My God, my God, why hast Thou forsaken me?" (Matt. 27:46). To Him this was the most appalling thing that could ever happen—the loss of the sense of the presence of God. Do we feel this deeply about it? Does it concern us as it ought to?

God does not always choose to remove the evil from us. He allows us to experience suffering and adversity, but He gives us the comfort of His presence in the midst of it.

337

His presence is the greatest blessing that we can experience in our Christian lives. With Him, we can face any kind of suffering or affliction. Without Him, we become weak and are unable to stand the pressure. We need to pray, "deliver me from the loss of the consciousness of Thy presence."

Removal of Evil, or Comfort
In the Presence of Evil

One thing that we need to keep in mind about God's deliverance is that it is relative. The fact that He delivers us from sickness doesn't mean that we will never be sick again. Just because He heals us from some illness doesn't mean that we are going to avoid the ultimate experience of death. When He delivers us from poverty and gives us the money we need in a particular situation, that doesn't mean that from then on we are never going to have another financial need. His deliverances are relative, not absolute. The removal of a specific evil at a certain point of time in our life is no guarantee that we may not encounter that same problem at another time in the future.

There are actually two ways in which God can deliver us. The first is the immediate and direct deliverance that He gives by the abrupt removal of the evil that is afflicting us. For instance, someone may be gossiping about us, maligning us and hurting our reputation. If God chooses to do so, He can quickly eliminate that person. He can take his life and thereby deliver us from the evil that he is committing against us. That is deliverance by the direct removal of evil.

However, the Lord doesn't usually take the evil away so abruptly and absolutely. He leaves it and permits us to experience it, up to a certain point determined by His sovereign will, in order to humble us and test us. Psalm

30:5 presents a consoling truth: "For his anger endureth but a moment; in his favor is life: weeping may endure for a night, but joy cometh in the morning." God's deliverance may not be immediate. It may take a little while. He may allow sorrow "for a night," but deliverance "cometh in the morning." Remember that God may test us, but it is not His purpose to break us.

Another way that God may effect deliverance in our lives is through mingling His comforts with our affliction, in order to give us the grace that we need to bear it. For example, suppose the Lord permits a serious illness in your life. While you are suffering weakness and pain, He gives you the fellowship of a very dear Christian friend who will uphold you in prayer and will draw you closer to God by his strengthening words and his kind deeds. God is effecting deliverance by mingling comfort with your affliction.

The most wonderful illustration of this in the Scriptures is God's deliverance of Joseph. You remember how his brothers treated him, how they hated him and tried to kill him, then finally sold him into slavery. When he was taken to Egypt he was placed in a position of great honor and responsibility. Then an evil woman lied about him and he was thrown into prison for a crime he had not committed. God didn't deliver Joseph immediately, nor did He immediately punish those who had blighted his innocent name. Yet while he was in prison God brought him many alleviations to help him forget his miseries.

Joseph named his firstborn son "Manasseh," which means "forgetting." Genesis 41:51 says, "And Joseph called the name of the firstborn Manasseh: For God, saith he, hath made me forget all my toil, and all my father's house." Not only that, he named his second son "Ephraim," which means "fruitful." Genesis 41:52 says, "And the name of the second called he Ephraim: For God hath caused me to be fruitful in the land of my affliction." God had mingled His comforts with Joseph's afflictions, so that He caused him to forget his miseries. Then He made Joseph fruitful and blessed him greatly in the very place where he was sorely afflicted.

In Psalm 94:19 the Psalmist says, "In the multitude of my thoughts within me thy comforts delight my soul." Actually "thoughts" here means the doubts and sorrows that he had in his heart. In the midst of these depressed thoughts, God's comforts delighted and refreshed his soul. When you are in affliction, seek God's comfort. He sweetens poisonous experiences and influences with His wonderful grace. Mingling comfort with affliction is one way that He answers this prayer, "Deliver us from evil."

God Effects Deliverance
Through Giving Us Patience
To Bear Our Trials

A woman who was very impatient began to pray earnestly that God would give her more patience. Suddenly, it seemed that her life was filled with all kinds of trouble, grief, and perplexities. She was baffled by this sudden outbreak of problems, and sought some comfort and counsel from a friend. During the course of the conversation she mentioned that she had recently been praying for patience. Her friend said, "Don't you see? God is only answering your prayers, for you have asked for patience, and the Bible says that 'tribulation worketh patience' " (Rom. 5:3).

We need to be aware of the fact that one way God often uses to effect deliverance is by giving us the patience we need to bear up under our trials and adversities. Have you ever thought of patience as a virtue? It is not something that is natural to sinful man, it is God–given. But God doesn't give us this grace wrapped up in a neat little package dropped down out of the sky. It is something that has to be developed within us over a long period of time. In fact, it is a process that goes on throughout our whole lifetime, a process of development that God effects through the experiencing of tribulation and suffering.

The fact is that if it were not for suffering, adversity, and trials we would never develop this wonderful virtue of patience. Patience brings with it resignation to the will of God, teaching us submission to His working in our lives. The development of our character is God's primary concern, and these virtues of patience, resignation, and submission are very precious in His sight. They cannot exist without God–given faith and hope. The virtues of faith and hope are best exercised and strengthened in the midst of trial, persecution, and suffering.

Can you imagine how much harder it would be if we were always living in circumstances that never opposed our wills and desires? We would be almost beyond management! The trials and sufferings God allows us to experience serve to humble us and teach us to be more loving, if we respond to them in faith and with the right attitude.

Another reason He permits them is to cause us to look up to Him. I wonder sometimes whether the name of God would ever be on our lips if He gave us health and abundance all the time. I doubt it very much. Prayer, the exercise of faith, and the realization of our dependence upon God usually come when we have reached the end of our own resources and strength. Nor are we as thankful as we ought to be for the many blessings God constantly pours out upon us. Times of sickness and trouble cause us to appreciate better the good health and prosperity we have enjoyed at other times. Any calamity is more than compensated to us if it teaches us patience in the day of adversity, and we learn "in patience to possess our souls."

If It Were Not for Suffering, Would We Ever Think of Heaven?

A young couple who had recently lost a beautiful baby girl were sharing their grief with their pastor. The heartbroken young mother said, "You know, it's strange, but before our little girl died, I never gave heaven a thought. Now I find myself thinking of it many times during the day, and wondering what it is like, and thinking of the day when I will see my little one again."

The pastor said gently, "No, my dear, it isn't strange at all. The reason you think of heaven so much now is that you have a treasure there, and 'Where your treasure is, there will your heart be also.'"

Who among us would ever think of heaven, if it were not for suffering? God doesn't want us to view this world as our ultimate rest or our best home. He wants to wean us from this earth and its transitory pleasures and joys, and turn our eyes toward heavenly and eternal joys.

I believe that if it were not for the suffering and pain we experience here we would never want to leave this earth. We would just settle down and enjoy it, and therefore we would have no desire for heaven. How we cling to this earthly life! We see people who are suffering all sorts of agonies, or are crippled and deformed, and yet they are clinging to life with all their might, and the last thing most of them want to hear about is leaving this earth and going on to another sphere of existence. We don't want to quit this world, we want to stay on in spite of our suffering. It seems to be the best that we know, and we human beings are so prone to cling to the known and familiar, aren't we?

The Word of God tells us that the best for the child of God is yet to come. It is not to be found in this world, but in the next. So that our hearts may not become too attached to this world and this life, He permits evil in the form of suffering, affliction, and adversity to come into our lives. He doesn't take it all away, for He doesn't want us to get too comfortable down here.

There is a beautiful passage in the Bible, Deuteronomy 32:11, 12, which gives a touching picture of the mother eagle teaching her young offspring to fly. She hovers over the warm, comfortable nest where the young birds have been so content and she begins to jerk at it and tear it to pieces. She flutters her wings over the nest to try to agitate the eaglets, and she keeps on until she has them all stirred up and completely frustrated. She tears at the nest until it is so messed up, and she nips at them until they are so upset, that they are ready to get out of there. All of a sudden, it doesn't seem nearly as desirable as it previously did! Finally, if they don't get out by themselves, she will kick them out of the nest with her powerful feet. They are so frightened and disturbed that by this time they are frantic. They don't know how to fly, so they find themselves falling helplessly through space.

What does the mother eagle do to them? She swoops underneath them and catches them upon her broad back. Then she tosses them off again, and continues to repeat this procedure until they finally begin to flutter their wings and gradually learn to hold themselves aloft. You see, the mother eagle knows that she must get her eaglets out of that nest, for if she doesn't they will never learn to fly, and they will eventually perish.

Likewise God, by the sufferings and sorrows of this earthly life, is "stirring up our nest," so to speak to "teach us to fly" to our heavenly home. He sometimes has to make that nest pretty uncomfortable in order to make us willing to leave it.

The saints of old were far more "heavenly–minded" than we Christians of this day. The Christian Mystics and the Puritans spoke often of this process, which they called "weaning." They knew that unless God brought these sufferings into our lives we would never become detached in spirit from this world. After all, God doesn't want us to leave this world as Lot's wife left Sodom, looking back over our shoulders and pining for what we are leaving behind. He wants us to go out like Abraham, leaving all the joys and pleasures and blessings that we have heretofore known, and looking for "a city which hath foundations, whose builder and maker is God" (Heb. 11:10).

There was an old saint who lay upon a bed of suffering. As visitors came she would pray for them and read the Bible to them, and then she would sing in her quavering voice some of the old hymns of the faith. One she often sang was this:

> My heavenly home is bright and fair,
> No pain nor death can enter there.
> Its glittering towers the sun outshine,
> That heavenly home shall soon be mine.
>
> I'm going home, I'm going home,
> I'm going home, to die no more!

Why was she so pleased at the prospect of "going home" to heaven? Because she had suffered so much down here that heaven would be a blessed release from pain and weariness.

Yes, God knows what He is doing. He has not told us too much about heaven, for if He did, this earth would lose all its charm and we would be so eager for the beauties and glories of heaven that we would not be content to remain here to do the work He has for us to do. Much of the glory of heaven will come as a great surprise to us, for He has not told us much about it.

On the other hand, He gives us enough suffering, pain, and sorrow to make us long to leave this world behind and to enter into the joy, peace, and rest of that world which is to come. By emptying us of the world, He fills us with Himself. He shows us while in the fire of affliction that "our light affliction, which is but for a moment, worketh for us a far more exceeding and eternal weight of glory" (2 Cor. 4:17).

Our desire should be for Him, whether in the midst of affliction or affluence. Let us live in His presence, in spite of all the evil that exists around us. And let us remember that the sufferings of this earth are only preparing us for the joys of heaven.

Two Conditions for Deliverance

There are two main conditions a person must meet in order to be delivered from his sinful habits and practices. The first is that he must really want to be delivered. He must recognize that Satan is his enemy and God's, and he must stop following after him. God does not deliver anyone as long as he follows Satan and listens to his suggestions. How our Lord fought against Satan in the wilderness! We must fight against him even as He did.

However, we must realize our inability to resist him or conquer him alone. None of us is strong enough to meet Satan in his own strength and wisdom, not even Christians. We must have the help of God. He alone can give us the strength and the power to be victorious over Satan.

Sometimes we pray for deliverance, but down in our hearts we don't truly want to do what is necessary to effect that deliverance. A smoker may say, "Lord, deliver me from the habit of smoking," but he goes on smoking. That's making a sham of prayer; he should just throw that cigarette away. Only then does he have the right to ask God to help him not to touch another one. God will never deliver us until we are really sincere about being delivered.

The second condition is that we must believe that God is able to deliver us. Sometimes when we pray for deliverance we don't really believe God can help us, so we just repeat the same prayer over and over, using words that are really meaningless. Prayer means absolutely nothing if we do not have the faith that God can and will help us. This doubt that the sinner can be delivered from his sin lurks in many hearts. No wonder their lives go down in defeat.

Nicodemus, a ruler of the Jews, came to Jesus by night to find the way of salvation. Jesus said, "Ye must be born again." Immediately a doubt flashed into his mind, and he thought, "How can an old man like me be born–again?" The Lord insisted that although it was a miracle, it could be done. He went on to say that flesh and blood cannot inherit the kingdom of God. There must be a radical change.

God can work this change in you just as He has worked it in millions of others. But when you come to Him and ask Him to save you, you must believe that He can and will do it. This is not something that can be accomplished by human effort, only God can accomplish it.

Jeremiah 13:23 asks, "Can the Ethiopian change his skin, or the leopard his spots?" Can those who are chained by sin be liberated? Yes, they can, and that includes you. But you must really want to be delivered, and you must believe that He can deliver you. Believe, and receive the deliverance that only He is able to give.

Put on the New Man

One thing that we need to understand about sin is that it is fearfully cumulative. Once you take one step downward, you will keep on going. You won't be able to stop the downward plunge, for one sin leads to another. You never know into what mire sin may drag you. It is like stepping into quicksand. The harder you struggle to get out, the more you are pulled downward.

No matter where you are, whether you are one of those who are safe in the Shepherd's fold or one of those wandering out in the wilderness, Satan is always seeking to get you to go lower and lower and deeper and deeper into sin. You may think that you are as low as you can possibly get, and that you have gone as far into sin as you can possibly go, but there is always a pit that is deeper still.

You need to pray, "Lord, deliver me from going further and deeper into sin than I have already gone. I have taken one step downward, rescue me from yet worse development of my sinful tendencies."

The downward plunge toward destruction starts with the thought–life. Our Lord told us that this was so. This is why we need to seek deliverance from evil thoughts. If we don't, the thought may soon become a purpose, and the purpose will soon become an action. If we don't ask the Lord to deliver us from thoughts of evil, we may have to ask Him later to pluck us out of the pit. Thought, purpose, act, is the sequence sin follows. If we allow thoughts to linger until they finally end in sinful actions, we may suffer irrevocable consequences.

For instance, if a person began drinking and injures his liver in the process, the fact that God delivers him from the evil of drinking does not mean that He will necessarily deliver him from the damage that has been done to his liver.

A preacher once demonstrated this truth to his congregation by bringing in a board that was driven full of nails. He took a hammer and pulled the nails out one by one, as he explained to his people that the nails represented sins we have committed, and that the board with all the nails pulled out represented what happens when we receive Christ. All our sins are taken away, and as far as God is concerned they are no longer there. "But," he said, "the holes that have been left in the board represent the sometimes permanent and irreversible effects of sin in our lives." God forgives sin, but He doesn't always "forgive" the consequences of those sins. However, such is His grace that even here He overrules and works all things for the ultimate good of those who love Him.

This prayer for deliverance from evil is only hypocrisy unless we are ready to prove its sincerity by offering to God our determined resolution and our constant watchfulness and resistance against sin. God's reply to this petition is, "I will protect you, but you must exercise watchfulness and caution. I do not protect you from that which you secretly desire."

There are times when we cannot be delivered without exercising our own efforts. Our deliverance is not something that God drops in our laps, so to speak; it needs our cooperation. We have to work for it. For instance, sometimes we have to repress our own feelings, which push us toward malice, gossip, and other forms of evil. Self–repression is one way of being delivered.

Many years ago an Indian who could speak very little English was converted to Christ. Later, telling his missionary friend about the conflict he was having between good and evil within himself, he said, "Indian have black dog inside. Him evil. Indian have white dog inside. Him good. Sometimes black dog and white dog have heap big fight."

The missionary asked, "Which one wins?"

The Indian replied, "The one that Indian say 'sic em!' to." He had learned that he had his part in deciding whether evil was going to win out or not. The side that we nurture, whether evil or good, will show itself stronger (Mark 7:14–23).

God told Adam and Eve not to eat of the tree of the knowledge of good and evil. It was their responsibility to stay away from it, for if they had not gone near it they would never have taken the fruit and eaten it. Eve approached it, she stood and gazed at it, and the thought process began to work. As she looked and thought, she was approached by the Tempter, who knew that she was ready to listen to him. What might the outcome have been if she had only stayed out of reach of temptation?

Deliverance from evil is not achieved through passivity. The Christian life is a life of cooperation with God. We may pray, "Lord, help me to deliver myself from evil. I'm not asking you to do it by Yourself Help me to do my part to achieve the victory." We thus declare our willingness to submit to God in order to be delivered.

God Provides Deliverance, But We Must Accept It

God not only wants to deliver us from future evil, or evil that is merely potential, but He is also concerned about delivering us from evil into which we may already have fallen. We must pray for deliverance from the evil that has overcome us. It is harder to be delivered from some sin that has already defeated us than to be kept from it in the first place, for innocence is easier kept than recovered. If Satan has been able to get you, it is harder to get away from him than it would have been to keep out of the sin in the beginning. So we ask for forgiveness for the past, as well as strength for the future.

A preacher received a note from a parishioner that said, "I am weary of repentance." What that person meant was that he was constantly committing the same sin and "repenting" of it, then going right back into it. That is hardly true repentance. It is "repentance that needs to be repented of."

Remember that when we pray, "Deliver us from evil," we cannot place the entire responsibility on God. We have our part to do also. Recently I had the experience of dealing with someone who was schizophrenic, and I learned that one of the symptoms of insanity is refusal to take one's medicine. Some people who suffer from certain psychoses have a hard time getting well because of this. Doctors and hospital workers today cannot even force the patient to take needed medicine, because they are afraid of lawsuits. Can you imagine a doctor who is sane depending upon the consent and cooperation of an insane patient for his necessary treatment? It's sad but true, doctors cannot force even insane patients to take medication against their will.

This is a picture of our moral and spiritual state of "insanity" in our stubborn refusal to take the medicine that God has prescribed for us. That "medicine" would bring us spiritual health, for it would provide forgiveness for past sins and victory against future sins. But just as psychotic or schizophrenic persons must submit to taking the prescribed medicine if they want to get well, so must sinners submit to God's remedy, which is the acceptance by faith of the salvation He provides through the blood of Jesus Christ shed upon the cross.

That is the remedy for our sin, and if we want to live in a state of spiritual health we must live continually in the moment–by–moment experience of the cleansing power of that blood. That is our protection from the presence and power of evil. First we must be delivered from the bondage of sin, then we need deliverance from the constant attacks of the evil one. We can have victory, but we must be willing to accept God's remedy.

Deliverance through the Word, Prayer, and a Vision of What Lies Ahead

We know that our Lord encountered the evil one many times throughout His life here on earth. The most well–known of these encounters took place during His forty days in the wilderness, when by three different temptations Satan tried to induce Him to act independently of the will of His Father, and thus to sin. One thing we must understand is that in this encounter the Lord Jesus did not meet Satan on the ground of His deity, but on the ground of His humanity. He used no resources or weapons that are not readily available to the weakest child of God.

Since this is so, it is important that we know what these resources and weapons are, so that we too can make effective use of them. The first weapon that our Lord used was the Word of God. He countered each of the three temptations recorded in the Gospels, not by argument or reasoning with the evil one, but by quoting verses from the Old Testament, prefacing each verse with the phrase, "It is written."

If we are successfully to resist Satan and the forces of evil, we too must know the Word of God and be skillful in our use of it. When someone is tempting you to deviate from the right path, why not quote some pertinent Bible verses to them, instead of trying to argue with them in your own wisdom, or resist them in your own strength? They might even be converted through your sharing those verses with them.

It is absolutely imperative that we not only read and study the Word of God, but also that we hide it in our hearts through memorization. When we do this we are fortifying ourselves with "ammunition," so to speak, that will be of great value in our future confrontations with the evil one. The Psalmist said in Psalms 119:11, "Thy word have I hid in my heart, that I might not sin against thee."

Secondly, our Lord used the weapon of prayer. We know that His life was permeated and saturated with prayer. As we noted at the beginning of this book, His prayer life was so outstanding that it made a profound impression upon His disciples, who had opportunity to observe it. He rose up early in the morning so that He could have much time alone with His Father in prayer. He prayed before every major decision and event of His life, and He prayed constantly as He moved among the people, always "looking up to heaven" as He ministered to them and met their needs. He devoted a great deal of His teaching to the subject of prayer, constantly encouraging and exhorting the weary and the needy to bring their petitions to One who promised to hear and answer. One of His favorite portrayals of the Father, through His teaching and His parables, was that of One who delights to answer prayer, and has pledged Himself to do so when we meet His conditions. Even on the cross, when He was in agony, He prayed for the very ones responsible for nailing Him there. How much prayer meant to Him!

The question has been asked: "If the Son of God, who was perfect and sinless, and who had the Holy Spirit without measure, felt such a need of spending much time alone with His Father, should we who are so weak, sinful, and full of self consider it of less importance? Far from needing it less, do we not need it much, much more?"

The times when we find it hardest to pray, and the times when we find the least enjoyment and pleasure in prayer, are the times when we really need it most. Yet so often we become discouraged when the going gets rough, and we slack up in our prayer life, instead of intensifying it as we should do. In the hour of temptation, when we are being attacked by the evil one, prayer is our greatest source of strength and one of our greatest weapons. It is here that the battle is either won or lost.

The third thing that enabled our Lord to withstand the onslaughts of the evil one was His vision of what lay beyond His sufferings on the cross. Hebrews 12:2 says, "Who for the joy that was set before him endured the cross, despising the shame, and is set down at the right hand of the throne of God." He looked ahead and saw the millions of souls who would be redeemed through His sufferings. He saw the ultimate triumph of God's purpose, and the ultimate establishment of His kingdom here on earth. He saw, beyond the shame and the pain of the cross, the glory of His resurrection, ascension, and eventual enthronement as King of kings and Lord of lords over the whole creation of God.

We also may be strengthened against the evil one by the vision of the glory that lies ahead of us. It is common knowledge to all who have ever run in any sort of race that one backward glance may mean defeat. The runner must always look ahead, never backward.

A young farm lad was having his first experience at plowing. He had watched his father plow many times and had noted that his furrows were always perfectly straight. He had thought it would be easy, but to his chagrin he found that he could not plow a straight furrow. He kept looking back over his shoulder at the crooked mess he was making of the field. At last he gave up and went to find his father. "Dad," he said, "I've watched you plow many times, and it always looked so easy that I couldn't wait to try it. I was so sure that I could plow like that, too, but I can't do it to save me. What is the secret?"

"Son," said the farmer, "the secret is this—never look back. When I am plowing, I pick out a landmark up ahead of me, maybe a tree, or a rock and I walk straight toward that object. I don't worry about the furrow behind me, for I know that if I keep my eye on that goal out in front of me, and walk straight toward it, then my furrows will be straight. But you must never look back."

Likewise, we must set our sights on what lies ahead of us, and not keep looking back to what is behind us. Look to that day when you will see God and be forever in His presence. Look to the time when you will receive a glorified body "like unto his glorious body," and this earthly body of weakness and pain and weariness will be gone forever. Look into the future with the eye of hopeful expectation until you catch a gleam from the golden gates of the New Jerusalem. Even if you are facing the evil of death itself, it can only serve to bring you into the presence of God, if you are one of His. Thus even death becomes your gain instead of your loss.

The resources that our Lord used were the Word of God, prayer, and a vision of the future glory that awaited Him. Through them He was victorious over the evil one, and through them we, also, shall gain the victory.

Past Deliverances and Future Expectations

"**W**hy are you so sure that God is going to help you in the future?" a cynic asked a Christian. "Because," said the Christian, "I know how He has helped me in the past." As we look back at the troubles, trials and sufferings through which we have already safely passed, we are encouraged in regard to those we shall have to face in the future.

There is an interesting incident in 1 Samuel, chapter seven, about a battle between the Philistines and the children of Israel. As the Philistines were coming up to attack them, the Israelites prayed and cried to the Lord for deliverance. The prophet Samuel offered a sacrifice to the Lord on behalf of the people. As a result, the Lord heard and delivered them through a miraculous intervention. In order to commemorate this victory, Samuel did something significant. 1 Samuel 7:12 says, "Then Samuel took a stone, and set it between Mizpah and Shen, and called the name of it Eben–ezer, saying, Hitherto hath the Lord helped us."

In the old hymn, "Come Thou Fount of Every Blessing," the author based one stanza on this incident:

> Here I raise mine Ebenezer,
> Hither by Thy help I'm come;

And I hope, by Thy good pleasure,
Safely to arrive at home.
                    —Robert Robinson

Just so, as we look back at the way God has led and
delivered, every one of us could, and should, "raise an
Ebenezer" in our own lives, saying, "Hitherto hath the Lord
helped me."

Over and over we have proven the truth of 1 Corinthians
10:13: "There hath no temptation taken you but such as is
common to man; but God is faithful, who will not suffer
you to be tempted above that ye are able, but will with the
temptation also make a way to escape, that ye may be able
to bear it."

As we have considered this petition, "Deliver us from
evil," we have learned that both the evil that is in the
world, and the evil one himself, are realities we dare not
ignore. We have seen that the evil that is the common
experience of all has come about through the entrance of
sin into the world. We have looked at some of the evils
from which we need deliverance, and considered some of
the ways in which God effects deliverance and some of the
resources available to us as we confront the evil that is
within us and around us.

As we look back to the past we see the many times
God has graciously delivered us. As we look to the future
we're assured that His goodness and mercy shall continue
to follow us, all the days of our lives, as the Psalmist says in
Psalm 23. None of us can know what the future holds, for
God has mercifully hidden it from us. As one has said, "The
past belongs to history and the future belongs to God."
However, we do know that as long as we continue to live
in this world we shall have tribulation, as our Lord has told
us.

Job 5:18, 19 contains a blessed word of assurance for us concerning the future. It says: "For he maketh sore, and bindeth up: he woundeth, and his hands make whole. He shall deliver thee in six troubles; yea, in seven there shall no evil touch thee." Because of past deliverances, we have expectations of hope for the future. We are strengthened and encouraged by the realization that if we in Christ do our part by faith, and if we trust Him to do His, our God will deliver us from all evil.

SECTION X

The Doxology

God Is Now Reigning

The doxology at the end of the Lord's Prayer brings about some very necessary concluding thoughts. Prayer is but man's wish. This is why it is called in Greek *proseuchē* made up of the preposition *pros,* "to," and *euchē,* to "vow or wish." *Euchē* comes from *eu* meaning "well" and the verb *cheō,* to "pour out." It is a vow or wish poured out to God.

In the Lord's Prayer we are taught to wish from our Heavenly Father the following:

His name to be made holy by us.
His kingdom to come.
His will to be done on earth as it is done in heaven.
Our bread to be provided by Him.
Our debts to be forgiven by Him.
Not to be led and left alone in facing temptation.
To be snatched by Him from the claws of the evil one.

There is a sincerity about every request. It is a wish by us that God's character and provision be manifested in and through our lives in a world having evil influences. Satan and his followers don't want God's name set apart as holy, God's kingdom to prevail, or God's will executed. They don't want us adequately and daily provided with bread, nor do they want to see us liberated from the guilt and power of sin. They want us to be tripped by Satan and fall as we experience inevitable temptations.

God is going to triumph some day and we shall triumph with Him. His righteousness will be established. But how about the here and now? Does God reign as King now in the sinful world in which we dwell? Is prayer only a wish for a future state or is God's reign to be acknowledged in us and among us at this present time? Prayer is for our present need of God's presence and provision now that we are constantly bumping into temptation and Satan's activity is so fierce.

This is the reason the doxology culminates the Lord's Prayer not with a wish for the future, but a statement of fact of what God, our Heavenly Father, is now. "For thine is the kingdom!"—not "May thy kingdom come," as the second petition of the Lord's Prayer expresses the wish of the heart.

It seems that the Lord's teaching gave the Pharisees of His day the wrong concept that the hope of the Christian and his wish is only for a future state when God's kingdom was going to be imposed. You recall on one instance the Lord Jesus was asked by them, "When is the kingdom of God coming?" (Luke 17:20). They thought it only in the future. Observe what the Lord answered them, "The kingdom is coming not with observation (visibly)." That's what their idea of God's kingdom was—a king with an earthly throne whose rule could be visibly observed. "Neither shall they say, Lo here! Or, lo there! For, behold, the kingdom of God is within you."

True, God is going to reign some day in a way that the existence of evil will be excluded from our earth "when all things shall be subdued unto him" (1 Cor. 15:28). "For he must reign, till he hath put all enemies under his feet" (1 Cor. 15:25). We also shall reign on the earth (Rev. 5:10). One

day great voices in heaven will be heard saying, "The kingdoms of the world are become the kingdoms of our Lord,
and of his Christ, and he shall reign forever and ever" (Rev.
11:15). The day is coming when the twenty–four elders will
say: "We give thee thanks, O Lord God Almighty, which art,
and wast, and art to come; because thou hast taken to thee
thy great power, and hast reigned" (Rev. 11:17). "And I
heard as it were the voice of a great multitude, and as the
voice of many waters, and as the voice of mighty thunder-
ings, saying, Alleluia: for the Lord God omnipotent
reigneth" (Rev. 19:6).

For this glorious reign of our God in the future and for
our reigning together with Him (Rev. 22:5) we have no
doubt and we pray with certainty. Our wish is without
wavering. But how about now? Is not God on the throne?
Yes, he is. And that is what His doxology at the end of this
model prayer reminds us: "For thine is (here and now) the
kingdom." The Lord Jesus Himself said, "For behold the
kingdom of God is within you," and this in spite of the
existence of sin, temptation and the evil one. If victory
were not possible here and now, why pray? It is possible.
God gives His own peace in the midst of turmoil. The kingdom of the future is going to be total peace and righteousness, but now it is peace within our own hearts.

Why Do We Pray?

We pray because we feel inadequate in coping with the realities and pressures all about us. We realize that beyond us there is One who created us and who is able to sustain us no matter what happens around us. One of the greatest misunderstandings of the purpose of prayer is seen in a little boy's remark to his mother. His conduct made her suspect that he did not pray. When she expressed her fear to him, the little boy said, "Yes, I do. I pray every night that God will make you and Pa like my ways better." For most people, prayer is for the purpose of persuading God to like their ways and give them what they think they need most. And our Lord's concern was lest we would misunderstand the purpose of prayer.

Thus in the prayer He taught us, we have:

- The concept of His Fatherhood—"Our Father."
- The necessity of our exhibiting His holiness— "Hallowed be thy name."
- Our wish for the coming of His kingdom—"Thy kingdom come."
- Our dedication to the execution of His will—"Thy will be done."

And then He gave recognition to our expression of dependence on Him for our material sustenance in giving us our daily food: "Give us this day our daily bread." Then comes our dependence for our moral victory upon His sustaining power:

– Forgive us as we forgive.
– Lead us not into temptation.
– Deliver us from evil.

As you pray, recognize three things:

1. That above you and all around you there is a Holy God whose sovereignty must prevail in your own life and in the corporate life of the world in which you live.
2. That you have material needs for your body.
3. That you have moral needs for your immaterial part of soul–spirit.

We pray because we choose to recognize God and the fact that He can meet our needs. The Lord Jesus taught us in the Lord's Prayer to freely express our desire concerning God's participation in our lives, in the prevalence of His Fatherly interest, His holiness and His Sovereignty. We are then to ask His help in providing for our physical needs and in endowing us with moral victories.

But in the doxology we have a statement of fact: "For thine is the kingdom, and the power, and the glory, forever. Amen." It is as if we were saying, "We have prayed but our prayer would have been a sheer mockery if it were not based on the fact that God is now and shall ever be the most powerful and glorious King." Whether we get our way or not, He is still King. Whether His power is demonstrated in our lives or not, He is still all-powerful. Whether our lives and that of the universe and manhood adequately reveals His glory, all that He is in Himself, He is still the all–glorious creator and sustainer of all things and all people. Our state of being does not determine His existence and sovereignty. What He is, He is in Himself and we do not contribute to His excellency in any way. Herein is His kingdom different from any other kingdom. He is not a king proclaimed as such by His subjects, but His sovereignty is inherent. God is not like a politician whose standing depends on the fidelity of his followers or the whims of the populace. The process does not begin from the bottom to the top, from men to God, but from God to men. It is as if we were saying at the end of our prayers: No matter what are the visible results of prayer, Thine is forever the kingdom, the power and the glory.

God can, therefore, be influenced by our will, especially when these pertain to our own relationship with Him. At the same time, it is God's planned will that evil be endured during this age of grace when the kingdom of God is not established as an externally imposed visible kingdom, but as the reign of God within our believing hearts. And because of the toleration of evil here and now, prayer here and now is an absolute necessity. Evil can rule all around us, and yet we can declare that God's is the kingdom, the power and the glory. A paradox? No. A reality. The reality of evil abounding as contrasted with God reigning and giving us victory against it. Evil is free to act, but it is not free to dominate us.

The paradox is that a Christian can live in a sinful environment as if in a prison, yet feel free because within him reigns God supremely. As stone walls do not make a prison, the absence of them does not constitute freedom. Liberty is a state of the soul. When God is King within we are free. Our prayers are so influenced by His nature within us that our petitions rarely miss His will for us. How fine then is the couplet:

> "Our wills are ours, we know not how,
> Our wills are ours, to make them Thine."

In prayer we exercise freedom of will. We come to God asking Him whatever we wish. Prayer is primarily the liberty to appropriate those blessings which only a moral being can enjoy. To the degree we refrain from accepting the moral and spiritual assets that God offers, to the same degree we refrain from exercising our freedom. Prayer is an instrument to help us appropriate as much of God for ourselves as possible.

Why does God not exercise His Kingly power to check us when we exercise our will wrongfully? Because if He were to restrain our freedom that would virtually mean its destruction. He would be taking back with one hand what He gave with the other. God will not limit our choice to begin with, and even when we misuse this privilege, He will not step in to withdraw it. In the same way, God will not object to our endeavor to influence Him through prayer.

Why Is the Doxology Omitted by Some?

This doxology at the end of the Lord's Prayer is disputed by some as not spoken by Christ Himself but as being a later addition by those who used the prayer. Some say it is patterned after David's praise of God in 1 Chronicles 29:11. The doxology is omitted by some manuscripts, and all those of the Vulgate. Certain Greek and Latin Fathers omit it in their expositions of the Lord's Prayer.

There is evidence indicating that the Lord's Prayer was used by the early church in its corporate worship, this is why it is considered by some as a prayer for the fellowship of believers instead of the individual believer. It became a practice, therefore, that the body of the prayer was repeated by the congregation and the conclusion by the one leading the service. Because of this separation of the Doxology from the rest of the Lord's Prayer, it began to be considered by some Christians as a man–made response and not part of the original prayer spoken by Christ. This probably is the reason why it is missing from some ten Greek manuscripts and from most of the manuscripts of the Latin versions. And this may be the very reason why some of the church Fathers do not mention it when commenting on the Lord's Prayer (See Edward F. Hills, *The King James Version Defended!* The Christian Research Press, 1984:97–102).

After considerable study on the subject, we have concluded that no matter whether these are words of Christ Himself or the early believers in response to Christ's model prayer, they are important and are in general agreement with the rest of the teaching of the New Testament. Therefore, they are worthy of study and of repetition by us. I personally consider them as having been pronounced by our Lord as a part of the corpus of the Prayer.

No prayer is complete without the acknowledgement that is found in the words "For Thine is the kingdom, and the power and the glory." It is interesting to note that the doxology in the Greek text begins with the particle or conjunction *hoti* meaning "for, because, wherefore." This conjunction introducing the doxology contains the reasons why we should pray to God and why we may expect an answer when we pray. When we apply for something, we must give the reasons. When we come to God in prayer, we should mention why our prayer should be granted. There are some basic arguments we must present. First we must never imagine that there is any merit in our prayers. Second, we must never argue with God to grant us something that is clearly stated in His Word as not pleasing to Him. Third, we must believe that, as James Drummond says, "God may have left certain things dependent on human petition." This constitutes one of the greatest difficulties of prayer. Can my prayers so influence God that He may change His mind? This subject is examined in the next chapter. It has the meaning of "Yes, indeed, thine is the kingdom, the power, and the glory." It is an affirmation of God's sovereignty. He is to be worshiped no matter what the seeming result of prayer. If you get less than you expected from God, you cannot turn away from Him and stop worshipping Him. You must worship God not for what you feel He has done for you but for what He is, the King of the universe and of all mankind. He was, is, and will be sovereign. He is designated the One who was, is, and will be.

———

What Is the Purpose of Prayer?

To realize that God is King no matter what the circumstances, because of or in spite of our prayers, is the real purpose of prayer. In the first place, when we pray, we do so because we realize that He is King, that He has power, that He has glory, which means that He has demonstrated enough of His power that we can recognize Him for who and what He is. When we are in need we go to someone who can help us. A subject may go to his king. A weak person goes to the one who has strength. Prayer is a mute recognition of our inadequacy and of God's ability and readiness to help us. But a subject does not always receive all that he desires from His king. It is his prerogative to ask. But it is also the king's privilege to give in the measure he deems proper in view of the total need of all his other subjects. He can also deny the requests of his subjects. Whatever the response of the king, the attitude of the subject should never be that he ceases to consider him king, and such is prayer. It is the recognition of need. It is coming to God as King. We can ask whatever we want. God will judge our character by what we ask even as a parent determines his child's character by the nature, propriety and extent of his requests. God, being King Almighty and at the same time Father, will use His wisdom in granting or denying our requests. Whatever He does toward us and our prayers, we ought to look in His face and say, "Yes, indeed, you are still King, most powerful and glorious!"

There is great danger of thinking of God as less than He is when we pray and don't receive what we believe we ought to have. There is a wonderful mural painting illustrative of God's sovereignty in spite of His seeming inactivity in some instances of history, even as in our present when sin seems to abound in spite of the prayers of the saints. This painting depicts the Jews brought into subjection to the heathen. To the left stands Pharaoh, exquisite, deadly cruel. In one hand he lifts the scourge, and with the other he grasps the hair of the captives. On the right is the Assyrian king, duller, heavier, with knotted limbs pressing down the yoke on the poor prisoners. But supplicating hands are raised up to heaven and Jehovah lends His ear to the cry of His people. The cherubim fly before Him, their wings glowing crimson. They hide His face, but from behind the wings issue His arms. The slender Pharaoh is repressed by the mere impact of His finger. The brute force of the Assyrian is held in a grasp by God's tremendous power.

There are evil rulers in the world. Sin predominates. The Christians, squeezed from every side, pray, "Lead us not into temptation! Deliver us from evil!" As you look at the powerful of the world and what they do to the cause of Christ you wonder whether there is a God almighty and sovereign. Remember, it is in the midst of evil rulers and Satan's activity that we must recognize that God has not abdicated His kingdom. "For thine *is* the kingdom."

The Danger of Answered Prayers: Can We Command God's Power?

T he doxology is also necessary for the person who seems to be very successful in his prayer life in as far as receiving from God much of what he requests. Such a person's danger is to unconsciously turn prayer and supplication into an attempt to command God's omnipotence. It is this person who no longer considers it necessary to pray "Thy will be done" because he thinks he knows what God's will is at all times and therefore he can demand it of God. To such a person God becomes an errand boy and is deprived of His sovereignty. Unconsciously, such a person may shout with his demeanor and pride, "Mine is the kingdom, power and glory." Woe unto the person who can say to others, "Let me pray for you for I can get what I want from God!" Such a person cannot end his prayer "For thine is the kingdom the power and the glory." God's sovereignty is not on the auction block. His power is given not for permanent and indiscriminate demonstration of self but only as a sign toward verification of His sovereignty.

The only one who has inherent, unrestricted authority and power is the Lord Jesus Christ. That's the last thing He told His disciples before He ascended to heaven when He saw them in Galilee in His resurrection body: "Unto *me* [not to you] is given all authority [*pasa* which means every kind of authority and all of it put together] in heaven and on

377

earth" (Matt. 28:18). On occasions to enable them to accomplish certain tasks, He endowed His disciples with power to preach the kingdom of God and heal the sick and cast out demons (Luke 9:1–6). Observe, however, that it was always to preach the kingdom of God, that the kingdom at all times was God's and He was King and therefore, the exercise of their power was under the restrictiveness of His sovereign will. Only as we understand the restricted nature of the authority and power placed in God's prophets and Christ's disciples can we understand why they were sometimes able to perform healings and miracles and sometimes they were not. Look at Paul the Apostle. No one doubts the genuineness of his miracles: striking a man blind in Cyprus (Acts 13:11), healing a cripple at Lystra (Acts 14:8–10), casting out a demon from a girl in Philippi (Acts 16:16–18). In Ephesus people were bringing handkerchiefs from him to sick persons and healing ensued (Acts 19:11–12). At Troas, Paul raised Eutychus who fell from the window and died. But as Paul is taken by boat from Caesarea to Rome, he cannot still the fury of the sea. He does not free himself from his captors in Rome. When Timothy suffers from his stomach, he does not heal him but tells him to take a little wine. Because he could then end his prayers no longer with the doxology "Yes, indeed, thine is the kingdom, the power and the glory." He as much says so in 2 Corinthians chapter twelve when he recounts his being caught into paradise: "It is not expedient for me, doubtless, to glory . . . of myself I will not glory, but in mine infirmities. And lest I should be exalted above measure through the abundance of the revelations there was given to me a thorn in the flesh, the messenger of Satan to buffet me, lest I should be exalted above measure. For this thing I besought the Lord thrice, that it might depart from me. And he said unto me, My grace is sufficient for thee" (2 Cor. 12:1, 5, 7–9).

Recognizing Evil and God's Ability to Deliver Us

This doxology through the particle *hoti.* "therefore or wherefore," stands in contrast to what has immediately preceded it: "And deliver us from evil." Nevertheless, this evil from which we are asking to be delivered does not involve our exercising of personal sovereignty in the world or in our own lives. "Deliver us from evil, the evil one, Satan; nevertheless, the kingdom is not Satan's, it is thine, and thine is the power and the glory."

One of the things that Satan tried to do was to persuade Jesus that the kingdoms of the world were his (Satan's). Immediately after His baptism Satan tempted Him. He took Him to a high mountain near Jericho and showed Him all the kingdoms of the world in a moment of time. "And the devil said unto him, All this power will I give thee, and the glory of them; for that is delivered unto me, and to whomsoever I will I give it" (Luke 4:5). That was Satan's endeavor to usurp what was Christ's already. The kingdoms of the world were Christ's when He was born in a stable in Bethlehem. Even Herod recognized this, hence his endeavor to kill a "baby king." They were Christ's when His enemies were spitting on His face, were jeering Him, were crucifying Him. Jesus answered and said unto Satan "Away with you, Satan" (Matt. 4:10).

The word which follows *hoti* "therefore or wherefore" in the doxology is the possessive genitive *sou* (from *su*), "thou or thine," as if to indicate that the kingdom and the power and the glory have always been God's, part of His very nature and character. There has never been a time that God was not characterized by these qualities. This possessive genitive is differentiated from the dative which is usual in the doxologies using the noun form which shows more plainly what God is about to make His very own. It does not say *hoti autō,* "for unto Him," but "for thine." It is more direct. This is not a wish on the part of the one praying that God may assert Himself and assume sovereignty, power and glory, but it is an affirmation that the One to whom prayer is offered has always possessed as His very own these qualities. This is the reason why the verb *estin,* "is" is used. It is not that God's may *be* the kingdom, the power and the glory, but God's *is* the kingdom, the power and the glory.

Why in This Order:
Kingdom, Power, Glory?

W hy are these three characteristics placed in this order: kingdom, power, glory? Kingdom indicates God's rank and office. A king is the supreme ruler. That supreme rule, however, is not a democratic one. He is not a supreme ruler because His creatures have placed Him in that high position. He has placed Himself there. It is not a kingdom by vote or by acclamation, but by inherent personal power. And then the third characterization of glory is the recognition of who He is. The Greek word is *doxa* from the verb *dokeō* which means "to think, to recognize." God through His power is to be recognized as to who He is. He is to be recognized as such through His answers to our prayers.

For how long has God been characterized as a powerful, glorious King?—always. But this in Greek can be expressed either with the word *aiōn*, "age" in the singular which is more common—"unto the age," *eis ton aiōna,* or with the word "age" in the plural, *eis tous aiōnas*. The expression *eis ton aiōna* in the singular means "long, measureless time." But the fact that it is in the plural allows the liberty to assume that the idea of successive, measurable ages is intended "unto the ages," as they succeed each other. In other words, there may be certain ages in time when we may be tempted to believe that God can not be considered as King, that His power is altogether hidden and He is not attributed any glory, any due recognition of majesty and grandeur. His power may not be as apparent in one age as in another, but nevertheless there has never been and there never will be an age when God has not been sovereign with power and glory.

Why Do We Close Our Prayers With the Word "Amen"?

The Lord's Prayer closes with the word "Amen." This was the word with which the praise of God was attested to in response to a doxology (1 Chr. 16:36; Neh. 8:6) as at the end of the doxologies of the first four books of the Psalms (Ps 41:13; 72:19; 89:52; 106:48). It indicates that what is said is true and valid. Generally it was used in response to any prayer or praise uttered by another. The concluding "Amen" signified concurrence.

The Lord Jesus used the word "Amen" before His sayings 30 times in Matthew, 13 times in Mark and 6 times in Luke. Luke also used *alēthōs*, "truly," in 9:27; 12:44; 21:3 and *ep' alētheias* "of a truth" in Luke 4:25, and John also used it 25 times in his Gospel. What he wanted to convey by its use was that His words are reliable and true. Interestingly enough, in spite of the fact that these sayings are of varied individual content, they all have to do with the history of the kingdom of God bound up with His person.

Christian prayers, doxologies, as also Jewish prayers, mostly end with "Amen." Paul, in presenting his argument that whatever is said in the worship service at Corinth should be understood, says that it should be so because otherwise how will a hearer in the assembly say "Amen" give a vocal concurrence of what is being said (1 Cor. 14:16).

Finally it is interesting to note that in Rev. 3:14 the Lord Jesus is called the Amen, the witness, the true one (literal Greek translation).

He presents Himself as the reliable and true witness of God. What He came to be and do is exactly what the Father wanted done down here on earth. We could thus say that every time we close our prayers with the word "Amen," we close with one of the many names of Christ as if saying that we pray in Christ's name. Thus we subjugate that which we have prayed to God's scrutiny. If our prayer is to show forth the true character of the Lord Jesus, then let it be answered. If it is not, we shall be just as content for God to demonstrate that He is King. He is all–powerful and capable of making Himself shine forth so that He is truly recognized for who He is and what He stands for. That is the ultimate purpose of prayer: not that we may have our own way but that God may show forth that He is King, most powerful and most glorious.

How Much Can My Prayer Influence God in Changing His Mind?

If God is responsible for all that man does, then is He also responsible for the evil man does? The big question is where does God's responsibility end and man's begin? God permits man to will to do certain things for which he must bear the responsibility.

Why pray if our prayers are only bucking a God who has already made up His mind about everything? His purposes will be accomplished whether we pray or not. Is prayer an attempt to change the inevitable? If the inevitable is unchangeable, then prayer is an exercise in futility.

We pray, "Deliver me from evil." God may deliver us or He may not. Conversely we say "His will be done." And at the end of our petitions, we must praise Him by saying, "For Thine is the kingdom, and the power and the glory."

The first thing we must recognize is that no one knows God's purposes except He, Himself. God's plans in their minutest details are made as He hears our prayers. His will is never lived in total disregard of ours.

God gave man freedom to choose whether or not to eat of the fruit of a certain tree. His will was that man might obey but had He forced him to do so, it would not have been man's choice and the result could not have been called obedience. There is evil in the world. The existence of evil did not involve God as directly creating it, but resulting from the availability of choice. One could not have obedience if there were not the possibility of disobedience. Without the possibility of obedience or disobedience, there could be no fellowship with God. Man's obedience would be that of an emotionless puppet—his actions and movements controlled from above. The existence of evil is therefore a necessary concomitant of good.

Man was made a creature of choice. He was thus created in the image of God, a moral being, one who could exercise the choice of will. If God forces men to do only what He wants him to do, then he is not a moral being but a machine. Only a moral being can pray or praise. That is what he chooses to do. God, in asking us to pray, is telling us that we have a will that can be expressed toward Him and that can be activated into action. We are thus responsible for our actions if we are free to act. If we are not, we cannot bear the responsibility. That which man chooses to do, he must also bear the responsibility for doing.

When we declare at the end of our prayers that God is King, sovereign, we do not absolve ourselves of the responsibility of the actions we chose to perform. Furthermore, God, although sovereign, is not responsible for the evil in the world caused, not by His will, but by man's choice of evil.

God, in imparting to man the ability to choose, also gives him the responsibility of his choice, although God at all times predetermines the consequences of the choice man makes. Man may work and have money or he may choose to steal. His work has certain rewards predetermined by society. Stealing may become man's choice. If apprehended and convicted, he must submit to the punishment of the law. He does not determine the consequences of his own actions. When God gives man freedom, He reduces His own control of him. I do the same as a parent.

My child is fully under my control when as a little baby he or she cannot exercise any choice. But as he grows, my authority as parent is reduced in proportion as his ability to choose for himself is increased.

God as King has given authority to man to make more and more choices. Man must bear the responsibility of the choices he makes. God therefore compels man as a creature of His own making even as a father does his child. But the time comes when man constitutes a challenge to God's authority, even as a grown child to his father's. As I can exercise my will in doing evil against the will of God, so can I exercise my will in influencing God to do His will for my life. Therefore we can say that God's preordination and predetermination of things is such that it cannot but be affected by our prayers. He is most eager to hear our petitions, even as a father is happy to listen to his children's requests whatever they may be. Of course. He never abdicates His parental right to sift our requests. He allows His purposes to be modified in their details as far as they affect our own individual lives, but always within His general foretold plan for all humanity and the world.

GREEK–ENGLISH INDEX

Greek	*English*	*Scripture*	*Page*
a	without		214, 218, 239
adikēma	criminal act, result of injustice	Acts 18:14; 24:20; Rev. 18:5	214
adikeō	to do injustice	Acts 7:24; 1 Cor. 6:7; 2 Cor. 7:12	214, 215
adikia	unrighteousness, injustice	Luke 13:27; 16:9, 11; 18:6; John 7:18; Acts 1:18; 8:23; Rom. 1:18, 29, 2:8, 3:5, 6:13, 9:14; 1 Cor. 12:13; 13:6; 2 Thess. 2:10, 12; 2 Tim. 2:19; Heb. 8:12; James 3:6 2 Pet.2:13, 15; 1 John 1:9; 5:17	214, 215, 218
agathōsunē	provision, abundant	Rom. 15:14; Gal. 5:22; Eph. 5:9; 2 Thess. 1:11	82, 83
agnoēma	to ignore, to be ignorant, not to recognize		220, 221
agnoēmata,	error(s), unintentional	Acts 3:17; 1 Tim. 1:13; Heb. 10:26	219–221
agnoēmatōn	error, unintentional	Heb. 9:7	219

aiōn	age	Matt. 6:13	382
airō	to take away, to cover	John 1:29	229
akoē	hearing		218
alēthōs	truly	Luke 9:27; 12:44; 21:3	384
anakainizēn	to renew qualitatively	Heb. 6:6	223
anarchia	anarchy		215
anomia	lawlessness	Matt. 7:23; 13:41; 23:28, 24:12; Rom. 4:7, 6:19; 2 Cor. 6:14; 2 Thess. 2:7; Titus 2:14; Heb. 1:9; 8:12, 10:17; 1 John 3:4	215–217
anomian	lawlessness	1 John 3:4	216, 217
anomōs	unrighteously	Rom. 2:12; 3:21; 1 Thess. 2:8	209
anthrōpos	man		32
apechō	have one's reward in full	Matt. 6:2	4, 5
apechousin	have one's reward in full	Matt. 6:5	5
aphē	to forgive, to remove from oneself	1 John 1:9	241
aphiēmi	forgive		229
aphēkamen	we forgave, to forgive	Matt. 6:12 (UBS)	270
aphes, see *aphiēmi*	forgive		229

SCRIPTURE INDEX

399